In Darkest England
NOW

In Darkest England
NOW

A Salvation Army survey of religious and social conditions in Britain eighty years after William Booth's blue-print for salvation – with a preface by
GENERAL ERIK WICKBERG

HODDER AND STOUGHTON
LONDON SYDNEY AUCKLAND TORONTO

Contents

PART THREE Ministry for Women and Girls

PART FOUR In Darkest England Now

PART FIVE The Soldier

Preface

CHARLES BOOTH, THE great investigator of poverty in East London, published the first volume of his *Life and Labour of the London Poor* in 1889. William Booth, founder of The Salvation Army, brought out his *In Darkest England and the Way Out*, in 1890. At the time William Booth's book attracted the most attention, and considerable controversy, but with the passing of time, and in recent years, the work of the sociologist has stolen the thunder of the Salvationist.

At the time the two men were mistaken for each other; indeed, occasionally, they still are. Yet all they had in common was their surname. They never met and in belief and method they were poles apart.

The social scientist insisted that one must define poverty, count and classify the poor, find out what keeps them poor, and how they react to their poverty. Not for nothing was Charles Booth President of the Statistical Society.

The Salvationist Booth, on the other hand, though he made a rough estimate that a tenth of the population was below the poverty line, never felt it necessary to classify them or argue the cause of poverty. If a man is drowning, he said, you throw him a rope. Argue how he came to be in such a precarious position and it will be too late. William Booth, like his Master, looked on the multitude with compassion: 'Go for souls', he commanded his Salvation Army soldiers. 'Go for souls, and go for the worst.'

The 'father of sociology' believed that religiously motivated approaches to social problems were irrelevant, usually insincere, and certainly incompetent. It would be by laws enacted that the people would be saved. Give the aged their pensions, the children their schools; pull down the slums and provide better homes, a greatly improved public health service, libraries, and a beautiful environment. It was a humanitarian programme. If Jerusalem were to be built in England's green and pleasant land, it must be a material city. Any resemblance to the city of God would be coincidental.

Alas, as this book shows, man cannot live by bread alone, nor by bread and butter, nor by the most enlightened social security. Beatrice Webb was related to Charles Booth, and helped him with his monumental research. She wrote, in *My Apprenticeship* (1926), 'In these latter days of deep disillusionment it is hard to understand the naive belief of the most vigorous minds of the seventies and eighties, that it was by science and science alone that all human misery ultimately would be swept away.'

Now it has been suggested to me that the time has come to publish the Salvationist reaffirmation of William Booth's thesis, *In Darkest England Now*, in 1974. At the time the book first came out, Professor Thomas Huxley furiously attacked General Booth in the columns of *The Times*–and not only his book, but his personal integrity as well. On that issue, time has given its verdict to the General. We here claim that time has also decided for William Booth, and against Charles Booth.

We agree that it is good to classify the poor, count them and make the best possible provision for them. We are wholeheartedly for Britain's Welfare State, but we insist that, inevitably, something vital is left out. One needs more than hard facts, good laws and State aid. As we seek to show in the following pages, the heart is also needed. The thirteen-year-old schoolgirls, mothers of illegitimate children, who are in our care require more than social security. The alcoholic who tries to stop drinking, who succeeds for a while, then fails, and tries, and fails again and again, must defeat the statisticians and the social scientists. The homeless, the unemployable, the host of mentally retarded, the drug addict and many others all come to The Salvation Army for aid.

Yet it is not the poor alone who need our ministrations. The exhortation 'Go for souls and go for the worst' does not tell us to address our efforts to the socially deprived to the exclusion of the affluent. Sinfulness is not a social classification. Rising living standards bear little or no relation to moral standards, leave alone

Christian ones. Alas, sometimes it seems to me that the more people have of this world's goods, the less they think of the God who is the giver of all gifts. So that, when we think of 'Darkest England', we are not concerned with the poor as such.

At the heart of all we do is insistence on the need of salvation for all. Although the emphasis in our work may change here and there from direct evangelism to community social service, the motivation is the same and will remain so. We witness to a power beyond ourselves, a power that can change men and women: the saving power of Christ.

We shall go on singing and witnessing, praising God and inviting men and women to accept salvation up and down the land, on street corners, seaside beaches and village greens. The Army band is not going to give way to soup kitchens. We have always believed in the helping hand and we have also always believed that we must preach the gospel. We must sound out our trumpet-calls to conversion.

In the series of interviews which follow, the attempt is made to show how these new times affect William Booth's original vision of *In Darkest England and the Way Out*. Though the opinions given do not necessarily represent the views of The Salvation Army, they all come from officers and soldiers engaged in the Salvation War, as William Booth often termed it.

I take this opportunity of expressing my thanks to all who have been concerned with the production of this book. I should add that all the statements in it do not necessarily represent the official viewpoint of The Salvation Army.

Erik Wickberg
May 1973.

PART ONE

Corps Life

CHAPTER ONE

The New Hunger

'MAN CANNOT LIVE by bread alone.' Commissioner Kaare Westergaard, in charge of Salvation Army evangelical operations in Britain, speaks of the new social challenge to the Army and how hundreds of corps are responding to it.

Times change, Commissioner. The Army in Britain has always concentrated on the evangelical ministry; the priority has always been soul-saving. I know this is harder these days but do you still get people converted in the old-time way?

Yes. Not in the large numbers of earlier times but, thank God, people are still being saved. Only the other day we had a great victory in this way: only one man, but typical of many similar contemporary cases. The man was invited to the meetings again and again and at last he came. He did not like them at first but he kept coming until the time came when he knelt at the Mercy Seat. He stood before the people, in the newly-renovated hall, in full Army uniform, to give a glowing testimony to the power of Christ in his life. There are many, many others. Throughout the whole of the British Territory we receive the most heartening stories of people being converted.

In Yorkshire, at Malton, there is a young Lieutenant who wrote me: 'Dear Commissioner, Could you find time to write four letters to four new soldiers who are to be sworn-in here on March 18th?' This is wonderful! For if you knew The Salvation Army in Malton, a hard, struggling battlefield for us, you would realise that the conversion of these four people is something of a miracle. They are all in full uniform and help to swell the considerable force of new Salvation soldiery, not large enough, but sufficient to cause us to thank God for present mercies.

At present there seems to be an explosion of corps community and social work in your territory. This is ironic because Britain, the motherland of all those Salvation Army territories abroad, is now learning from the Americans, the Canadians, the Australians and others that corps work can be in part social work, whereas before they were exclusively evangelistic citadels. Would you comment on this?

Coming back to Britain after ten years on the Continent I would say without hesitation that the most noticeable change in the pattern of corps life is along the lines you mention. In re-establishing contact with corps I knew years ago, I find that in almost every instance a programme of community service has been introduced. I look upon it as a very good sign. I don't think that it is consciously an imitation of the American style or of any other overseas countries. People are just not so meeting-conscious as they were in our early days. Then, they used to come to the Army on Sunday, Monday, Tuesday and any night of the week. There was very little in their homes to keep them there and they did not have the wide range of interests they have now—the car, the T.V., the radio . . . We had to find something to take the place of all these abundant week-night meetings and I think that that is partly where the community service comes in.

Also, I would like to think we have made a discovery of a need—deep, sometimes tragic, but different from the lines of that old Darkest England of 1890. The need is not now for bread and cocoa, for old clothes and free meals—there's still some demand for that—but, in the main, the new deprived people are those of whom it was said, 'You never had it so good.' In the midst of relative affluence there is a hunger of the spirit, there is loneliness, mental depression, marital discord, adolescent unrest, and the plight of the aged, who have better pensions but who know well the meaning of the words of Jesus when He said, 'Man cannot live by bread alone.'

Does this mean that your people have become social workers? General Booth would not have approved of that!

Not at all; we maintain the Founder's aim—go for souls. The new tactics put The Salvation Army in touch with all sorts of people of whom we knew nothing previously. Over a period of years I think the Army turned in upon itself. We had a strategy, but less and less chance to accomplish it. Now, with community services, we have found a mission in this new sector of public need. The new 'down and out' may be the middle-class housewife who drinks, or the compulsive gambler; there are many maladies in the affluent society.

You are doing great things among the old folk?
Yes. The over-sixty clubs are part of our community service. A week ago I spent the week-end at Sunbury with leaders of these clubs. We had to have two week-end conferences because there are so many leaders. Though this work is a comparatively recent innovation in Britain, we have 550 registered clubs with 58,000 members. Many of these elderly people had no previous association with The Salvation Army. Furthermore, they all represent a link with a family, with children and grandchildren and, indeed, through the work of these clubs some of the younger people are now attending the meetings.

Isn't there a dichotomy here between these younger evangelical innovators and the older, preacher-ministerial men? These latter see their work as attracting folk to the citadel to hear them preach, to share in worship, in praise with the band and songsters. Now, they ask what are you doing for those 58,000 old folks? You provide them with a club—what is that to do with soul-saving?
I have heard that view expressed. But I insist that the clubs have everything to do with soul-saving. We create a fellowship, we share recreation and other interests for these old folk. In many instances, they are lonely people. This we do in the purposes of Christ and always with the soul-saving objective of The Salvation Army in mind.

I personally have removed from my mind any objections to our new tactics which divide our methods into direct and indirect evangelism. You have recorded interviews, I know, with numerous officers who find that the social-service approach is the Christian approach. These officers are winning people to God and they will not accept that their method is inferior to preaching.

To preach, to proclaim the gospel by word of mouth is no more effective than to proclaim the gospel by the service of one's hands or one's feet. Some of our preachers would have difficulty in producing results equal to those of our people engaged in community service.

This leads me to another problem which arises from what you have been saying. There are corps where it is traditional now, within the short space of a hundred years, for a large band and songster brigade to play to themselves and their Salvationist friends and relations unto the third and fourth generation. They keep to their Army way—it is quite a ritual. Where this conservatism resides in the people of the corps and the officer wishes to have this new 'outreach' you mentioned, what can we do? Must we leave it?

No, we cannot just leave it. In some instances the position is as you say. But on the other hand there are signs of improvement, evidence of a new approach. In recent years many of our bands and songster brigades have moved into eventide and convalescent homes and hospitals. There they exercise a ministry of music and song. After a programme, they will break up and visit the inmates or patients in the various institutions. There are thousands of splendid men and women in our bands and songster brigades and many of them are alive to the new challenge.

At Chelmsford some weeks ago I met the Mayor and members of the Appeals Committee for money for our £165,000 building. We received compensation when our present hall came into a road-widening scheme, but we need a lot more money. I went to see the site where they had already begun to dig the foundations. Now Chelmsford, as you know, has a band tradition. One thinks of the band at Chelmsford in the same way as of the Regent Hall, Chalk Farm or Tottenham Citadel bands. Now, judge my surprise and delight when I discovered from the architect's plans that there is no band or songster room, as such, in the planned building. The band and songsters recognise that in these days you cannot demand floor space where a band can store its music and instruments during the week, and where they can hang their caps and coats on Sundays. There are 'all-purposes' rooms which will be used for community services during the week and into which the band will put its paraphernalia as needed. When you get a bandmaster, bandsmen and local officers of the Chelmsford tradition to support such a plan, then that is an encouraging sign.

Some of your young people, the better educated and radical, including university undergraduates, say that the average bandsman is just a member of a club and if he were deprived of this special interest of his, he would probably not be with us at all. What do you think?

There is perhaps an element of truth in it as applied to a minority. But the bands of this territory have done much to retain the men, to maintain the strong masculinity in Salvation Army corps. For that I am grateful! I remember going to Monkwearmouth where we have one of our finest Salvation Army bands and sitting in the officers' room when the vicar of the district came in to greet me. He said, 'Commissioner, how I envy the officer here at Monkwearmouth his fine Salvation Army band! How I wish, when I am in the parish church, that I had, seated in front of the pulpit on a Sunday morning, a crowd of men in number and in quality like the men here in Monkwearmouth Band.'

This is a point we could apply to many places. It ill-becomes our young people to criticise the role our bands have played in providing an outlet of service for men Salvationists.

Yet, having said that, I will admit that one of our difficulties in the past has been that we have not had enough variety of forms of service into which we could invite our men as an addition to their brass-band duties. But with the increase in community service there are signs that we shall be enabled to employ some of our men in these social-service expressions.

You could not accept that those men who are very interested in brass bands, and relatively inactive in any other area, are not sincere and dedicated?

No, not at all. I think they are hard-working, genuine Christians. Some of them have been led to believe that their only outlet of service in a corps is as bandsmen.

Is it still the case that the would-be Salvation soldier voluntarily signs a covenant, a promise that he will not drink?
Yes, so if he does drink that is a breach of contract, a breach of promise.

It is the same with the 'no gambling' rule. When we had a Salvationist winning a car in a raffle, I made it my business to put my hand upon the pulse of The Salvation Army in Britain. I wanted to discover whether there should be some modification of our attitude. I did not want my own strong feelings, my own deep convictions, to sway my administration if in fact they were merely personal. But the pulse of the Army in this matter supported my point of view. I want our officers to feel that if any breach of the rule occurs and this comes to light, they must deal firmly with it and that there is 100 per cent support for them from National Headquarters.

There is an acute lack of officers—you are calling out retired officers to take charge of corps and you have corps that are without officers. There is cold comfort in the fact that this problem is common to all the churches. It seems to be a world problem. But how does it affect your command? How do you propose to solve it?
It might be solved by a dramatic, large intake of candidates for officership, but I cannot see that happening in the immediate future. To make matters worse, we are just now affected by the many retirements arising from the very large training sessions that we had in the 1920s. Then we had 500–600 cadets per session—they are now about sixty-five, the retirement age. As far as the intake of cadets is concerned, we shall do rather better this year than we did last. We expect about 100 new cadets—not enough, but better than last year.

We try to cope with the situation as best we can. We have approximately 1,000 corps in the British Territory; of those over 200 are without officers. About 100 of these corps are looked after by auxiliary officers. These are experienced soldiers, many of them retired from business, who feel that they could give a period of service as officers. We have worked out a course of training and I look to that to help us considerably.

We are also pursuing our policy of merging certain corps that are in close proximity. Lower Openshaw and Manchester Temple have now become Manchester Citadel. Middlesbrough West-end and Middlesbrough Central are now Middlesbrough West-Central. There are many other instances. I do not mention these cases as full-scale advances, but at least they show that we are acting to meet a serious situation.

Is it working effectively?
Yes, especially when we bring about the merger in a new building. It is also essential for the sake of the traditions and susceptibilities of the people of the two merged corps to give the new corps a new name. For example, the Borough and Kennington Lane Corps became Southwark. It has a psychological effect.

Then we have to close certain corps. Some are registered when there has not been any viable Salvation Army activity for years. This is a sad decision to make and sad for some of the people involved. But, again, all the churches are having to face this and we must face it—it is no use pretending.

Some small corps are to have society status. Take, for instance, Thornton Heath. Less than a mile away is West Croydon. Now we must say to the strong Thornton Heath Corps, 'You must be "mother and father" to West Croydon Corps. We realise that you cannot support a full-scale programme, but at least do a Sunday night meeting, a home league and a Sunday-school.'

Then we are now working out what we call a group command. Probably the first experiment will be at Ipswich where about eight corps will be grouped together. Something like six officers will be appointed, not to any specific corps but to the group command, of course with the aid of the local Salvationists.

Where do your lay-workers come in on this? As you know, for a century or so, the Methodists had great success with them. At Basildon the Captain said to one of her converts, 'Would you act as a pastoral visitor?' She pays her and the system works well.
I have asked Captain Keith Banks of Clapton Congress Hall to speak to the British officers about this employment of lay-people full time—salaried lay-people, to help him in his corps work at Congress Hall. I visualise the time when most of our corps will have

a full-time social-worker and perhaps a full-time youth-worker, working under the direction of the corps council and the Commanding Officer.

What about The Salvation Army in Northern Ireland?
We have wonderful Salvationist forces there, who have the respect of both sides in that conflict. The work is so hard that we give officers the option of coming out after a set period. We say, 'You and your wife must need a break. Do you think you should come away now and take an appointment elsewhere?' The remarkable and moving fact is that many of the officers insist on remaining. We have lost a lot of Army property, of course, and we are trying to help them to acquire new properties where possible. Belfast Citadel was completely demolished as a result of that bomb explosion some time ago. It is not thought that the people who used the bombs intended to destroy Salvation Army property, but our citadel was in close proximity to a building that belonged to the Co-operative Society.

You have been arranging work among Ugandan Asians?
Some of our officers have distinguished themselves in this field. I went last week to Newbury at the invitation of Brigadier-General Bates, who is responsible for a very large camp where they had between 3–4,000 Asians, and he paid a warm tribute to the Army. When the Asians first got in, he could get no one to help, even with the cleaning of the camp. It had been standing empty for eight years after the American Air Force had used it. Some of the people sent up from the Employment Exchanges refused the work because they were afraid that these Asians coming in would take the housing and the jobs they needed themselves. So they went on strike. But our Major Albert Stevenson and his wife came up to see how Brigadier-General Bates was getting on. He told the Major his predicament and the Major said, 'Look, leave it with me. I will get people up to clean.' He gathered together the people from the corps and the members from the ministers' fraternal. For two weeks they set to and cleaned the camp.

When the Asians took possession of the camp he and his wife became the welfare officers. They have done a wonderful job there. When I went down I saw 350 of the Ugandan Asian children in school. One of the Headmaster's assistants took me down to the college where fifty teenagers are pursuing further education. I spoke to the parents and when, at the invitation of the Rector of Newbury, I used the parish church for a meeting at night I enrolled two new soldiers of The Salvation Army in front of the high altar of the church and under the Army flag. In the congregation there were about fifty or sixty Asian families. Major Frank Ward, of Hemel Hempstead, earned high praise from Brigadier-General Bates because he, more than any other person, had helped to find accommodation for Asian families. There was warm praise, too, for our Men's Social Services and our Goodwill Department for donating blankets and articles of furniture to the Asians.

How is the Army integrating with coloured immigrants?
Well, go to Catford, a stronghold of Army traditionalism. Look at the singing company. Fifty per cent of them are coloured children. It is more difficult to get their parents integrated into the corps. But we are producing future cosmopolitan corps; there is no doubt about that at all.

CHAPTER TWO

Modern Babylon

'MODERN BABYLON IS a mild description,' the Officer responsible for Salvation Army operations in London's West End reports:

What do you think about the relationship of Victorian-style evangelical work of the sort William Booth was so good at and the social service to which he came reluctantly and late in life?
As far as I am concerned, community social service is not an alternative to the gospel but an expression of it. Although in our social work we are not always able to wag a Bible under people's noses, we are none the less working in Christ's name to rehabilitate the whole man, physically, mentally and spiritually. If The Salvation Army loses sight of this spiritual dimension we have lost our way. The social and the evangelical are two sides of the same coin. We must cherish both in our thinking.

Then why is it necessary in a society which has never had it so good, where there is a minimum subsistence level fixed by the State, and where many avenues of assistance exist to abolish poverty, where the local authority has a statutory obligation to prevent homelessness? Why do you have to do your social work in London in these modern times?
The welfare state is a very good thing as a broad principle but there are forms of need that can better be met by those who are not part of the bureaucracy of the State. There are many forms of service which can be better met by those outside the statutory services. I

would agree, though, that there is need for better co-ordination and more mutual respect between the statutory bodies and the voluntary bodies. There is often a tendency on each side to discredit the other. Statutory workers sometimes refer to the voluntary people as 'do-gooders', which has uncomplimentary connotations. The voluntary people are equally scathing about those in the statutory services.

Is it your experience that the authorities who, by statute and custom, ought to help you, do in fact help you?
As far as youth work is concerned we are in receipt of grant aid, but we provide people with the academic qualifications. Sometimes the person who has the academic qualification does not succeed as well as the person who lacks such qualifications but has something else in terms of devotion and personality.

Are you required to know the law with regard to what you may expect in grant aid and what you may not expect?
We are learning to find our way about the maze of corridors of power. It is a maze, believe me. One can become frustrated by the way one is passed from one official to the next, with nobody wanting to make a final decision. Having said that, I acknowledge gratefully that we are in receipt of considerable financial assistance with our youth work. In addition, we are to open temporary accommodation for young people at risk in London and we are seeking grant aid for this.

What do you mean by 'at risk'?
On the soup runs and at railway stations we often meet the youngster who has come to London looking for a job and a fresh start. Sometimes this is from an area of high unemployment, or there has been a break in the family. Often these young people come to London with the naive notion that once they arrive there their problems are at an end. Sometimes they haven't a clue where to go. They have no money and they are easy game for confidence tricksters and worse. The moral dangers are tremendous, especially for girls.

As newcomers they are specially vulnerable, for if they do not have an address they do not qualify for social security benefits?

That is so. I had a man in my office this morning, a Czechoslovakian. He is not the rough and ready type, and he had found our Army hostels, the typical hostel, more than he could take. He had been walking about for the last three days and nights and was just at the end of himself when he came to us. He has now been taken in at our Booth House and, having spent a night there, will qualify for social security.

In our advice bureau we have an arrangement with hotels which send every week a list of jobs that are vacant: dishwashers, porters and so on. Some of these offer accommodation, so we are able to use these places as temporary 'pads' and help the 'down and out' in that way.

Part of your 'beat' is in the West End—is it the sexual jungle it is alleged to be—the 'swinging' city?
Our experience suggests that it is as bad as its reputation, or worse. Pornographic books and magazines, 'blue' films, call girls, nude shows, homosexuality—the lot. Contrary to what many permissive people forecast, the lifting of restrictions, the so called 'healthy' freedom, has made matters much worse. There is more perversion as well as straight promiscuity. Drugs are widely used and inflict enormous damage. The V.D. rate is high. What W. T. Stead called 'the Maiden Tribute of Modern Babylon' is a mild description of what is happening in London now.

We have recently begun a counselling service to be manned by qualified people with experience in helping drug addicts and sexual deviants. There are many people who come within the scope of our ministry who have those problems. Some men and women who kneel at the Penitent-form at Regent Hall have these and other acute difficulties. They need help.

Was it just a romantic illusion that, in the old days, we used to say that their 'sins rolled away', they were 'washed in the blood', they were 'made new'? They got up there, on the spot, and said, 'I am saved!' Now you suggest therapy, clinical treatment, psychiatric advice by qualified experts. Have we lost faith in the Penitent-form?
No. These things are not mutually exclusive, but rather complementary. In the past year I have seen people whose lives are radically

altered as a result of what happened at the Penitent-form. A man who is working with us at the moment stood near the open-air meeting and he was invited to come along to the Army. He was an actor doing small parts for the I.B.A. and some script-writing. He had his first contact with the Army at a drug-centre. A cadet invited the man to the hall and had the nerve to say, 'Sit near the front; you may want to go to the Penitent-form.' The man retorted with a couple of four-letter words. Yet later he did as he was recommended. He sat near the front and he did kneel at the Penitent-form. The whole direction of that man's life was altered. Some weeks before Christmas he was in hospital, having had a heart attack. A doctor inquired, 'Do you smoke?' 'No,' he said. The doctor had reasons to be suspicious of this. 'Used you to smoke?' he went on. 'When did you give it up?' 'April 7th,' the man replied. 'I smoked sixty or seventy a day until that day. That was when I gave my heart to Christ.' It was all true and the doctor was much impressed.

Are you not a little discomfited that William Booth's old adage, 'Go for souls and go for the worst', is less quoted? You know now that with many people this is but part of a complicated process of salvation which may take quite a long time?

No. This does not depress me. I have always believed that while there may be an instant crisis there must also be a process. For some people things are much simpler. There are people who come to the Penitent-form, and afterwards there is no need to arrange psychiatric treatment or anything of that nature. The direction of their life has been changed.

Many of these people help each other. Take Harry, as an example. He is a middle-aged man, once a jockey. One day he was walking down Oxford Street and heard the band play a tune which struck a chord in his memory. He followed the band to the hall and after some weeks knelt at the Penitent-form. His family said to him, 'What has happened to you?' That was more than a year ago. He is now a Salvationist and a radiantly happy man. He is coming with me on a tour of the Holy Land in a few weeks' time. He has not needed any help but the Bible, prayer, our fellowship and his own faith.

Another example is a woman who has worked for members of the

Royal Family and others in 'high society'. She is now housekeeper to someone with an address in an exclusive block of flats – very high-class indeed. As she walked her dog in Green Park on Sunday she used to meet a Salvationist on the way to the Regent Hall, our citadel. Eventually the woman attended our meeting. After many weeks, she said, 'You know, I should go and kneel at the front; but I could never do it.'

One Sunday night, into our hall, into the gallery where the woman sat, within a yard of her, another woman came – a methylated-spirits drinker. She kept interrupting the meeting in a rowdy fashion. One or two of our people tried to restrain her but not to evict her, for that would have caused even more disturbance. I remember thinking that anyone who was in that part of the building was not going to get much out of that Service. Yet it was from that noisy place, within a yard of the drunken woman, that the woman came out to the Penitent-form – the woman who had said she could never do it. She told me, 'It was as though someone put a hand on my shoulder.' As a result of that conversion, but merely incidentally, we have had a donation to our funds, and the woman's employer has himself been to meetings. This convert now wears our uniform. She engages in hospital visitation every Sunday afternoon, proving to be highly suited for hospital work.

What about your wealthy and distinguished 'parishioners'? They include the dwellers at Buckingham Palace as well as other exclusive places. They don't need your social work – do they acknowledge your existence?

Some of them do – even the Queen herself – not only with money but with more substantial support. We have been invited to the Palace. The Queen showed us that she was most concerned and well informed about the work we are doing. When my wife and I were at a reception at Lancaster House, the Duke of Edinburgh talked to us for some time. He asked some pertinent questions. One was, 'Tell me: do you find that if you put up hostels which are too posh, the really poor people feel uncomfortable?' My reply was that if the hostel was too elaborate we would appeal to a different kind of clientele but we must never forget those in the most dire need. His reply to that, I remember, was, 'I would know the feeling. When I want to come into the house with mud on my boots I feel I am not wanted.'

Do you work for, or believe in, the existence of what William Booth called, 'the submerged tenth?'
My terms of reference are rather wider. Oddly enough, I feel that needy people may not need money. On Christmas Day we provide a luncheon and entertainment for about 300 people who would otherwise be on their own. Many people ring up to ask 'Can we help?' Two men who helped last year were quite wealthy. One came in a Jensen car. He was out all night helping us to distribute 600 parcels of food and clothes for people sleeping out. He was up working with us all of Christmas Eve night, and after an hour or two of sleep on Christmas Day he came to wash up and work like a trojan all day with our needy people. He is by no means the only well-to-do among the not-idle rich who show interest and give practical help. One woman, an internationally famous surgeon, has been on our 'staff' on Christmas Days. She has helped with the washing up and said 'It has been the best Christmas Day I have ever known'.

Some people who help are, of course, helping themselves. Money and security are not enough of themselves. One of our helpers is a property developer. He counts himself one of us, although I cannot see him wearing Salvation Army uniform! What happens, I think, is that there is fulfilment in helping others, and perhaps assuagement of loneliness or some other sort of lack in their own lives.

People of all kinds come to us. Perhaps our Sunday-night congregation (500–600 souls) is the most cosmopolitan in London. There will be a sprinkling of the highbrow, the middle class, and students, but it always includes the poor. There are odd people and the slightly drunk. They are not only tolerated but woe betide anyone who shows intolerance towards them.

One man who comes to us was a surgeon, but an alcoholic. He has been in and out of prison and he is in prison at the moment. For ten years he would come to the Rink. He often interfered with the meetings, shouting obscene comments and abuse at us as we marched outside. But he is accepted by our people; they care about him. I am proud of the Army when I remember that.

Do you think we need bringing up-to-date—more in line with modern conditions?
The Founder is supposed to have said, 'Let there be adaptation of method but continuity of principle.' In many ways we have been slow to change and when we have changed, sometimes we have changed for the wrong reason. Some have asserted that an open-air meeting is not effective and then we cut it out and put nothing in its place. That is not worthy of us. In some places the only change that has taken place is a diminishing of activity, the lessening of out-thrust, rather than a changing of tactics and expression.

I certainly think that we need to be more careful of our use of time-honoured phrases, meaningful to us but mumbo-jumbo to those who are not versed in our ways.

Our great need is for a new baptism of conviction. Some of us go through the motions of evangelism without being evangelical. We have always gone out at ten, two, and six-thirty on Sundays. But do we care very much about the people who are there? We can become mechanical, we can grind to a halt.

What about your wife—what is her status? There is some criticism in the Army these days that women do not achieve female ministry in the Catherine Booth sense, and that many women, even if they achieve it, lose it when they marry.
Some of the ablest women do lose their officership, or rather let it be submerged in the officership of their husbands. Some women, who in their own right would be leaders, very good leaders, are overshadowed, wrongly overshadowed, by men who are not their equals.

Does marriage invalidate the concept of female ministry?
It probably modifies it, but in some ways it can enrich it. A married woman's ministry can be enriched by experience of domestic life, of childbearing, of family life. But often, during the years when the children are small, she needs to devote herself to them. Then, having got out of the run of public work she is content to let her husband carry on.

Do the people at Regent Hall look on your wife as a part of the ministry?

Yes. My wife preaches only occasionally, but every Sunday she takes part in meetings: she runs the over-sixty club and she goes visiting with me. She contacts the people around the open-air meetings and helps in many other ways.

. . .

THE DOG DID NOT ASK QUESTIONS: An officer in London's West End talks to some of his 'clients', using a tape recorder.

George, you have spent quite a long time in the West-End scene. What brought you to London in the first place?

I came to get work, partly because I felt rejected by my own provincial society and also because of the fantasies that the idea of London gave me. These I had from magazines and books. I came from a hospital in Kent. From sixteen up to the age of twenty I suffered one form or another of nervous breakdown. I've only known my mother for the past three or four years. I was adopted as a child. My father died and I was shoved into a children's home. I had a complete mental breakdown at the age of six. I fell victim to a homosexual who raped me. I was just learning how to read and write at the age of sixteen. But always I was mentally off-balance.

When I left school it was discovered that I couldn't cope with the outside world. As I was cracking up they put me in hospital. But some efficient bureaucrat was saying, 'Well, look, he now seems O.K. Why the hell doesn't he get out and earn a living?' So out I go into the society that doesn't want to give me a chance. To get a job and make headway you are always fighting against your unfavourable background. You cannot get references and consequently, before any organisation agrees to help you, you must hit rock-bottom. It is a vicious circle, really. Before you can be helped up you have to be down and out. But you never get over such a fall. When I came to London I became involved in the homosexual scene and pornography. I took part in photographic sessions and blue films. It took quite an amount of drugs to keep me going.

I left London, went to Oxford and the Church Army helped me. I met a girl and for a time I got on pretty well until she discovered that I was taking drugs. I was put into a clinic for three months. One of the night-nurses there was actually killed. There were always fights. With another fellow I broke into surgeries, and brought 'gear' back to the clinic; it was through us supplying gear that we were caught. I was lucky not to go before Quarter Sessions. I was asked to give evidence and I had to leave Oxford because I was known to the police. Eventually I went to Brighton and in the hostel there was a dog. He didn't even know me. He didn't know what I was. He didn't ask questions. I would take him out for a walk, and he accepted me as I was. 'Why can't human beings be like this?' I asked myself. 'Why can't people show love as this dog does? Why must they always see the bad in me?' That is why I reject society. I no longer want to go back to it. I don't feel I could face up to it. I don't suppose I shall reach even thirty years of age. I shall be twenty-four in March.

The impression I have of the Sally Ann is that it is not enough to play bands on the streets and get people to come to the service, and persuade sinners to kneel at the Penitent-form and get them converted and all that. It is when you show love like The Salvation Army has to me. That changes a person and it means more to God. It is the showing of love, rather than sermons, or words, that makes all the difference. Emotionally the band here at the Regent Hall moves me in a way that I don't feel when I'm 'stoned' on drugs. I realise that there's something missing in me. It hits you like a rock. You think, 'I cannot face up to it.' I cannot trust myself and I cannot trust other people.

I worked in a convalescent home for about three years when I was recovering from a mental breakdown. The hours I worked were pretty long but I enjoyed it; it gave me satisfaction. When the Matron discovered that I had had a mental breakdown she decided she could no longer risk keeping me. You can't trust people . . .

You can't trust some doctors. A large number of people have drug problems in London because doctors are giving patients two- or four-week prescriptions. You take a person who is on tranquillisers. He gets very depressed. He thinks, 'Yes, I'll take one', and before he knows where he is he has taken the lot. Doctors sell 'gear' to people with drug problems, you know that, rather than give a prescription; they are absolutely 'bent'. And not only in London. Southampton seems a very quiet town but when I went there not long ago I was astonished. I lived in derelict houses and the number of streets I walked down that teemed with prostitutes and drug addicts was incredible. The amount of drug trafficking that goes on in Southampton is tremendous. It is a main port for drugs. One fellow offered me over 3,000 tablets of dexadrine. He said they were quite easy to sell and so they were. We started off in Bournemouth, then went to Eastbourne and from Eastbourne came to London. If you come direct to London you are asking for trouble.

Doesn't it worry you that by pushing these drugs you are getting others into the same situation as yourself?
Sometimes you feel you are doing somebody a favour. Besides, you often feel you don't give two damns for anyone. I feel that with some of my friends I am doing them a hell of a favour in giving them the stuff. Sometimes you feel that you are pushing somebody into a grave that has a nothingness that some call eternity.

Is there any connection between prostitution and pornography, or prostitution and drugs?
Yes, and also between drugs and some sorts of pop songs. If you listen to some of the records you find them singing about drugs. One very popular song is 'Brown Sugar', which is recognised as Lebanese 'hash'.

But prostitution is often a matter of poverty. I know a girl at the moment. She was homeless. She went to Social Security but she could not get any money. It was virtually useless trying, as she had no address. Eventually she got so browned off she decided she could not carry on. She couldn't sleep on the station for long; she was always shoved on. She could not sleep out in the cold all the time. So eventually she decided to sell herself for the money to buy a kip and some grub. It's as simple as that . . .

'George' is real; he is still alive and he has by no means told all his story. There are hundreds like him in the dark side of London.

. . .

THE BEST SOUP IN THE BUSINESS—but it is not enough.

You are a Salvationist?
Yes. I am a convert of about two years ago.

How did it happen?
I first attended the Army when I was at college. A friend had been staying in Cambria House, which we knew as the cheapest hostel around. She became involved in work going on at the Regent Hall Corps, Oxford Street. They were short of help with their all-night club. We were sharing a flat together, so I went down with her. There I happened to bump into a young man, who is now my husband. Mainly because he attended the meeting on Sunday, I attended as well. We were married about eighteen months ago, after I became a Salvationist. My husband was a lifelong Salvationist.

What sort of religious background did you have?
My mother sent me to Sunday-school at the Methodist Church until I was about fourteen. Then I began to think things out for myself. At the Army I met Christians who seemed to have a faith that mattered, that meant something to them. I could not dismiss it and in the end I accepted it for myself.

What college were you attending?
A speech-therapy training college; I was in my final year. That was when it happened. I did not have any instant dramatic conversion. It was gradual. There was a sermon in particular. One of the points was, 'You cannot sit on the fence for the rest of your life. You must decide whether you are for Jesus or against Him.' That was something I had been doing for a long time, sitting on the fence. When I got 'off the fence' and committed myself as a Christian it was wonderful but difficult to explain.

What is your present job?
For the past two years now I have been working as a speech-therapist for the Inner London Education Authority. Until three months ago I was working in clinics and special schools for the sub-normal, dividing my time between the clinics and the schools and doing a lot of travelling round. Three months ago I changed my job. I am now a full-time speech therapist working five days a week in a new school for the physically handicapped.

Then how do you find time to work for the 'dossers'?

Well, I didn't think I was involved enough and the need really is urgent. Twice a week a soup-van goes out from Regent Hall – about five people all night. About midnight we go to places where people are sleeping out. Other teams are doing this, also, and we co-ordinate to some extent to avoid doing the same areas. We go to Victoria Station, Mortimer Street, Euston and Charing Cross Stations.

Are there many in need of this soup and whatever you have?
Victoria Station, about half-a-dozen people. But they are 'regulars'. At Mortimer Street Employment Exchange people queue up for casual labour jobs the next day. There's normally about half-a-dozen people there, starting a queue for the next day, when we arrive just after midnight. At Euston Station there's up to twenty people; about a third of them are habitual dossers. A lot of them have drink or other psychological problems. We see these every week. There's a large floating population of casual labourers, who are homeless. People come down from the north, especially young people. London is still very much a 'magnet', a city with streets paved with gold.

But the real thing is disillusionment and misery. Hotel accommodation is hard to get and costs a fortune. If you sleep out for a couple of nights you get dirty and untidy, and then you can't get a job. If you do get a job, as happens to most people, there's no pay until the end of the week. So it's a hungry time, sleeping out for the first week at least before they begin to get on their feet. Many do make the grade – get on their feet eventually. Then they disappear from the stations and other places. Of course, others go under . . . We don't really know what happens to them.

A few come back. One lad in particular reappeared and asked how we were getting on. But he would not tell us what he was doing. He was well dressed . . .

Others down at Charing Cross, older people, habitual dossers, sleep out regularly. These are the typical dossers. A lot of them are alcoholics. Some could not work if they had the chance. They will not settle in a hostel. They could not live at home. These are the old style 'down and outs' for whom one must have compassion. It is so hard to love them. They are sometimes verminous; their clothes are fusty; their health is bad; one imagines that they are part of that same submerged tenth William Booth saw sleeping out on the benches by the Thames about a hundred years ago. It has been stated that there are 30,000 sleeping out in Britain now.

It is said that many of them are mentally affected; that if they were rescued and put in hostels many of them would just die. They are homeless by choice. Would you agree?
No. They are not there by choice. I agree that many have not settled in hostels because of their problems. They must be out; they must be on the move; they could not cope with community life. They are 'loners'; put them in an institution and it feels like a prison to them. But they want help. I have met one man who lives that way by choice, but when you see the sort of life most of them lead; they do not choose to sleep out in the streets, in the cold and the wet. No, hardly any of them.

You might be saying that you don't think they should be allowed the choice, even if it is their choice. Such a life should be forbidden to anyone for any reasons?
They need psychological and social aid. Taking them off the streets and putting them in a hostel would not work at all. It does not deal with their problem. They cannot exist indoors; they cannot live with other people. Some sort of rehabilitation process is necessary where it would work gradually. One would get them indoors in special conditions in small groups. The people in charge would understand their problems.

Do you think the Army could help with such a difficult and expensive project? It would be expensive in terms of money and man-power.
I would like to see the Army do more for this 'lost' legion. We could provide more accommodation and do more on the streets. One voluntary agency has full-time workers with these men. They go out every night of the week and really get to know them; then they can sort out the ones they feel can benefit by being taken inside and helped in homes, in small groups. Full-time workers are hard to find, but they would do better than volunteers, one evening a week. There's much follow-up work to be done. We often meet people with whom we cannot cope in the half-hour available. They require

more time, more skill. Some are not going to improve, but I think a lot would. I would like to see the Army do more in this way. The problem is large at the moment. We have counted eighty men in one night sleeping at Charing Cross Station and thirty to forty at Euston.

Is it much, do you think – a bowl of soup?
The soup is to warm them up. But the real work is to find newcomers, to help those who can be helped, especially young people. We send some to the Regent Hall for extra aid. We can give clothes; we can find a hostel; we suggest where they can find work. Often you can only give superficial help. But as I said earlier, I feel I ought to get more involved in it.

Are you paid for this work?
No, the soup-van costs money and the soup more than you might imagine. We have been trying to make it more nutritious. If the thing is worth doing it is worth doing with proper soup. Our clients are good judges.

Is it good? Give-away stuff can be atrocious.
We have a reputation for having the best soup! We also give bread, as much as they want, and two cups of soup if requested.

You say that the young are your chief concern? What of the old people?
Many are very old and used to this hopeless, homeless way of life. Some have alcoholic problems; it is difficult to distinguish between an alcoholic and one who drinks heavily. Some are in the catering trade on a casual basis. This is a trade with a large labour turnover. It is one of the less difficult trades to get into when a person hasn't a permanent job or much skill. Some of it is organised on a day-to-day basis. You can turn up tomorrow and start that morning. Much is very low grade, such as dish-washing. It is a very low wage, even though you may put in sixteen hours' work in a day. Then the next day you may have to queue up again to get a job. This is wrong. Some men have to queue all night, sleeping in the street, just to get a day's money. They are willing to work. They should be protected,

and that part of the catering trade should be better organised, just as it is for those with training and skill.

Should more Salvation Army lay-workers help as you do? Or should the work be done by officers?
Certainly, lay-people should be more involved in the Army's work. Some could give a full-time service, as does happen abroad. But on our soup-run we are never short of helpers. The man who runs our group is often turning people down. If you have more than five or six in a team the 'dossers' won't come near. They prefer the same sized group, and people they know.

Many Salvationists prefer to worship at the citadel on Sunday, sing in the songsters. No other involvement–no social service.

The only Army I know is the Regent Hall. I have never sung in the songsters and never had much to do with bands. There is plenty of opportunity to become involved. The bandsmen make music for God; the songsters sing for God and they bless the people, and thousands hear them outside as we march along the crowded streets. We have differing gifts and we must serve God in differing ways. I am keen on the Army remaining 'a church', not becoming a social centre. We need not throw the baby away with the bath water. We can have a social conscience and help the dossers and the lonely and the aged and the young without discarding those other expressions of Salvationism that so many people care about.

. . .

THE MENTALLY HANDICAPPED: A Salvationist worker at The Salvation Army 'Gateway' Club for mentally handicapped young people at the Regent Hall in London describes her work.

Primarily the young people are here for recreational activities: table-tennis, billiards and five-pin football. They play ludo, do jigsaw puzzles; they read, they paint. Some of the girls, with a little more ability, sometimes do cooking–normally a sort of 'do it yourself' cake which, in our coffee break, we sometimes eat, depending upon what it looks like. In the main they do quite well. They also sew, do basket-work, knitting and anything useful which keeps them amused and occupied.

There is a wide range of abilities. Some are much more handicapped than others. One will sit down and do some sort of puzzle over and over again: another will read the same page in a book, never turning to the next. None would hold their own in a normal youth club.

The physical ages range between twenty-one and forty. Mental ages would be about eleven to fifteen. Some cannot add one and one. Others can just write their name, and that is all.

Two men helpers collect the children. They collect them in the minibus which holds fourteen.

At one special Army service our 'children' sang and surprised many people by their responsible behaviour and by the sweetness of their song. They are not always in perfect tune, but then not many ordinary people can sing in good tune. If they are told over and over again what to learn they learn. Pop records they will listen to again and again because they are on all day. Many of these records are simple and primitive and they latch on to their minds.

Some of them you cannot tease. They would get over-excited. Yet one has to be firm with them. If you are foolishly kind they can get excited and quite out-of-hand.

There is scope for more clubs of this kind. They must be affiliated to the Association for Gateway Clubs who examine the various activities during the course of the year. We are helped by the interest of workers from the Westminster City Council. The centre of London is very short of clubs like this to which our 'children' can be affiliated. Ordinary children are catered for adequately; they have day nurseries and schooling. But these mental children are just out of that bracket. Some of the parents have died—so our club-members are kept by sisters or brothers. Some were quite literally turned out—from exhaustion, I should think—because they had no one who could cope or no one who cared. But even those who are fortunate enough to have responsible parents or other relatives need somewhere where they can have a break from their home environment, and their custodians appreciate the break, too.

We are going, a week on Tuesday, to see *Sleeping Beauty on Ice* at the Wembley Pool. It should be quite hair-raising. It is very important that these people should not be cut off from society. The Social Services ought to re-organise their role with regard to these people, to find a means of accepting them. They have nothing, and in some cases nobody. It is a reproach to us all that in a few years the 'children' we have will have nobody and they will live the rest of their lives in geriatric wards. To me that is terrible.

With more resources and staff more of them could be helped to develop skills. Some could be taught at their day centres, not to run a home – obviously that is beyond them – but they could have flatlets, the same as are provided for elderly people. There could be resident nurses and staff to look after them. They could have their own room where they could make a cup of tea; they could sew on buttons; they could wash their own clothes, under supervision. It would be fine for them. Certainly some fifty or sixty per cent could manage on their own, just to do ordinary things, nothing complicated or difficult.

This would be so much better, more humane and civilised, than institutionalising them. They have this mental condition now, and they are going to have a more serious mental condition when they are sent into a hostel. Of course, it is a challenge and one so terrible that we usually choose to ignore it. But soon our 'children' will have nobody to care for them because parents grow old and pass on. Other relatives have their own lives to live.

In the early days of the Army we were able to influence legislation in a number of fields. Today the Army should not only set up clubs for the mentally handicapped but also seek to bring pressure to bear to alter the national situation. If there were only enough people who believed in the cause and would work hard for it, something might be achieved. It would cost a lot of money but lack of experience is not an insurmountable barrier.

. . .

ANOTHER SALVATIONIST concerned with the care of mentally handicapped children in London's West End speaks of her experiences.

Concerning the mentally handicapped child, I have found that some of the mothers are so terribly harassed that everything is forgotten apart from the condition of the child. This seriously affects family life. All begins well with the joy of a child's birth. But as this infant grows the tragic situation becomes apparent. Sometimes the parents ask each other who was to blame. Wrong reasons are given, suspicions are aroused, and accusations are made. They do not take expert advice from anyone, and often they get so involved with the handicapped child that they lose their love for each other. Over the years husband and wife gradually drift apart. Other members of the family, the brothers and sisters, are also sufferers—every relationship within the home seems to be poisoned. When a daughter or son brings home a friend, perhaps someone they are courting, the presence of the 'mental' adult-child sitting there, who may have to use the toilet and things like that in the presence of all is painful and embarrassing. Often the other young people hurry to leave home.

It would be better for the child to be in some kind of institution or home. But one problem is that, over the years, the parents have become dependent on the child. They have to build their whole life round the handicapped child; they come to depend on it. This is wonderful, but in other ways it is catastrophic. They have lost friends; they have not been able to get baby-sitters; the wife has 'let herself go'—no time to go to the hairdresser. Often the parents have no outside interest—they have withdrawn into their lonely, sad, world.

In some flats, tenements, and old, shared houses living conditions are bad. If there were more space—a garden, room to walk and play—it would be better for the afflicted child. But the parents cling to it as it clings to them—a kind of symbiosis. For these shattered adults 'This is your life', just looking after the child, who may be, in physical terms, thirty years of age, but mentally an infant.

We started the special Mental Care Unit at the Regent Hall about eight years ago. The Commanding Officer had met the mother of one of these mentally crippled children. He had seen how over the years she had become more and more broken. The idea was to make a 'break' for a parent, if only for one day a week. We collect the 'boys' and 'girls' (many of whom are of adult years). The mother is therefore freed from about ten o'clock in the morning until four or four-thirty in the afternoon. This means she can have a friend round, with normal conversation about the ordinary things in life. Or she can pop out to the supermarket or hairdresser. The parents find that this helps them to continue through the week, and they look forward to the next week with its interlude of freedom.

During the eight years we have been operating this silent service some local councils have been following our example to some extent. Similar centres now exist in two or three other places. But unfortunately they close when the children reach the age of sixteen. But many of these poor mental victims now have a longer life-span. Where the twenties was about their life expectancy, they now go on into the thirties, forties and sometimes even fifties. This is because of the drugs that are used. We need to be concerned all along the extra miles.

Some of these families are being rehoused by being put into reconditioned tenements, or modern flats, with all mod-cons, such as lovely bathrooms. Yet they only have, in the majority of cases, one living-room. This causes extra problems. It isn't that the normal members of the family want to shun the handicapped relative, but they do need a break and there is little privacy. How can family friction be avoided when one member comes home from a hard day's work to find a heap sitting on the floor? He has to be fed, or taken out to the toilet. Sometimes nerves and emotions cannot stand the strain. Jesus, you remember, found the devils in the man on the cliff top and sent them hurtling into the sea. But more often the devils are in us as we encounter this terrible disability of mental sickness. We are in need of strength and unceasing compassion so that we can serve these afflicted children.

CHAPTER THREE

The Penitent-form in a Box

As AN EXAMPLE of the new kind of Salvation Army evangelical outreach, Basildon in Essex, a new town, is an excellent example. The Captain in charge has been in her present post for seven years – a long time by Salvation Army standards – and expects to stay longer, for she has much more to do.

The Captain is another 'throwback' to Harold Begbie's 'Angel Adjutant' of Edwardian times, except that the social conditions she encounters do not as a rule include drunkenness, wife-beating, crime and extreme poverty.

But first consider the young woman who is engaged in this splendid and highly-successful work.

Her father was a Baptist minister. She joined The Salvation Army when in her early twenties, and not long afterwards entered the Training College. She was content in the Baptist Church except that she felt it was very much a man's world and she, without knowing it, wanted a ministry of women. She had worked in a children's home for a number of years, was yet another with the Florence Nightingale–Mary Slessor syndrome and the 'do-good' urge that is often a mark of female adolescence.

She had been glad to be away from home where she had to go to church regularly, but soon realised that worship, fellowship and service are necessary to Christian development. For her the Army made things different. It was not conversion, for as a Baptist she believed in conversion. She was baptised at the age of thirteen, so she felt herself to be a truly committed Christian before she threw in her lot with the Army. What was new was opportunity as a woman to serve and have responsibility. The woman officer at the local corps seemed to be able to win great respect because of the responsibility she had. To hear her speaking with skill, commanding attention from the men as well as the women, impressed her greatly. She enjoyed the clapping of hands and the 'noisy worship' of the Salvationists to which she was unaccustomed. It was wonderful to see young Salvationists in their uniform, completely dedicated. The desire to dedicate herself in the same way became over-powering. She knelt at the Penitent-form, without feeling the guilt and remorse that some associate with that place. She did not feel wicked, but she did want to be good and it was clear to her that a woman could be very useful in God's service in The Salvation Army. But female ministry is in one way the opposite of women's liberation. She felt that she could work with The Salvation Army and be respected as a woman – equal with men. But there were constraining factors as well as liberating ones. She had worked for a time with the Faith Mission in open-air and door-to-door ministry, so she had a good idea as to the life Salvationism might involve for her.

But most girls, as they grow into womanhood, dream of marriage and having children of their own. Many women officers in The Salvation Army do not marry. Sometimes this is from choice and sometimes it is for lack of opportunity. The ratio of women to men officers in the Army is more than two to one.

The Captain says she felt a definite call to officership and she counted the cost. 'If God intended me to marry it would have to be in the ranks of the Army. I was prepared to take a chance on that.'

It is early yet but she was asked 'Do you regret it?' 'Not at all,' she answered, 'I have been happy, very happy.'

As a Baptist minister's daughter, with little experience of the Army, did you find the going hard, the discipline?

When I arrived at the Training College the first object placed in my hand was a flag. I was to carry it at the head of the march. But I felt conspicuous and embarrassed. I had never marched in my life before. At home if you didn't clap your hands in the meetings it didn't matter. In the Training College if I was the only one not clapping hands it seemed to be a crime. I was very shy, very unsure of myself. I wasn't used to Army ways. But after about six months I began to fit in and really felt part of the Army. At the end of training I was commissioned a Lieutenant and sent to a corps in Durham.

My position as Lieutenant to a Commanding Officer, a woman, did not prove irksome to me. At the Training College I observed orders and regulations. I was new to the Army and observed the 'drill'. As the second officer I had responsibility to help the Major who had served for twenty years or more. If she was tired I did all I could to help.

My first command was in Huntingdonshire. It was a very small corps with terrible quarters. I was alone. The house seemed likely to fall down and it was dirty. On arrival I had to move out and live elsewhere while the young folk in the corps helped me to repair, decorate and refurnish the quarters.

Then we had a marvellous time. At first the congregations were small and we sought to win new people by holding many family services. On an estate not far from the citadel I visited hundreds of homes. About forty children began to attend, and, as is often the case, where the children go, the parents follow. Just as things were moving I was appointed to B . . ., which is a small country village. I discovered afterwards that the Divisional Commander had noticed that I was thinner – wasting away through overwork, or so he thought. There would not be so much to do. I lived alone in an idyllic little cottage; there was a pleasant congregation; a band and songsters; and the local officers were most helpful. It was too pleasant! There was little opportunity to reach the people who needed to be saved. It is possible even in modern England to win people to our meetings and even to the Penitent-form. I found that attendances increased considerably. We had 'youth crushes' and we invited the youth from other churches. This stirred things up. The Army hall became a central point of youth activity. Instead of the bell-ringers going to a pub, they would come to the Army youth get-together. We had a marvellous time. One of the questions asked often and answered sometimes was, 'What is a Christian?' In facing up to that I feel that some young people were helped.

You were alone, you were working hard, although supposed to take it easier. What did your work-load include? What would be the programme?
Monday morning was always correspondence time. On Monday afternoon I visited a Borstal Institution. I interviewed some of the boys there and sometimes took a brass band with me for meetings conducted there – about ninety-two boys. Tuesday was home league day (women's meeting). There was the over-sixty club on another day. We had timbrel rehearsals for young people, junior soldiers' club, classes at Sunday-school and a youth group. I visited about thirty-four public houses each week. There was usually a friendly reception at the pubs. I was treated with courtesy and made many friends there. The ministry of Salvation Army women in public houses seems to show how decent the average man is, for all his booze and his occasional swear-word.

Naturally in a war, you do not always win. I have had my share of defeat. My next corps, which I will not name, was a reversal for me. There was a feud among sections of the people – part Irish and part Scots. This situation is not new – it is even found in the Bible – but I was very disappointed because it held up the work. Sometimes it was difficult to hold one's head up as a Salvationist. People said to me, 'If that's your Army, I don't want to come.' Of course, such lapses can be put right and God will forgive – and forget. But we should not pretend they do not happen. There are black-sheep Salvationists as there are black sheep in all other flocks. What makes me happy is the thought that, as the Bible says, it is the one black sheep who is the special concern of Jesus and the one He does most to save. In the end we had a shake-up at this corps. Some 'heads had to roll in the basket', so to speak, and I was very unpopular. Yet surgery must often precede healing. I prayed about it and felt that God guided my actions. They gave me police protection on one occasion. After this clean-up, almost disbanding the corps, we began to build again. God gave us wonderful success. New people threw in their lot with us. We built up the children's work. Once a month the hall was packed for family services. Then I was appointed to Basildon New Town, my present appointment.

This new assignment was especially dramatic because really there was not a corps – just a plan and a site. No citadel had been built.

The Salvation Army in Basildon was just a project and a dicey one at that.

I went to a corps in Essex, which is actually three and a half miles away. At that place there was a very dilapidated building, a few Salvationists, a small band and some young people's work.

At some corps our people do not seem to have much understanding of what the Army is all about. If you clap your hands and shout at the top of your voice, you are there. Then you are a good Salvationist. The spiritual side of The Salvation Army does not come through. The good life, the joyful life should not be mistaken for a mere clapping of hands. Of course, I have to watch that my more formal chapel upbringing is not unduly influencing me here.

The war will not go right if our soldiers are not in good heart, sound in their principles of Salvationism. I have found some who drink, although the Army is strongly teetotal. They thought it did not matter if they drank a little in secret. Also, we have a responsibility to dress properly and conduct ourselves in a manner worthy of The Salvation Army. Sometimes I found Salvationists who were not clean, not tidy, not careful in the way they spoke, not living in accord with the 'Articles of War' that we all sign before we can be accepted as Salvationists.

A lot of this had to be dealt with before we could make a start to build a corps from scratch, and again, it was not a very nice thing to have to do. I wanted the people, but we must all have the new birth, the gospel of Christ to match the present age. I did not want any worn-out faith, dead hopes, and frustration that amounted to a state of backsliding. I asked God to give us all a new heart and a new strength to meet this challenge of new times.

My first two years were spent trying to teach and foster this new spirit. Some could not give up the old corps—I lost almost all.

We went to the vacant site where the new Army centre was to be built. When the men put in their shovels to start digging the foundations, many prayers were uttered and we asked God to strengthen our faith. I went on to the estate asking the people if they knew what was happening about the proposed hall. Most said they were delighted to know that the Army was coming. We started a Sunday-school in the local elderly people's day-centre, which was loaned to us by the authorities of the new town, only a stone's throw from our own site. We also began adult meetings here.

Of course, I kept watching—and praying—for the new building which seemed to be a long time rising out of the bare earth. When it was completed I think it was one of the best Salvation Army halls ever seen: but then I am prejudiced! It was a large part of the fulfilment of my ideas. It is designed as a community centre and that is wonderful. If an ordinary Salvation Army hall had been built in Basildon, we would not have had opportunity to do the valuable community work we are doing.

Instead of the usual citadel, with a big platform for the band and songsters, with set seats, and just a small kitchen in the back, plus songster room, our hall is a lovely, all-purpose hall designed by Alan Vince—a most beautiful building, with a moveable platform, designed by Salvation Army architects. Our Mercy Seat folds up into a box and so it cannot be misused in any way.

We have a hatch leading from the main hall into the kitchen, which is a reasonable size. There is an office, which is used for counselling people, and the highly important lounge—what would old William Booth think of that, I wonder? This lounge has fitted carpet and about twenty easy chairs; there are coffee tables and other modern fixtures which make it a most lovely room in which to relax. It is the sort of building that lends itself to community work.

At Laindon, before I went into the corps, my predecessor had started a club for physically handicapped people. We sought to develop this club to make it a pleasant whole-day club where they could have a good dinner served and a nice tea later. We arranged transport, a big coach, to bring them in. It was necessary for me to drive the ambulance at that time—a terrible contraption: the bottom was ready to fall out. In this I used to bring the worst immobile cases.

So we had a Sunday-school functioning and this club for the physically handicapped. Then we started the home league (women's meeting). It was informal and held in the lounge. One thing I learned from American friends and from study of American methods—I always begin functions in our centre with meals or refreshments. The psychological benefits are enormous. The home league ladies come in about one o'clock for a 2.30 meeting. They sit and knit and chat, with hot scones and tea, as soon as they arrive, and then we have the informal home league meeting.

Then we decided we ought to do something more for handicapped people. Many of them never attend church. This was the outing of the week, and we ought to undertake religious ministry that would be helpful. So we started the home league for the physically handicapped. We also decided it was important to have something for young women; these found it very difficult to mix with the older ladies. Shakespeare says something about the incompatibility of age and youth, doesn't he? We therefore started a young wives' group. Many of the parents of children in the Sunday-school were interested. This young wives' group has been meeting now for about three years.

We also founded a morning nursery (ages from three to five), and about thirty-five children attend this. Of course, skilled staff are employed to run this. We also accept a number of socially-deprived children – we don't make any charge for them. Children from broken homes are sometimes sent to us.

In conjunction with the cradle roll – William Booth came to feel that you cannot enlist them too young – we began a mother and baby club, on Thursday afternoons, for mothers with babies under school age. All children have their names on the cradle roll. It is a link between home and nursery and Sunday-school. As the children get to know us they are prepared to go into the nursery when they reach the age for it. From the mother and baby club the latest development is the gingerbread group. This is part of a national movement on behalf of the single-handed parents – mothers with their children, or fathers with their children; divorced, separated, and unmarried mums and dads. This is a supportive group, a form of group therapy. The adults, both men and women, meet in the lounge and the children are cared for by our Salvationists in the main hall. We have not had any unwed parents come yet, but they are welcome.

The Probation Service holds a therapy group for prisoners' wives in our lounge. We support this group by our presence and also by transporting prisoners' wives and children to visit the husbands in prison and by arranging holidays for the family when they leave prison.

You are 'the Angel Captain' behind this work. But what help have you, what staff?
No angel I! There are full-time community workers, a young woman visitor and case worker, and a retired Salvation Army officer comes in on three days a week. He is good at clerical work. We finance all this ourselves. I also have casual staff for a few hours a day. The nursery staff is paid by us, as are the cleaners. In all about twelve people are employed. You say you pay for it at this Basildon corps and Community Centre. We make a charge for the nursery, though we give a number of places free. Then the local people support us through our terrific pub-booming round. New converts are out on the round. The men and women are supposed to buy the *War Cry* and the *Young Soldier* and some do take these papers. But more of them just use the papers as a means of giving money to The Salvation Army for the work. It is wonderful, really.

And what about this Penitent-form in a box? I do not think William Booth would have approved of that!
I think he would if he could see how we use it – how marvellous it is. We have had about fifty people kneel at it. We made twenty-four new Salvation soldiers during the first eighteen months. Thanks be to God! Ever since, there has been a gradual coming, and more people have decided to enlist as Salvationists.

From community service a corps has been built. As people are saved they automatically enter into community service with one aim – to win others for Christ.

CHAPTER FOUR

They Never Had it so Good

A YOUNG OFFICER-WIFE speaks of another type of problem: getting the conservative people of her corps to adapt to new techniques.

Tell us about your corps, in a place where, judged by our history, the Army ought not to thrive—in a rich Surrey setting, amid relative affluence and social stability. Can you, with a university degree in social history, reconcile it with William Booth's ideas?

We are in the wealthiest suburban borough in the country, but the corps is situated in the industrial part of the borough, the place where the work is done. It is on the edge of a new, working-class housing estate. Tenants pay £7 for a four-bedroomed, centrally-heated council house. The corps is an old one, established in the 1890s. At the moment the soldiery come from the small segments of house-owners, or from the older established council estates. They are working people, who either own their own houses or have lived in council houses for many years. So they are not professional people in the accepted, middle-class sense: not white-collar workers, but bakers, roundsmen, lorry-drivers, minor clerks, factory workers. They are steady, respectable, workers. I would call them working-class people.

How does the corps justify its existence there, except as a little community of Christians, which was not William Booth's idea of a Salvation Army corps?

It is possible to explain the existence of the corps by the fact that people who are most likely to remain Salvationists, and establish a little corps like ours, are respectable, established working-class people, with Georgian, Edwardian and even Victorian traditions. Our great sorrow is that the Army as a community, and as a Christian fellowship, does not relate to the folk on our doorstep who are the new 'brash' working class, the building workers, the wives who go out to work at the factories in the evenings as soon as their husbands come in. Forty pounds a week and more comes into the home. There's colour telly, Danish furniture, but not a book, or a good record, or a good picture in a house. It is the new materialistic, 'never-had-it-so-good' working class. The Army seems irrelevant to them. We find it difficult to bridge the gap, and William Booth would have been hard put to it to bridge it, also.

Do the children come to Sunday-school?
Some do, and they can come if they want to. They are not sent. Parents do not feel that a place of worship is really necessary.

Do they have their children christened in church or anything like that?
I would think that the majority of them would not bother. But they are quite friendly, although they keep their distance. We puzzle them. They are not quite sure what we are on about and they are not willing to join in. When we first went to the corps about two years ago, we were invited to a meeting by the Residents' Committee. It was held in the top room of a public house. My husband and I, who are in charge of the corps, joined in a discussion of how the children on the estate could be better catered for. We offered to start a junior club for children and a torchbearer group for older teen-ager types, but we would need help with staffing because our own people were not able to do it at that time of day. But we didn't get any help at all. There were numerous promises, but when it came to it, the people didn't turn up. I think this is not their fault; it is because they don't understand us. To them we are strangers. We have a different way of life. We come in from outside in our cars; we march out sometimes to our open-air meetings, we go back into our building for our meetings. They look and even listen a bit, but there is no communication.

You are frustrated by this? Have you given them up?
No. We keep trying. I went from house to house on the estate recently to publicise a young wives' club which had just been started at our hall. At some of the homes where young housewives live they were very friendly. 'Oh yes,' they said, 'this is wonderful.' But they did not come!

Perhaps their husbands would have a say in that?
Yes. Perhaps they are 'captive' wives. This is quite a problem. The young wives are left at home to look after the children, and when the husband comes home he has plans. They often go out at night. Then there is the perennial T.V., and social visits between neighbours. They all have cars. It is not as if they were socially deprived.

Do you think lack of religion affects behaviour?
Just as it would on a London working-class estate. Sometimes there is heavy drinking; the men go out to the pub leaving their wives at home; the wives go off to work in the week-time. There is sexual permissiveness of course—that is a sign of the times—a Victorian survival! But this sort of thing is accepted very much more than it was. The teenage daughter stays in the home; the baby is brought up as one of the family. The younger children are just delighted that a new baby is coming. There is no moral stigma attached; no public disapproval. A lot of their bewilderment with the Army arises from what they see as our out-moded moral preoccupations. They think they would not fit in with us and we would not approve of them.

Do you think we give people a guilt feeling? Are we too censorious, too puritanical?
Not deliberately, but we do practise a much more rigid way of life. We conform to a different social standard. Many of our working-class folk have middle-class ideas. It is the old problem—we are very respectable and perhaps proud. Our people are teetotal; they do not gamble or smoke; they are not sexually permissive. They live by the Army's austere principles and they are, in some cases, moving up the social scale.

We have quite a number of youngish couples in the corps; the majority of our soldiery, our active soldiery, would be in the twenty-to-thirty age group. The young men are establishing their work-pattern, building up their career, buying houses. One or two of them are going to move into the professional classes as they get older.

Are Salvationists sufficiently concerned about the agnostic jungle? The materialism, the religious indifference?
We should be rather disturbed when we come to our Sunday activities and go into the hall, and find 'we' are all there but 'they' are not. We feel no sense of sorrow that the folk on our doorstep are not involved in any way in what we are doing. We have the atmosphere of a club.

I wouldn't want to denigrate our Salvationists. Their sincerity cannot be questioned. But they do not stop to think; they accept routine far too easily and are shy about the message they have to proclaim.

Please don't be offended, but William Booth would place the responsibility for changing this attitude upon you and your husband. Do you try?
Oh, most certainly. But we feel we must move as our people move. We can seek to lead but we cannot force. I feel quite strongly that we ought to develop a much more community-minded corps. My husband isn't entirely with me in this – he is an evangelist, basically. He wants to make our meetings and our witness much more relevant, and I agree with this, obviously. But when the establishment, for example of a play-group, is mooted, or anything which would help to bridge the social gap between 'them' and 'us', then our own corps folk don't see the relevance of it. Some would say, 'We cannot have our sacred building used for such a purpose.' There used to be a youth club held. But the young people created mess and noise and the cleaners objected and the thing closed.

But they are coming round to it. It takes time and wisdom and much patience. We must not force people into something, but we must persuade in the end. One difficulty is that we are 'transients' – we move on but they remain.

How long do you think you may stay at your present appointment?
We hoped for five years; we have been here nearly two.

Will you have time for this 'break-out', this 'jump over the wall'?
It has taken us all the time so far to get through to our own people. To some extent now they are with us, but we are very much hampered by the traditional corps programme. Now we both feel very strongly about this. Because of conditions in the corps, so much depends upon the corps officers. This leaves very little time for the new things we want to do.

Are any of these corps activities dispensable?
No. But some ought to be run by soldiers. For example, the junior clubs ought to be run by the soldiery. The over-sixty club ought to be run by the people in the corps and the home league (women's meeting) also. Everything that happens between Sunday and Sunday is our responsibility. We have local officers, of course, for the band and the songsters, the corps cadets, and the traditional corps activities. But the activities which affect outside people are run by us. Until we can get rid of some of this work-load we are unable to try new ventures.

Why do you think your people are hesitant?
They lack confidence in themselves. They must believe that they have something to say. As it is, some of our people do not feel they have a message people need. I am not sure that a greater number of people would come to the meetings even if we solved this problem.

But isn't that irrelevant?
Yes. What matters is whether we can affect them in this basic way. We can save girls from having illegitimate babies, not by free contraceptives on the National Health Service, but by a better life-style. We can help unhappily married people; we can stop marriages breaking up; we can put new, better ideas into the minds of teenagers; we can care for the aged; we can bring something into the lives of people who are lonely . . .

But will your husband accept that? A preacher may come to feel that the alpha and omega of his work is how many folk will come to listen.
Oh, no! He is not that sort of preacher. He would be happy if he could feel that there was a healing ministry given to him, a wider

mission than there is at present. We are happy when people come to the meetings because we feel very strongly that The Salvation Army corps ought to be a fellowship of spirit-filled men and women. This in itself is a healing ministry. A proportion of our congregation would be people who need to come to the meeting, not to hear the sermon but simply to be with friendly people, where their own problems and needs are absorbed and shared, and where spiritual healing is found. So however we reach out to the people in their homes and their social living, the meetings and worship would still have a vital part to play.

Whilst we feel that the approach to the 'never-had-it-so-good' community must be through community service, we know also that the message of the gospel, presented in a relevant, up-to-date way, is our greatest gift to them. To try to hide this in our relationship with them would be a very great folly.

A good Salvationist is quite something. From the preacher's platform, in the pubs with the War Cry *or in the club for housewives—it is one and the same thing?*

Yes. We have to do it through the corps. We are corps officers. We love our people. We want their spiritual good. So we have got to do it with them, slowly if necessary—we need five years at least.

We rejoice to see growing signs of concern and a greater reality in prayer among our own people, which makes us very happy. We retain great hopes for the future of the Army in this area.

CHAPTER FIVE

Shop Manager to Officer

What brought you into officership at such a comparatively late age?
It's a long story and goes back many years. Doris, my wife, will have her own contribution to make to it. Eighteen years back I had heard the call for officership in the Army. I discussed it with Doris but she felt that it was not for her. But it came back again. I tried to rationalise these 'calls'. Perhaps I was physically low or discouraged or had an argument with the boss. But somehow this reasoning did not stop my unease. I made some progress in the company and my income and prospects were good. But that call was still there. In the end I saw everything I did as a substitute for or escape from officership. A customer would say, 'Can I talk to you for a minute?' Then I would find myself being 'father confessor' as a sort of priest.

Can I ask Doris about this call?
Well, Alan was very unhappy. I felt that he should be an officer, and that I was doing wrong in not helping him more and encouraging him. I realised that a decision must be made one way or another. For me it was stepping out blindly in faith, because I couldn't see myself as the officer's wife.

Alan, what difference has this made in your life?
Of course it has changed it completely. The children are left to themselves a lot more; but they are older now. Doris helps with the platform work. She is now at ease; she can give an address.

Doris, what about that vanished affluence? How do you manage on an officer's allowance?

If anything it is easier! In our well-paid days we had so many commitments, and had to spend so much to 'keep up with the Jones' that we lived up to our income, whereas now it is so much more important to live within it that I find I can do it and it is much easier.

You, Alan, have you any regrets? Would you do the same again?
Without question I would do the same again. I am happy. There is a tremendous amount of personal satisfaction. As officers with a simple standard of material life, we do not have any problems financially. The only regrets I have are personal, very ordinary ones, to do with music for instance. Perhaps I can do better in this field later.

Do you think the age for entry into training should be raised?
I think that single people, in the main, enter too young, under twenty-five. But for married people we thought, when we were in training, that the best way was to be what the training staff call 'single marrieds', married couples without children.

What has happened to your corps in your eighteen months?
When we came, there was the over-sixty club at an outpost, about four miles away. This still runs; about forty people gather. Sunday meetings then were eight to twelve people in the morning; Sunday-school virtually non-existent; there were three children present on our first Sunday. For the Sunday evening meeting six to nine attended. About eight women attended the week-day home league. Now congregations have improved, but statistics are no measure of success. They are the criteria of success I used in my business employment. Figures were the all-important proof of success. You earned more money by taking more money in the store. Christ does not measure success in that way. But it can be said, for what it is worth, that more people now attend the various Sunday and week-day meetings.

What about new activities?
We had a most unusual opportunity here. We were able to create a programme from scratch. In subsequent corps we may have to

accept the *status quo*. It has been our joy to create 'something out of nothing' at this place. The over-sixty club at the corps has been running for about eighteen months. It has an attendance of about eighty-five people – one of the largest in the district. There are about one hundred and seventy-five members. This has helped the corps, because some of these old folk now come regularly to the meetings. We began a luncheon club, which was initially held one day a week, then two days a week. We serve one hundred meals a week now on two days. The home league (women's meeting) attendances have increased as a result of the luncheon-club activities. We began a junior club on Wednesday nights which has flourished. We don't quite know why! It is amazing to see the members tearing about, doing the odd bit of handicraft here and there, letting off steam. We now hold this on two evenings a week. It is unmanageable otherwise, because of its size. We have begun a separate girls' club and boys' club. The children's work seems to prosper, too. We gave out twenty-five prizes this year – three prizes last year.

Improvements have been made to the property. The meeting-hall was a very gloomy place. The first thing was to get rid of the old-fashioned forms and buy some chairs. A nearby corps fitted new chairs; we bought their old ones. We have lowered the ceiling some fifteen feet; there is new fluorescent lighting and sanded and polished wood-block floors. We are now in the process of changing the heating, which was an old coke-fired boiler, to an oil-fired system.

Then are you satisfied?

There are always 'downs' as well as 'ups'. The thing that concerns me, and I mean it in a kindly way, is that I would like to have seen more of an improvement in the spiritual life of the people. A new ceiling, a polished floor is something, but the ministry with people is the supreme aim. That is the reason for our call.

Do you think that service to the community or building up the spiritual lives of your people is the more important task?

It is difficult to choose. They are inter-related. Building up the Army is important, because spreading the gospel depends on having people with high spiritual morale. We spread the gospel through our life and work for Christ.

Any other problems?
Relatively mild ones. Sometimes when I prepare what I feel is an adequate sermon-address for a meeting and get up to preach this profound appeal on Sunday night, I see some people fidgeting and I think, 'What is this all about?' There may be one or two deaf old ladies at the back. Did they hear what I said? This kind of thing is the test—the burning fiery furnace. But they are the testings that any officer or minister might get at any corps, church or chapel.

How long would you like to stay?
That is difficult to answer. I am a believer in longer terms for corps officers. After a year they wanted to move us on, but we felt that we ought to stay at least two years. This corps has been open for forty-four years. Its seeming failure is due, in my opinion, in no small way to the fact that during that time forty-six officers have been stationed here. We shall be creating history—we shall be the longest-serving officers in the history of the corps. If one knew one had five years, one could work with young people, hold them, and have time to see them grow up. There are several aspects of this corps that lead me to feel that I would like to be here a long time. On the other hand there are other factors—those people I was telling you about. But they are relatively unimportant and I will edge off that platform.

What do you think is the greatest difficulty facing the Army in Britain today?
Shortage of man-power and officer-power. That is the greatest difficulty for us in Britain.

Then sometimes I have a gloomy feeling about the Army and our so-called autocracy. Here I am a sort of autocrat. But in larger corps it is difficult for the Commanding Officer to be an autocrat in our democratic society. He has to be the man in between the Army hierarchy operating a system of autocracy and the corps which operates. If it possesses a corps council under a democratic system, he is 'between the devil and the deep blue sea'! I see that as a problem, but don't ask me to solve it for you. I thought this one through before officership and before soldiership in the Army.

Of course, we do have a one-man autocrat, but I am assured it doesn't work like that. The General has his Advisory Council. So he isn't autocratic in the strict sense of the word. But I think there could still be consultation—up and down. I know there is a good deal now, though some of it may be merely nominal. There could be even more. Communication up and down is most necessary. But it is coming—as it has come and is coming in the British Army on which our administrative system is modelled.

What do you think is the opinion of the man in the street about the Army today?
By virtue of regular public-house visitation I think we are as near as we can get to the man in the street. The Army holds a very affectionate place in the hearts of people. But I am not too sure that we treat this as seriously as we should or that they consider us as seriously as they should. They recognise us for our good works, our cup of tea at the scene of the disaster. They give us a couple of bob for what we 'did in the war' or when 'my sister was born in your hospital'. It is affectionate and good humoured but not for the best and most significant reasons.

Doris, *what do you think of women's place in the Army?*
I am content to play the part of second-in-command. But I do realise that the Army gives marvellous opportunities to women. They can play a prominent part, equal to men's. Catherine Booth established a Salvationist Women's Lib more than a century ago. We have officer friends, a married couple, and the wife is not content to be in the background. She says that she and her husband have a fifty-fifty relationship in the running of everything. Mine is a different role but at least it is of my choosing.

Do you think the Army should relax some of its strict rules in these more tolerant permissive days?
No. I had some different ideas, about our teetotalism particularly. But now that I am older, I can see it in true perspective. I hope the Army will not relax any of its standards.

Finally, Alan, *is this vocation of officership what you expected it to be? Was your training for it adequate?*
I find myself with more paperwork and financial detail than I

expected, but that is because I do not have a full quota of local officers.

With regard to training, the short answer must be 'No'. Academically the training was very good and I was not up to it. As far as field training was concerned – the practical side – I felt it was – I was going to use the word abysmal – inadequate. It did not prepare me for the work that I had to do. The first need we saw when we came to this area was for an over-sixty club and a luncheon club. But we hadn't the foggiest notion of how to set about starting one, or how to keep it going; yet the first thing we had to do when we came here was just that.

CHAPTER SIX

Community Service in North London

How old are you?
Twenty-six.

How long married?
Just over four years.

William Booth would not have approved of your getting married at twenty-two.
I needed the money; I thought it was the sensible thing to do. I was at Glasgow and we both wanted to enter The Salvation Army college as married cadets.

Are you a 'born and bred' Salvationist?
Yes. My parents were local officers in a mining town outside Glasgow. My father has just retired after fifty-one years as a coal miner, and he has been a Salvationist all his life. My sister is an officer, too.

What sort of a man is your father?
If he hadn't been a Salvationist he would have been a communist, I think. During the great depression his brother would march with the communist flute band and my dad would march with The Salvation Army band. They would wave to each other as they passed by. He was a staunch union member. Perhaps he had reservations about some things they did but he remained union-minded.

Did he send you to university so that you could become a Salvation Army officer?
No, though he knew when I went to university that I was going to be a Salvation Army officer. He left school at fourteen. The only thing for him was the coal-mine. When I had the chance to go to university he wanted it as much as I did.

Why did you become an officer?
It is not easy to say why. I rejected my parents' beliefs but remained in the Army because it was fun. It was trendy to reject God.

But you did not in fact lose your faith?
No. Somebody said, 'You ought to read *The Screwtape Letters*'; and I did. I owe the beginnings of my Christian faith on a personal basis to the reading of C. S. Lewis. Nothing in my life has influenced me so much as he has.

You went through with this intention of becoming an officer after graduating—where does the young lady come in?
We used to go regularly for holidays to Bournemouth. I met her when her folks were stationed there as officers in charge of the corps. I was about fifteen. Looking back, I think the original impetus for officership may have come from Margaret, who is now my wife. I never forgot her, even though I was only fifteen. It was a typical holiday romance. When Boscombe Songsters came to Scotland I met her again. She thought officership was a great life. Her parents were in it and she knew both sides of it.

What about the economics of getting married at twenty-two?
We hadn't a clue how we were going to manage. I was at university. We had no place to live, apart from our parents' homes, and that we did not want. But the way opened up. We had started a coffee-bar in our corps. There we met a young couple who said, 'This is marvellous. We are not Salvationists, but can we join and help you in this work?' The young wife was a display artist at a large store. Through them we got lodgings and in due course we went into training. We were both happy in training.

Your corps work is a mixture of straight evangelistic work and indirect evangelistic work, social service? You do not feel that the social side is a diversion of your ministry?
It can be. There is a struggle to balance the two. But it is not just social work. We are seeking to help the complete man – or woman – spiritually as well as materially. The paper-work is a burden.

Don't you have clerical help?
My wife carries the clerical load.

Couldn't you have a secretary on a part-time basis? Is it a matter of cost?
I should think so – yes.

Some Army officers have clerical help paid for by the local authority and in the United States it is commonplace for an officer to have a full-time professional secretary.
A good idea. It may come, especially at community centre corps – it must come.

Tell me what social services you deploy?
There is a luncheon club, which is run by our Army people. The cook is paid; the others are volunteers. We have over-all supervision, look after the accounts and act as chaplains. For five days a week we do meals for sixty-five to seventy old people. The cost to the old folk is 6p per day. The local council gives us an extra 10p and certain expenses.

Do the local council people take readily to this idea?
Yes. There was a desperate need for such services in the district. Indeed there is a demand for them all over the country and where we will not do them then the other voluntary agencies or churches do.

We don't have an over-sixty club as such – with the day programme for the old people it would be very difficult. We have got an active Sunday-school, with good prospects. There are a lot of new flats going up round the hall. We have a very good cub pack of about thirty boys and a recently formed scout troop. My wife has begun a singing company and a timbrel brigade. Shortage of leaders holds us back.

Apart from financial help, must you have professional help at all: inspectors, people like that?
They should come and inspect the premises' hygiene and so on to make sure that everything is in order. Certain standards have to be met—cleanliness and public health. You have to have so many toilets per person, for instance. But they know our hall is new; everything is up to scratch. So we are not troubled much.

Do you have many people with personal problems, apart from the need for a good meal and social fellowship?
Regularly we have folk coming for consultation, not only old people. A lot of people come over from Ireland. Many have no job, nowhere to stay. Obviously they need help. I give them what help I can. If it is beyond me I send them to the town hall. The next building to ours is the Social Security office. Sometimes I take needy people in and explain the position.

Then there are many squatters in the area. Some who have no food come to us. We try to help. I take them to buy food. I make sure the money is spent on food.

How do you get to know the people you cater for?
Well, lunches are served at twelve o'clock. People arrive any time from eleven o'clock and most stay until one o'clock each day. So we have an opportunity to get to know their needs. We also visit them in their homes.

Your staff, all, apart from the cook, unpaid volunteers, must work long and hard?
They are there from about ten in the morning until two o'clock in the afternoon.

And they do this five days a week?
Yes. A couple of these people are not Salvationists but wanted to be associated with the good work.

What else in the way of social service?
In our hall each day, not fully operated by us, but under our over-all supervision, is a therapy class for mentally-disturbed old people. A local-authority qualified physiotherapist is in professional control. We are involved in that we try to make these people part of our pastoral concern. One of the men recently moved into a new flat. He had very little furniture and no bed-clothing. We helped by getting him a table and four chairs, curtains and bed-clothing—and we hope to do more for him.

Part of the equipment at the therapy centre for the aged is a fifteen-seater mini-bus. This is used to bring patients or clients every day. The local council gives us an allowance to pay the driver, and also a substantial grant for the purchase of the bus.

What sort of people are in this service?
All are O.A.P.s and some have had mental breakdowns; others are inadequate in some way. There is much loneliness and very profound personal problems that they bear with great fortitude. One woman has a husband dying of cancer. The only cheerful companionship she can look for is when she comes to this centre.

What do they find that makes their journey worth while?
Well, they have their lunch with us. We have television, but oddly it is very rarely used. They prefer to talk to each other. That makes a change for them.

Do they get the chance to talk to you?
I always make a point of going round and speaking to them, individually if I can.

Do you think your other work, your 'straight' Salvation Army ministry—your preaching from the platform, looking after the children in the Sunday-school—suffers because of this social work?
It does if I do not get up early enough in the morning—if I get up later than 6.30 a.m., as I sometimes do, then my study and preparation for the meetings is adversely affected.

Normally you would get up at what time?
6.30 a.m. as a rule.

What time do you knock off?
The straight corps work I finish about 9 o'clock. But if, after visitation or attending band practice, songster practice, cubs or other sections, I do some study, the day will finish at 11 p.m.

Too many hours! The trade unions would not stand for it. Neither would the factory inspectors! What are your study subjects?
The second part of the Certificate of Religious Knowledge of London University. I have permission to work towards doing the B.D. eventually.

What about the Salvationists in the corps, your orthodox-type Salvationists? Do they resent this social work of yours? Isn't it a bit much having these old folk around and having your time and attention taken up so much?
I don't think they resent it. They are glad that when they are asked what The Salvation Army does, they can point to our social work. They are glad we are involved in the community, and pleased to be associated with it.

What about the coloured people?
A good number of coloured people are in our corps and are well integrated. There is little tension over colour in the area.

Do they become English-style Salvationists?
A Jamaican woman in the corps is a songster; her Salvationism is excellent. Her two children sing in the singing company and attend the Sunday-school. We have two African Salvationists also, both of whom were Salvationists before they came to England, which is probably significant. We have numbers of coloured children in the Sunday-school.

Though many of the newly-arrived Africans and West Indians are Christians, they do not attend the Army in large numbers. Do you know why?

We did have a Jamaican family, a boy and a girl of seventeen and eighteen, and four other members of the family, all likeable children. But their parents have taken them away and send them to what is, more or less, an exclusively West Indian church. I think the parents were suspicious of the Army. I'm not sure why. We visited them on a number of occasions but they would not invite us into their home.

It is not because of reserve or hostility in your congregation?
There is no hostility. But perhaps we are too 'stiff and starchy'. We imagine ourselves to be very free and easy in the Army. But we can be solemn and very stereotyped.

But you are the officer in charge. You can make your meetings as free and noisy as you like?
Yes, I am a fairly noisy type! But if I changed the pattern of the meetings to please immigrant people and displeased all the others, it would not be good policy. One can only do such a thing gradually.

Are the West Indian, African, and Asian people well-disposed towards you? Do they support the Army when it appeals for funds?
Yes. One has to explain what The Salvation Army is and what it does to deserve support. When I explain that we are Christians, that part of our commitment is caring for people, all people, then they are ready to support financially and are most friendly.

Do you think the Army can expect to survive in an area which may become more heavily populated by coloured immigrants?
Yes. But we shall have to work for it and do some re-thinking. We must thrash out new policy; we must get close to these people; we must achieve real integration in the corps. We must take more trouble in the language area.

By and large my people are trying to face up to the challenge. I spoke to the coloured people in the corps and said, 'I come from a different environment; there are relatively few coloured immigrants in Glasgow. So I need your help; please advise me how we ought to deal with this problem. I am trying to learn; I am trying to understand their ways of thinking.'

What will happen to your work when you leave? A man may be convinced that community social service can be part of his ministry. But he may go, and if he has carried it on his shoulders it may collapse. Suppose his successor doesn't have his view of the ministry, but is of a more orthodox evangelistic viewpoint, is it not possible that what you have done might collapse?
It could happen. But there are safeguards. One is that Salvation Army officers must stay for longer periods. I would like to stay for another two years anyway. I will give of my very best. I will hold nothing back. I must never think, 'This is my first corps, so I will only be here for a year.' This work is long-term work; we must stay and do it well. Another safeguard, and I am sure the Army command knows this, is that the officer who succeeds me will be chosen to carry on from where I leave off.

Do you think Army officers are sufficiently aware of the need to delegate responsibility so that much of the administrative work could be done by local people? These are not subject to changes of appointment every three years or so?
Yes, I think we must do more of this, but much depends on the local people.

CHAPTER SEVEN

New Weapons on an Old Battlefield

FORMERLY AN ASYLUM for Orphans, the Clapton Congress Hall in north-east London became a major battlefield for Salvationists in 1882. There, in the huge citadel, thousands of men, women and children knelt at the Penitent-form and thousands of cadets were trained and commissioned as officers. In Victorian times the work was in line with William Booth's original idea that salvation of itself was sufficient to cure man's ills. But now diversification has become necessary.

You are the Captain in charge of the Clapton Congress Hall and have been there for three years. What events and family background preceded this? My father and mother are Salvationists. I entered training at nineteen. I registered my decision to become a Salvation Army officer when I was twelve. I wanted to be a Salvation Army officer-doctor, and later I dreamed of being a missionary and going to China, preaching the gospel to the millions there. I never ceased to have a strong desire to preach the gospel. Now I have firm and somewhat different convictions as to what a corps officer's vocation is. I believe there is more to it than preaching. Jesus ministered to the total man: body, mind and spirit.

Preaching, often to the converted, and visiting one's own people in their homes is only part of the gospel. Something vital is missing. The full gospel for the whole man ministers to his physical, mental and spiritual need.

Do you think of it in terms of a social gospel?
No. It is just the gospel. I must not allocate my work into categories, evangelism one day, community work another. All the time, at any task, I am doing the work of an evangelist. The aim is to communicate Jesus. By the blessing of God I can do that as effectively sitting in the lounge with old folk, amidst their tobacco smoke and even amidst their curses and their arguments about the Common Market, as I can when preaching from the pulpit.

We have two hundred soldiers formed into band, songsters and various Salvation Army sections. They help with this concern for others in the community.

Can you tell us how this work is carried out?
Yes. I live on the building. This enables the Army to operate a twenty-four hour service. We have a luncheon club for elderly and needy citizens, and serve between fifty and sixty meals a day. From Monday to Friday we organise a play group for children. We have a long waiting-list for this. We provide for unsupported mothers, whose children are in particular need. There is a club for educationally sub-normal children which meets in our building but is not administered by The Salvation Army. However, we are closely involved in it. I am on the committee, and a number of Salvationists are involved in the operation of the club. Also we have a junior youth club, a senior youth club, a large over-sixty club, and a rest lounge, which is open all day for those people who may feel the need to sit and talk. Between nine in the morning and nine at night there is always a staff member in the office.

How is this work financed?
The personal giving of the Salvationists has increased considerably since we moved into our new buildings and since we began to carry out this kind of community service. We also receive grants from the local authority. At the moment we are granted £250 a year towards the costs of the luncheon club and £650 towards the play group. There have been no other grants. Other costs are financed out of Salvation Army funds. We are not in the red. People have given more liberally since our programme of community service began.

We employ two full-time staff in addition to the play-group

leaders and the luncheon-club supervisor. Of course, my wife and I are full-time workers too. The staff are Salvationists who receive a lieutenant's allowance, which is certainly not in the super-tax bracket. The corps is responsible for their rent.

Living on the premises with a telephone sounding off day and night—doesn't this make you feel a 'prisoner' to the work all the time?
As a Salvation Army officer I exist to serve the people. We sing, 'All my days and all my hours', and it would be wrong to pretend that there is no physical strain.

Are you able to get away from it sometimes?
We try to keep one full day a week free. The other six days of the week it is one task after another all day from early in the morning. After work at home I try to get down to the office by 9 o'clock. After that it is work in the office, or out on the district, or at the centre, with brief breaks for meals. Sometimes committees and councils take up some of the time.

It used to be said that the old Congress Hall was haunted by one of the orphans from the Asylum who came to a violent end there. Suppose you met the old warrior, William Booth, stalking his old battleground. Suppose he asked what you were doing to save souls. Are you not afraid he would be angry and think that his Army was off target?
No; I'd be happy to meet him! I am proud to carry on the fight he began. I believe he would be proud of his Army soldiers, and the war they wage. The tactics have changed and the weapons are different, but that is all. There is no departure from that love of souls, that great compassion for the needy that the Founder exemplified in his wonderful life.

But can you say that of such a project as a luncheon club?
Yes, I can. I know those fifty people in a very special way. To them I am the Salvation Army Captain. I have access to their homes, knowledge of their families; I share their problems and I pray that as time goes by they see Christ in it all.

But William Booth might judge the worth of your work on the number of penitents you saw; whether your old folk and young folk were 'saved'.

We would be quite content to have him judge us by that criterion, too. People have been saved. They now wear Salvation Army uniform. On a Sunday night ten or a dozen luncheon-club members are present in the meeting. In the majority of cases they did not attend a place of worship before they met the Army.

Do you think that this approach to the gospel—the 'gospel of Christ for the whole man'—is the way? The method of the Ministry of Social Security is simple and direct. If you remove the worst of poverty and provide a good health service, then the intrusion of religion is superfluous and complicating.

I dare say a lot of social service 'professionals' are religious, too. There's always room for honest religion. The Army recently held a conference at Sunbury Court at which officers engaged in this social-evangelical ministry spoke of their experience. We found that we had much in common, and that there is much room for development. The idea that the Army is bands playing brass instruments, marching behind the flag, and inviting people to be saved is not all the story.

My kind of Army is also the spiritual child of William Booth. It is part of his *Darkest England* dream fulfilled. And it can happen anywhere. There is need everywhere—elderly people who need care, young people who need interest, lonely people who need a friend. For me, wherever I was, this would be how I would interpret Christ's command to preach the gospel.

Could we have more information about your plans for Clapton and nearby Tottenham? You are responsible for that area, I believe?

Well, recently I applied to the local borough council for financial aid with our work. I have asked for a grant of £2,400 from the local authority. With money supplied by the Army this should finance growing community work. The evangelistic work will not be neglected.

At Tottenham we have a unique situation. The local authorities wanted us to increase our community service. Their experts went to great pains in drawing up a scheme and recommended that we should qualify for urban aid grants. Between £8,000 and £10,000 is being made available to us in Tottenham over a period of five years. There are no strings attached except that we keep the door open to all, without discrimination. It is going to be an important development, because the hall is situated on an 'island' of housing with a high percentage of coloured people.

We have made a survey of the area. There is need for a play group and for a luncheon club. We shall concentrate on these at first.

What is a luncheon club, Captain?

For the elderly, who come along every Monday to Friday for dinner. We serve lunch at 12.30. A man arrives about 11.45; he sits around the place, talks in the foyer if he wishes, and has a general chat around until dinner is served. Afterwards he can go home or relax in the lounge for the afternoon. He can watch T.V., play dominoes and other similar games. But mostly he likes to talk. We allow smoking. You will appreciate that this is the 'meals on wheels' service adapted for those who can 'come and get it'. Dinner costs 5p and is subsidised by the local authority, who provides it in pre-cooked large containers. Salvationists do the menial tasks, washing up, serving and so on.

I find that Salvationists have a wonderful sympathy and aptitude for helping these aged or otherwise needy people. We visit countless homes where the case-history begins with a telephone message, a neighbour's inquiry or some other small detail. But it often entails our involvement in family problems, personal crises, social suffering of many kinds. And we remember the words of Jesus, 'I am among you as He that serveth.'

CHAPTER EIGHT

From Coal Mine to Community Centre

I WAS ATTRACTED to the Army through the torchbearer youth club and was converted as a teenager in County Durham, in a little mining village. None of my family had anything to do with the Christian faith.

You were converted, but first of all there was a process of softening up in the youth club?
Exactly. I went there with friends. I enjoyed it; then the officer did what an officer should do; he interested me in the deeper side of the Army. I was definitely converted.

What does conversion mean to you?
Conversion to me means that God accepts me.

You went to the Penitent-form?
Yes. But it didn't quite work at first. I thought that the officer was some type of faith-healer. I waited for him to put his hands on me, to say 'the magic words' or something like that. It didn't work.

But you got the right thing in the end?
Yes.

What was your job?
A coal miner.

You lived as a Salvationist down the pits?
Yes.

You joined the band?
Yes, and the songster brigade and corps cadets. I was extremely happy as a Salvationist.

You had a girl friend?
Yes.

How did you come to be an officer?
From the time I was converted I felt that God wanted me to do something with my life, something worthwhile.

Was this because life is wretched as a coal miner?
Oh, no! I enjoyed coal mining. I was going for a manager's ticket. I spent five years at day classes and evening classes, and was quite well on my way towards that goal.

But you applied for officership?
Yes. But it didn't quite work out. My girl friend wasn't interested. So I put it off and we were married. I didn't mention it for two or three years. Then my wife raised the matter.

Had you felt that marriage would make officership impossible?
I had put it out of my mind altogether. I tried to substitute training for youth work and becoming a youth leader. I tried to lose myself in corps activity. But deep down in my heart I knew it was a poor substitute—nothing more.

Was there economic or domestic pressure—any sense of failure in your mining career which caused you both to think of officership?
Quite the contrary—I had taken a sandwich course for my under-manager's ticket. The National Coal Board was quite happy for me to be away for nine months at the local university and the Coal Board Training Centre. My parents and my work-mates thought it ridiculous for us to try for officership. We felt differently. We

entered the Training College in London, in 1962, as a married couple.

How did the training go?
At the time it was confusing. I had come from a physical industry. To sit and be lectured at, to read, to write, was not easy. But I went to learn what I could. I had much to learn.

Your wife was with you, of course. How did she get on?
She enjoyed it. She is a second-generation Salvationist. A lot of the things which she took for granted I found hard.

Did you agree not to have children during this time?
Yes. Until we had completed our term at the Training College.

Did this mean that you practised family planning or that you were separated from each other?
We practised family planning.

You didn't have scruples about this?
It was a reasonable request on the part of the college authorities. Training would have been impossible without some such proviso.

You were commissioned?
Yes, to a mining village in south Yorkshire. We were there one year. As it was a mining area we felt quite at home with the people. We knew how to approach them and how not to be offended by their straightforward speaking, a quality they share with most mining communities. I was able to put some of my mining experience to work by putting myself at the disposal of the colliery manager then as a minister of religion with underground training. If there was an accident I was quite happy to go down and be of what use I could.

Was there much religion—there among the miners?
Yes, religion often means something to a miner. Colliers have a reputation as heavy drinkers and much else that is profane, but some of the greatest saints I know have been converted miners.

Did you find that your own flock went their way with their religion, their self-discipline: no drinking, no gambling, no smoking and no womanising, while the mass of the village went its way, just admiring you and giving you 25p now and again?
No. That was not how it was. There was much understanding of our work, much friendliness and much fellow-feeling.

Were you deeply involved in village life?
As the village was small we could not be anything else. We ran the only youth centre in the village. It was attended by nearly a hundred youngsters and we had access to over a hundred homes from that source alone.

What about the old people, the lonely people?
Our over-sixty club grew overnight. It was launched while we were there and grew to over a hundred members. There was a community of retired miners who lived together in blocks of Coal Board houses. We had deeper influence among many of these people when they learned that we had come from mining stock, ourselves.

You didn't feel you were captain of the Salvation Army soldiers, but rather that you were the captain of the village itself?
Yes, I looked upon the whole of that village as a priest would look on his parish. I was welcome everywhere.

What of the village children?
The Sunday-school grew rapidly, as did a youth club and boys' band. We commissioned ten young bandsmen before we left.

What about money? Did you have food and a roof over your head?
Our first week's salary was about six shillings, our second about thirty-two shillings. We had to rely on money from headquarters, but we found, after a while, that more money came in.

You would have had a good salary as an N.C.B. under-manager. Did lack of money worry you?
Well, money has never worried us, from then until now. We went into our vocation with our eyes open.

We moved to another mining area, where we stayed one year. God blessed us again. We were happy there. But we felt, long before we came into training, that God needed us for youth work. I was converted as a teenager. So we began a torchbearer club and over one hundred young people joined.

What did these young folk find when they came?
In some respects it was a run-of-the-mill youth club—records, table-tennis, bar canteen, pot-holing, and mountain climbing. Some of the young people were saved—definitely converted. This club was teetotal, and no smoking took place.

Surely this was a bar to the youth activities?
Yes. But we had one hall, used for everything from worship to youth work. It would have been wrong to allow youngsters to smoke or drink in a place of worship. We lost some members, but most found that they could do without such indulgences for a couple of hours.

No defiance of these rules of yours?
There was the occasional smoking in the toilet, etc. One or two of the older Salvationists complained of such profane behaviour, but when they saw the results they agreed that the effort was justified.

Are you particularly shockable?
Well, it is in part a promiscuous society in which we live. But one must face these things to work amongst the young. I have worked among drug addicts—I am beyond shock, I think.

Do you feel that your old-time message of salvation applies to the drug addict, the young lay-about, the chap who sleeps around, and all the others?
Without a doubt. I try to serve about 300 young people every week in my present appointment, which has a youth centre. Many of them are quite lost—they need to be saved. I find that young folk want something stable, something to hang on to. Some need escape, or a crutch. That is why they use drugs and drink and sex.

What came after that?

Another mining village. In many ways it was like the other corps. But I found one difficulty – the small hall had been newly renovated and the local Salvationists would not let me start a youth club. My first instinct was to go ahead and start, for I was the Commanding Officer. But they were adamant. As I would only be there for a year, perhaps, there would be no point in starting such a club. I remember warning them that the corps would suffer because of this attitude. Today the corps is smaller than it was when I was there. But how can we have a future if we do not win and keep the young to replace older generations?

But the Army is autocratic, and you were the local commander-in-chief. You could have gone ahead without them.
Perhaps. But at that time I had only been out of college a couple of years, so I had little experience. I think I would do it now.

At this time I was the County Scout Chaplain for the South Yorks Scout Camp. It was here that the County Commissioner offered my wife and me a full-time job as Wardens of the County Scout Camp. I will confess that we were tempted, for we were suffering some frustration in our work at the corps. Then a miracle happened. The officer in charge of the Army's Goodwill Department came to see us, to question us. Looking back I can see he assessed our capabilities. As a result we were appointed to open a residential youth centre in a country town. This was our opening into youth work.

Tell us about that.
This was a new town and young men were moving into it to work in industry. They could find no accommodation. The corps officer there with the social welfare services planned a youth hostel. This was, to begin with, a battered house that had been derelict for many years. This youth residence opened in due course, and in the grounds was an old barn which we fitted as a youth centre both for young men at the residence and, for five nights a week, for other young people. There were over two hundred of them. We were there for five years, and to our great joy we saw thirty-two converts from the youth centre. Some went into the band, some went into the songsters. Some went to other churches. One of the most difficult boys was

converted and is now an officer in The Salvation Army. We had great joy!

Then, after nearly five years, we were appointed to the youth and community centre at Hoxton, London.

Are you a social worker or an evangelist?
In the purely social field one would get twice or three times as much salary as one gets in the Army. But in the Army one can serve the whole personality – physical, mental, spiritual.

But how is this concept regarded by teenagers in this rather cynical world? This business of religion, the Bible, saying your prayers, and living a clean life?
I don't think they are as cynical as they are made out to be. I have been to a number of pop-festivals to take charge of the Army's work there. There were 155,000 at Weeley when we put up 'the Jesus tents' there. We found youngsters not only coming for the free food and the clothing, or the shelter in 'the bad trip' tent. They also came to talk about God and religion and the world – 'love not war'. They talked of the Jesus folk, the Jesus cult and other such groups.

I meet a great number of young people today who believe that Jesus and the truth that He spoke are the most definite things in life today. More and more young people are turning to the Christian faith. I think it is because they have tried everything else.

At Hoxton, which is associated with Hugh Redwood and God in the Slums, *do you feel that you belong to that tradition at all?*
The Scriptures are very simple; my faith is very simple. This is what the majority of people want – to feel that somebody loves them, that somebody cares. This is the lesson of the Bible. Goodwill work is caring for people. The men and women who live in the flats and in the areas round about Hoxton need care and love. This is our work.

The Army said to me, 'Go there; try to meet the needs of the people. If an idea doesn't work, throw it out until you find something that does work.' There is no 'red tape'. We can cater for over a thousand people in our building each week.

What do you do? Who are these people?
The aim of the Centre is to meet social, spiritual and physical needs. We work with the local authority. We start from the beginning of a person's life. Our youngest members are two years old, in our day nursery, open from 8.30 a.m. until 5.30 p.m. They are cared for by a dedicated Christian staff—a full-time staff.

At the other end of the scale—with carpets, television and armchairs—are the old people—one member is ninety-four years of age. They sit in the warmth; they can snooze, play cards, watch television, have their lunch in the luncheon club. We cook seventy meals a day. We also have the Army activities; Sunday-school and the Army meeting which we call the 'family fellowship service'. We have a timbrel brigade, two home leagues, and the over-sixty club. We have a full-time chiropodist's clinic run by the local authority. There is an advice bureau open all day.

What sort of advice?
It may be the need for a rent-rebate form, a family-income supplementary form, and many others. People complete these forms in the office, with our help sometimes, and then we send them on their way—happy. There are those whose problems are deeper—some may need the Missing Persons' Bureau; others ask us to get in touch with firms about jobs. Some of these negotiations go on for weeks. Then there are the more profound needs of the lonely, the insecure, the depressed. There are high-rise flats around the Centre. Many of the older folks live in them. They feel cut off. They want to sit and talk, have a cup of coffee, and then they move on. We like to feel they feel better and that they will come again. Some of them we get to know well and we are able to help them in some major way. We visit many in their homes.

Do these people understand that there is a Christian drive behind this?
Of course. These men and women are quite happy to talk about The Salvation Army and what it stands for. Some don't always agree and tell us so. But mostly they understand what we are doing and why, even when they will not commit themselves.

The need for the Christian faith is now greater than ever before. People are lonely and empty inside. I find this in my work. Many want comfort; they want to be needed as individuals. Formal words are not enough. One must speak the word in Christ's name. The local authorities can cater for many needs, but they often prefer non-statutory work to help them in difficult parts of their programme.

The Founder would say 'Amen' to that. He knew that Parliamentary laws were not enough.

The local authorities often learn from us. One of the officers at Hoxton is a schools health visitor. About thirty sociology students train at our centre. I am a tutor in youth work for the Inner London Education Authority. They also pay my salary, which is considerably in excess of a Salvation Army officer's allowance. As is usual in the Army, the excess is used by the Army towards other costs of the Centre. I am quite happy about that. I should add that the local authority does finance much of the work we do. Yet, while we are thankful, we do this work for God. Oddly, I am sure the local authority experts know that as well as we do.

CHAPTER NINE

God in Northern Ireland

Have you been in the Army all your life?
No.

How did you become a Salvationist?
There is a small Salvation Army corps just round the corner from where I live. With some friends I used to go to Sunday-school as a child. But when I was about eleven I stopped—I was too old! But I used to meet the Salvationists going round the pubs on Saturday nights with the *War Cry*. They used to invite me to their meetings held on Sunday evenings. I used to say 'Too much to do' or something of the sort. My friends would ask me to go to a dance, but at this period something important happened to me. It was a kind of spiritual or emotional thing to do with growing up. I said to myself, 'I wonder, if I pray about it, would God do anything?' When I used to go to Sunday-school I used to pray. So one night I knelt down in my bed and I said, 'God, I don't know whether you are there or not, but if you are I want you to answer this prayer for me . . .' He did answer and I felt better and I knew what I had to do.

How old were you when this happened?
Eighteen, just coming up to eighteen. That Saturday night God answered my prayer. Nobody actually knew anything about it. I didn't tell anybody, but that Sunday, when my friends called for me to go to the dance, I told them that I had a date. I was going to The Salvation Army—that was my 'date'—the most wonderful date of my life. I kept my promise. I went to The Salvation Army, and the next week as well.

Nothing happened. But I just kept going every Sunday. I wanted to be religious, to be converted, but I was cold and nothing happened. This continued for about a year and then a group of cadets visited Ireland. After their last meeting was over they were talking to us, when I felt a great need to surrender at last. My friend went first and then I went forward to the Penitent-form. I said, 'God, forgive me.' From that time I continued going to The Salvation Army. I began to wear uniform and became a soldier.

Did your parents approve of this step?
My parents are not Christians but my mother thought it was all a bit of fun. She said it would soon wear off.

Didn't you have boy friends? Did you go to dances?
Yes, I did.

Yet you were not happy?
No.

Would you say that you were a very religious sort of girl?
I believed in God but I had no religious background. I didn't belong to a church.

And yet you wanted to be saved?
Yes, I really wanted to be saved.

But when one wants to be saved, one has a sense of something wrong—what was it that was wrong with you?
I did not feel I was wicked. I didn't think that going to a dance, or having a drink, was sin. In my prayers I said, 'Lord I'm not really a sinner; I don't do anybody any harm,' and the Lord just spoke to me and said, 'Thou shalt love the Lord thy God with all thy heart . . .' and then I realised that God wasn't first in my life and that was what made me a sinner. It wasn't what I was doing that put me in need of salvation but what I was not doing.

Do you believe that God can save Ireland?

Yes, I do.

Do you love Ireland? Do you love all the people, Catholics as well as Protestants?
I love the Catholics and I have had Catholic friends. I believe God will give peace to Ireland when the people turn to Him.

Do you think there is fault on both sides?
Yes. I have seen both sides do wrong and I have seen the Army and The Salvation Army go among the people and they have stopped shouting and throwing stones and fighting to let us move by safely.

Why do Christians fight, do you think?
It is not a Christian war. It is terrible that religion is blamed for it. If the people and the Parliament will turn to God and pray and accept God's way then the troubles could be solved and Ireland could have peace at last. Up to now it has been the will of men. But there will be no end until it is the will of God.

FROM LETTERS written by the same girl cadet during field training in Northern Ireland.

I was anxious about the groups of young people. One Saturday afternoon I went to speak to young men who were of a 'tartan gang'. They asked questions as they sat on the pavement; I spoke about Jesus. A drunk came up to demand that I sing 'The Old Rugged Cross'. I obliged. A crowd gathered, which brought the police who broke up the crowd. We were able to help the drunk, finding him clothes and arranging meals on wheels.

The trouble came at last to Larne. We heard word that someone had been shot and we decided to go down and see what, if anything, we could do. The police allowed us through the cordon into the street where most of the people were. The women and children were in a terrible state. While we were there the rioting began again. We helped with the wounded. A boy of about sixteen said, 'Please help me.' I took him indoors; he was bleeding profusely.

There was some crossfire and I fell to the ground. A man in front of me was shot. We entered the house where he lay and did what we could. Lieutenant went off to get a priest, for the wounded man was a Roman Catholic. We stayed with the people until 4.30 a.m. Next morning we visited the home of a Protestant who had been shot. His wife was in a terrible state of grief.

. . . A miracle happened last night. For over a month now we have had about twenty to twenty-five youths, eighteen to twenty years old, attending the meeting. We met them in the pubs when we were selling the Army papers. As you can imagine they are rough, and belong to one of the tartan gangs that have sprung up all over Ireland. Last night I talked to the leader of the group. Earlier, when I mentioned God or prayer, he would laugh. But last night he was not drunk. As I got up to go he said, 'Will you pray for me?' That was the miracle!

The Lieutenant in charge was invited to take tea with the Mayor, who had noted that Salvationists were able to talk to the young folk. He asked the Army to assist in the formation of a youth club to help keep the youths out of trouble.

When we were very short of funds we prayed, 'Lord, we must have money. It is up to you.' Later there was a knock on the door and we found a man standing there. He was dressed in a duffle coat and seemed to be a countryman. 'I want to make a donation to the Army,' he said. 'I have not brought it all, but here is £200.'

Two cuttings from the local newspaper show something of what the people felt:

BACKING FOR YOUTH CLUB

The Salvation Army in Larne are giving their backing to attempts to find a youth club for the town's tartan gang and other teen-agers.

Plans are well advanced to find premises for the youth club and The Salvation Army are taking part on a committee which has been set up to officially take possession of the premises when they are made available.

The residents of Ronald Street, Bryan Street and St. John's Place, wish to convey their sincere thanks and gratitude to the local branch of The Salvation Army for their devotion shown during the rioting in Larne's Night of Shame.

. . .

'GO' FOR SALVATIONISTS IN THE 'NO GO' AREAS: A young Salvation Army officer, stationed in London, visits Northern Ireland to conduct a Sunday-school anniversary.

My visit was preceded by a week of violence which involved, among other things, the throwing of a bomb into a bus full of workmen, and a one-day strike which resulted in a number of deaths during rioting.

The journey through the city revealed massive destruction. In some main streets there was barely a handful of shops still trading. Everyone entering the city centre was 'frisked'; troops and police were shoulder to shoulder. A demonstration by Ulster loyalists was awaited with great tension. In fact, it fizzled out that day, but the impression was one of a people trying to live as though there was nothing wrong. To cease from normal living would be regarded as defeat.

My first engagement was to distribute prizes for regular attendance to children who had attended a Belfast Salvation Army Sunday-school during 1972. As the Army hall was the only non-Catholic building in that part of the city, and as on either side the British Army were at their 'look-out' posts, it was felt that to take children into the area at night was foolhardy; so a Congregational school-room was used. A week earlier a sniper had used the roof of the Army hall while a meeting was in progress, and I was given a special welcome because of my willingness to journey from the relative safety of London. But far from feeling heroic, I felt proud of the way in which these Salvationists were living out their Christian faith.

'There aren't many prizes this year,' the Young People's Sergeant-Major informed me. 'Many parents won't let their children come into this area. We can appreciate their feelings.' But there were still 120 prizes to distribute. The number usually presented was about 400.

Open-air meetings were held in Catholic 'territory' and the march through Catholic streets up to the Army hall is a regular weekly fixture. I joined them outdoors. We stood on a spot of ground where 'there used to be a pub just a few weeks ago'. Our march was not one of defiance, not a gesture by the foolhardy, but rather positive action by people who had the 'good news' of Christ to proclaim.

The civil and security authorities had asked the Army to continue 'normal activities' in the area. Many streets of Belfast had become 'no-go' areas and it was only through peaceful activity, such as the Army carried out, that the situation was prevented from getting worse.

There was a profound desire for peace – peace which would allow people to worship freely, peace to enable Ireland to be a happier country. Sometimes there was an embarrassed feeling of need to apologise for fellow-countrymen. Bravely and with belief in the God who has promised His continued presence, they were living their lives, as Salvationists. They strive 'to love their neighbours as themselves' and count everyone worthy of the love of God. The situation is bound to have changed before this is read, but whatever the scene, the Army will be there with 'heart to God and hand to man'.

CHAPTER TEN

The Army's *Jesus Folk*

MAJOR JOHN GOWANS and Major John Larsson have collaborated successfully in Salvation Army music-drama productions which have been appreciated all over the world. Of course, The Salvation Army has been featured in musicals on the professional stage. *The Belle of New York* was one of the earliest. *Guys and Dolls*, based on the stories of Damon Runyan, had a Salvationist lassie heroine. But Gowans and Larsson are far and away the most successful Salvationists within The Salvation Army to use the 'musical' technique. It is as if they were adapting slightly a famous query attributed to William Booth, 'Why should the devil have all the best stage shows?' One of the Gowans-Larsson songs – 'How much more' – has won international acclaim and has been transmitted by the B.B.C. and numerous other broadcasting stations.

Major Larsson, about your work with Major John Gowans on 'musicals': how many have there been?
Three. *Take-over Bid* was first; then *Hosea;* and now, *Jesus Folk.*

Did you expect them to be so successful?
No. You have great hopes when you start off, but the fact that they were taken up so well in this country, and all round the world, really took us by surprise.

Had you planned it for a long time? Did it come out of the blue?

The first one was commissioned by the Youth Department. They wanted something for the 1968 Youth Year, perhaps in the style of Oberammergau. We suggested that the 'musical' would be a better proposition. Colonel Denis Hunter, then of the Youth Department, was a great impresario. He virtually 'sold' the thing before it was written, and then the whole thing just went off as easily as that.

Any opposition from the old guard? It was a modern, 'with-it' approach, quite unconventional.
Surprisingly little. We worked it out very carefully, trying to avoid needless alarm. Though the story of *Take-over Bid* is the contrast between youth and age, in the resolution of the play it is shown that youth doesn't necessarily have all the answers, but that all of us, young and old, are dependent upon God.

Was the story the work of you both?
Yes, we worked together on the story, and on the script. The lyrics are separate—John Gowans does these and I do the music, independently. This takes the longest time, getting the plot worked out, finding where the songs can be fitted, and what kind of songs we need.

Any straight dialogue, or is it all music as in opera?
Very much on the pattern of a straight musical. It goes from song to song but is bridged with dialogue, with a story-line running through it. *Jesus Folk*, the latest musical, moves out more. It has less of a plot, less dialogue, and much more music.

Any interest in this form outside the Army in the United Kingdom?
We get press cuttings from all over the world. In many cases it has quite revolutionised Army centres where it has been put on abroad. In the United States, in the Central Territory, the Royal Oak Corps put all their people to work on *Take-over Bid* and *Hosea*. In consequence they had a revival, bringing new families into the Army.

Some of the songs, I know, have become world-famous. One I heard

broadcast on T.V. appealed to me very much. It was taken up by numerous church people too. It was entitled, 'How much more'. Why was this so successful, do you think?
In each musical we try to plan that there will be a few songs that will stand on their own legs, even when completely divorced from the musical. 'How much more' is obviously one of those. It was intended to be one of those songs that would stand up on its own appeal. It was the theme-song of the musical. Hosea loved his wife, Gomer, who was a very wicked woman. If Hosea could forgive and love her, then how much more will God our Father love and forgive us? The tune is simple, and suitable for congregational use, and it is also a central theme of the Gospels.

Your latest, Jesus Folk*—has already had its première in a packed town-hall at Lewisham—every ticket sold out and people turned away. But what does the term 'Jesus Folk' mean?*
We chose the title because of current interest in the Jesus movement, and Jesus people. But the basic idea of the story is that the Jesus folk of New Testament times are the people who walked with Jesus. The Jesus folk of today are the Christians who follow Christ. In the play people come in, modern people with problems. They call on their counterparts from New Testament days—Zaccheus and Lazarus and the man with the paralysed hand, to tell what Jesus did, how He helped them. The basic message is that what He did then He can do today.

It is not particularly 'Army'?
Take-over Bid was Army. We reckoned, even though we hoped to reach non-Army people, that 80 per cent of each audience would be Army. By the time *Hosea* came along, the Army element was quite incidental. The venue was an Army youth club, for that gave us the colour of an occasional uniform, and the band thrown in. But the setting could have been anywhere. *Jesus Folk* has no Army connotation whatsoever. It is strictly a Bible story. We think it is going to be strengthened because of this. It might be taken up by outside dramatic groups. After all, the gospel is not sectarian. We would not like our plays to be sectarian.

You have had large numbers of people from other churches come to these shows?
Yes, churches have presented excerpts from the musicals, particularly *Hosea*. Our music has been used widely. But we don't push printed books of the musicals; we don't try and sell them; we don't advertise them. If churches happen to hear about them, all well and good. The *Jesus Folk* musical will be more readily available, because it is going to be published by the Army and will be on sale to the general public.

Would it not have been an advantage to have, as Joy Webb had, a commercial publisher? Some organisation with expertise to sell the musicals?
We think it would be good if Army musicals got to that point. The first two were distributed by the Youth Department, but the Army's publishers had their doubts about them as potential successes. But because they proved to be popular with the public they are now publishing the third. If Army music, generally, were made available to churches and other bodies we think it would be a good thing.

Have you had any feelings yourself, or encountered them in others, of shock or fear that you are breaking an old-time taboo on 'worldliness'? After all, you are using a medium which is entertainment. You are venturing into the arena of the world, the flesh and the devil—the theatre, the monopoly of Hollywood films. What's the difference between Shaw's Major Barbara, *which he wrote for profit, and your productions?*
The main difference is that our pieces are deliberately evangelistic. From an art point of view this is a weakness. But we are prepared to work within this narrow limit which sometimes irks us. It would be nice to produce a musical without having to say something, without having to preach a sermon. What has pleased us with the three productions, and despite the limitations, is that they seem to pack a strong punch. Particularly in *Hosea*, people are moved to tears. I can remember the first presentation which was before 2,000 officers. It started at 9.0 p.m. at Bognor Regis at officers' councils. It went on until about 11.30 p.m. It was late, and not the easiest of audiences. They had been travelling all day. At one point, with my back to the audience, because I was conducting the show, I thought that we had

lost the attention of the crowd. I could hear restless movement going on behind me. I discovered afterwards that it was caused by people reaching for handkerchiefs to blow their noses and wipe their eyes. They were greatly moved by what was happening on stage.

That is certainly a good Salvation Army way!
We always reckoned that we were following good Salvation Army tactics. General Orsborn's father showed films at the old Clapton Congress Hall, almost as soon as films were invented. It is our aim to attract people and, at the same time, present a message.

I think our strength in the early days was that we were not afraid of profane things and ideas. Our officers were secular in that sense, they weren't high priests. We took the gimmicks of the world and sanctified them. William Booth would move into areas that shocked ecclesiastically-minded people. He had no qualms about using a motor car for God's purpose—in 1906, when some people were still debating whether the infernal machine should be tolerated at all. He favoured the use of the lantern slide and the cinema and circus tent and the trumpet, even 'Champagne Charlie', the tune from the music hall and the Brewers Industry. It all came alike to him. He removed all taint by the use he made of it. You are a third generation Salvationist of Swedish origin. Are not the Scandinavians orthodox and austere in their attitude to these things? Will they not be shocked?
The problem is one of translation, as well. I know they are working on *Hosea* in Stockholm and thinking of *Jesus Folk* in Copenhagen.

PART TWO

Inside the Army

CHAPTER ELEVEN

Keeping The Army on The March

AUTOCRACY WAS FASHIONABLE when The Salvation Army was founded in the 1860s. There had been bloody revolution and other more or less fierce political pressures, on a world-wide scale, in a quest for democratic freedoms. Much of this failed, provoking reaction and oppression. William Booth was not a dictatorial type, and much too warm-hearted and reasonable to fill the bill as an autocrat of the Luther, Cromwell, Calvin, or John Knox sort.

A group of Booth's supporters, which included his wife, encouraged him to take personal control of The Christian Mission when it was losing momentum, and engaging in wrangling and interminable indecisive conferences, which Booth called 'talking shop'. He was, however, a reluctant dictator. The military analogy, which coincided with the Boothian *coup d'état*, helped to make a system in which William Booth would be supreme and all officer subordinates would have well-defined authority, from the General down to the newly-commissioned lieutenant.

The General's supreme authority presently included Booth's right to designate his own successor, and William Booth chose his eldest son, Bramwell, who was General from the time of his father's 'promotion to Glory', in 1912, until the year of his own passing in 1929. That was the year of a crisis of Army authority.

The first High Council was called. General Bramwell Booth was deposed and General Edward J. Higgins was elected his successor. Since that year, all Salvation Army Generals have been elected, rather in the manner of the election of the Pope by the College of

Cardinals. Press publicity for the 1929 High Council affair was enormous and numerous books have described it, notably *God's Soldier* by St. John Ervine, *Bramwell Booth* by Catherine Bramwell-Booth, and *Salvation Dynasty* by Brian Lunn. Volume Six of the Army's history, published in 1973 by Hodder and Stoughton, and written by Frederick Coutts gives a scholarly and reliable account of the affair.

The main issue in 1929 was undoubtedly the succession. In the twentieth century it did not seem reasonable that this should be by nomination alone. But, though the first High Council and succeeding modifications of the Army's constitution changed the method of a General's accession to control, it did little to diminish his authority once he was elected.

One new factor in the exercise of authority in The Salvation Army is the Advisory Council to the General, which came into being in 1949. This had been mooted long before, and might have been set up a decade earlier if the Second World War had not interrupted the consultative processes between Salvation Army leaders in many countries. Oddly, it was a General with a decidedly authoritative disposition who set it up, its membership to consist of seven Commissioners. They were to advise the General on a wide range of matters, which included the appointment of leading officers, the promotion or retirement of officers affecting membership of the High Council, the training of officers, doctrinal questions, policy for missionary endeavour and evangelistic work generally, changes to rules and regulations, and numerous matters arising therefrom.

An officer who serves on this Advisory Council has commented in the form of answers to questions:

Would you say that the General is still an autocrat?
To some extent I suppose he always will be, in that he has the sole oversight, direction and control of the Army, constitutionally. This must always be while the Deed of Constitution remains. It specifies that he has the sole oversight, direction and control, as the General for the time being of The Salvation Army.

Where does the Advisory Council fit into this picture?
It has no executive powers at all. It receives requests from the General for advice and recommendations. The General is then quite free to accept or not to accept.

Does this system of consultation refer only to decisions above a certain level?
The General can refer anything he wishes to the Advisory Council—anything on which he wishes to have advice.

But, in practice, does he consult the Advisory Council about leading appointments and about high ranks and responsibilities?
He is obliged to do that by the constitutional Minute of the Advisory Council. It is laid down there what he should refer to the Advisory Council—the first appointment of a Territorial Commander, for example. This is set down in the mode of procedure of the Advisory Council.

Does dissent take place between the General and the Advisory Council? Can the General ask your advice and then refuse to take it?
We can recommend that the General looks at it again.

Does he?
Sometimes! But he still has the final word. There is nothing mandatory about our recommendations.

Is there room in the Advisory Council itself for differences of opinion on what advice to give the General?
If any members differ from others they are quite free to present a minority report, and this does happen. There is another thing. At the time of his election by the High Council as General, he may give certain undertakings. Now he is not legally bound by these, but he is morally bound. Legally he has the sole oversight, direction and control of the Army. But morally he gives these undertakings on being elected. He says, I will do so and so, and so and so. One expects that he will do as he says, although this is not enforceable in law.

What sort of commitments would these be?

Changes in the Army's system of government, for example; changes in the Army's ranks system; changes in the Army's policy regarding evangelistic or social work.

The General then makes an election speech, like a politician?
Yes, if he wishes he makes certain promises, tells the High Council what kind of things he believes in. There is a list of questions prepared, and nominees are asked to answer these questions.

What about the Commissioners' Conference recently held in the United States? Was that an 'election commitment' by the General?
He did agree to hold a conference of Commissioners and to invite all Territorial Commanders.

What of the Chief of the Staff of the Army for the time being? Is he an executive officer with definite authority, or is he in the role of 'Lieutenant to the General', and his Personal Assistant?
No. He is the Chief Executive Officer of The Salvation Army, and he is also the second-in-command of The Salvation Army. When the General is absent from International Headquarters for more than a calendar month, he is obliged to give Power of Attorney to the Chief, who acts in his stead. This is a legal requirement.

In William Booth's day the General was the evangelist-in-chief par excellence, and the Chief of the Staff was the brilliant administrator. Does that situation still obtain?
Looking back at those who have been Chief of the Staff, we have had some more inclined to be prophets and evangelists than others. But the prophetic evangelist's function must remain with the General, whose service is to seek to save souls, to travel, to preach and inspire Salvationists throughout the world, whereas the function of the Chief of the Staff is to be chief executive officer. In recent years, however, the Chief has travelled considerably. Of course, any Army officer is an evangelist at all times.

But we assume that when he travels, he is travelling primarily to solve administrative problems and to talk over policies?
Leaders take advantage of his presence in a territory to discuss

problems. But at zonal conferences the Chief would very rarely, if ever, give a decision on the spot. The various matters would be discussed. He would sometimes turn to the International Secretary, who has his own responsibility, and ask his view and opinion; but then these recommendations would be gathered together in a report and implemented later on, after being given due consideration.

The military analogy, with the name 'Salvation Army', was a brilliantly inspired move of our early days. But is the military analogy still valid? We hear of 'boards' and 'councils'. They are not committees so-called, but are they committees under another name? Could we be in danger of becoming the very thing which William Booth abolished in 1878?
In the Founder's day he could cope, especially with the help of Railton and Bramwell. But the Army has outgrown that state; it has become too large for any one or two persons to deal with it administratively. Secondly, in an age of democracy, when there is a distaste for autocracy, the General has delegated authority at various levels. But even a Territorial Commander is controlled by a Memorandum of Appointment, which sets out his area of authority, and he must act on the General's authority, within these limits. So our military system, our ranks, our authority still operate even though we have boards and councils to assist in reaching decisions.

Britain's position in the world is different from those far-off days of 1878. The Salvation Army was created when London was the world metropolis, when it seemed quite natural that all roads should lead here. But now, with the U.S.A. as the superpower and London, at best, part of the so-called third world, is there any difficulty about 'internationalism' operated from London?
I have had many years' experience at International Headquarters here in London. I have neither seen nor heard any objections to the centralisation system of Army operations. This is the birthplace of the Army, and I am constantly surprised at the way people look at our homeland, the 'Old Country', as being the birthplace of the Army. They make their pilgrimage to Nottingham where William Booth was born, and Mile End Waste where The Salvation Army began. It is a revelation of the way people look towards London as the home of The Salvation Army.

Would you agree that at one time our internationalism was a bit unbalanced? Englishmen would be sent to posts abroad, so that our internationalism consisted of a large number of British officers holding executive responsibilities abroad, a British hierarchy. We know that at one time it became a matter for some comment abroad. The Queen of the Netherlands once asked the General, 'Can we have a Dutch Territorial Commander?'

The predominance of British officers, when it existed, was brought about because at that time they were the only officers who were ready. There is constant interchange. It is evident that this policy is gaining ground. We have a Swedish General, a Canadian Chief of the Staff here at International Headquarters and similar evidence of true internationalism in many parts of the world. It will increase more as men of various nations become available. In Africa and Asia we have a definite policy of appointing national officers to higher responsibilities.

There seem to be few nationals of the newly-independent countries among leading Salvation Army Commissioners. Will they qualify for these positions in due course?

Yes. We have had Commissioner Dahya, Commissioner Hasegawa, Commissioner Corputty; these are all nationals, as we call them. This explains in itself that where the man is available he can take the top positions. It goes without saying that in considering the merits of a man his colour is irrelevant.

Has The Salvation Army suffered because of its 'colour-blindness' in some countries?

It certainly creates problems for Headquarters when colour is a factor, a serious political factor. We must go along to some extent with the prevailing political wind. You cannot operate without Government permission, and even its aid.

Does the Army suffer greatly because of having to go along with Governments in such conditions?

This has not been so detrimental to us as you might imagine. You see, we have work among the Bantu, the black races of South Africa, and amongst the coloured population, the mixture of black and white. We have no work, or very little work, among the Indian population. But we also have work among the Europeans, the whites. This includes the Afrikaners, who are the descendants of old Dutch settlers, and the white Europeans. This is understood; our work is not interfered with. There are certain laws we have to keep and these are strictly enforced. It is the same in Rhodesia. Although we may not approve of the attitude of the Government, and sometimes of some of the African people, we are there for them, and we work on their behalf. We are trying to serve every branch of the community.

In Tanzania, Zambia, Kenya, or other territories where we have African governments, the old white regime is there on sufferance. Has the Army work in those countries greatly diminished?

On the contrary, we have gone on from strength to strength. In Kenya, an outstanding example, the Government is pressing us to do more. At this very moment I have a request from the officer-in-charge to open new Salvation Army operations in Kenya, and the Government is finding money to help us.

In Zambia our work is being encouraged and helped. In Nigeria and Ghana it is the same. There has been no adverse pressure upon us because of change from colonial to national leadership. It is recognised that the Army is trying to help people everywhere. The spirit of colonialism should not be present in any officer. We are known to be non-political. We may have differing views, but while we are working with a Government we do not join in the cross-currents of politics.

Isn't it true that some of our young people are critical of us, because we are not more of a protest or pressure group?

Yes, this is so. They feel we should march down the streets with banners. But I have often said to such young people that it is a much better course to remain and do our job. How can it help to protest, and then be put on the next ship home and have the Army closed down? It is best, I feel, to go along as best we can, maintaining our principles and serving the people. This we are doing. All over the world our man on the spot will seek to serve and save without any selfish aim and without regard to race, or creed, or colour.

CHAPTER TWELVE

Authority and Discipline

As the Chief of the Staff, Commissioner Arnold Brown is second only to the General in the command echelon of The Salvation Army. As a Canadian, he is familiar with the North American pattern of Salvationist operations in corps activities, where direct evangelism and the approach through community service is closely integrated. Now that the dual method is developing in Britain, we asked the Chief if this did not entail changes, among them the need for officers to have longer command terms.

There is little doubt in my mind that this will happen. The norm could well become a term of greater length. If you move a man within a short period of time that will be because of some emergency or particular necessity or unexpected circumstances. The corps officer will need to know not only his theology, his platform ministry and his pastoral cares, but he will also need to know local authority staff and municipal legislation and finance. He will need to know how to get funds and other local authority assistance. This will require some degree of stability in his appointment. Even more important, perhaps, he must be able to move from the spiritual to the social and from the social back to the spiritual without a wobble. Of course, as you will find elsewhere in these pages, Salvation Army officers insist that the spiritual and the social work are inseparable.

Will you need to explain with any sense of apology that this is a reversal of William Booth's idea? He would leave a man in one place for six months. Given a longer term, he was afraid the officer would settle down and become complacent. There would be too many local ties and local friends. Then he would not want to move.

That was the way of things in Victorian times. But improved educational standards among our officers, and an acceptance of the complex patterns of our work, make it possible, and necessary, in these modern times to allow longer periods in an appointment. We still have the option to move an officer at any time, but we accept that both our own people, the Salvationists, and the townsfolk and local authorities with whom we work expect continuity of command.

New social legislation is out of all recognition complex, when compared with that of William Booth's time. If the Army wanted to open a hostel in those days we took an old mill or factory, and the hostel could be operating within a day or two. No one would say you nay. That is not possible in these times. One must have outline planning and approval. There have to be feasibility studies. There are minimum ministry standards to be observed. Even in those corps where we use our own citadels as community centres, there has to be conformity with public health standards, if food is served or clubs are operated. Considerable sums of public money are involved. Getting this money and budgeting for its outlay, seeing that it is well spent and properly accounted for, is something that requires expertise and more time than formerly. All of us are still subject to marching orders, but not so frequently as in earlier days.

As the Chief of the Staff, you visit and deal with the Army in the United States, Australia, Scandinavia, India. But when the Army began in London, Britain was the world power on which the sun never set. British Salvation Army officers were sent to leading commands, perhaps because at that time they were the only suitable officers available. The Army in those days seemed to be The British Salvation Army abroad. Now, some say, Britain is not a leading world power; London is just another capital. Is the Army adjusting to this change?

In the early days, obviously, it was 'a British Salvation Army'. It began here; then British Salvationists emigrated and British leadership was appointed. These people made a profound impact. Eventually the Army became indigenous. But this took some time.

They tell me that in Germany there are still traces of a kind of translated English. Early Salvationists would say, 'I am glad I can say I am saved.' Literally translated this is not good German. They were trying to make things easy for the Founder and others from Britain. Very often the leader in Germany could not speak German. Generally that will not do today.

Nowadays there is a balanced, international Salvation Army, with headquarters in London, England. There is a Swedish General and I am a Canadian. You have American officers in charge of territories far from their own country. A Finn is in Canada as Chief Secretary. One could list dozens of such international appointments. The roster of appointments here at International Headquarters reads like a roll call at the United Nations!

This is bound to affect the number of leading ranks held by the British—particularly the rank of Commissioner?
There is a degree of change here, but it is not overwhelming. I don't think anyone sits down to prune the number of Commissioners who are British. If the balance were drastically disturbed, the Advisory Council to the General might ask, 'What are you doing?' or 'Are you aware this is happening?' The constitution says that the General has to maintain a minimum of twenty full Commissioners, plus the Chief of the Staff, in office at all times. How these twenty are spread around the world is a matter mostly of their relationship to a concentration of responsibility, not to their nationality. There was a necessity in early days for the Training Principal in London to be a Commissioner. He might have seven or eight hundred cadets —a large concentration of Salvation Army force and a tremendous responsibility. With reduced sessions, one has to have a different policy. In other parts of the world there is cadet strength not far below that of London, but the Training Principal may be a Major, Brigadier, Lieutenant-Colonel or Colonel. There is not, I repeat, any plan deliberately to reduce the number of Commissioners in Britain.

Sometimes there are factors other than Salvationist strength. For example, you have to take into account respect for a nation as such. We have an Officer Commanding for Belgium, and one for Italy. 'Why don't you tack these relatively small commands on to one of the larger territories?' we have been asked. 'Why don't you attach

Belgium to France and Italy to Switzerland? You have a leader in Switzerland, at the moment, who can speak Italian, and it has been done before.' This sounds very persuasive, but the point is that you take note of the nationhood of a people within precise geographical borders. When we forget this national aspect we may be reminded of our lapse by a prime minister, or a president, or a monarch in the countries concerned. It has happened.

The Army's International Headquarters is located in London by a process of history. The Army began here. A good deal of what happens in this 'head office', this 'pulse' of the Army, has been handed down from the very beginning. International Headquarters is a repository of Salvation Army administrative experience different from that of any Territorial Headquarters. Events have decided that; not any pro-British feeling.

Now, Chief, may I be topical and ask you about women's lib? The Army pioneered, in its own way, female ministry. Now there are suggestions that we are falling a little behind. If you were diminishing the number of Commissioners in Britain, the Women's Social Services might not have a woman Commissioner. Then you might not have a woman Commissioner anywhere in the world.

Yes, this matter of female ministry is of great significance to us, and equality of opportunity must be faithfully and intelligently preserved. We are proud of the Army's record. But some women, like some men, have said 'no' to increased responsibility. Many take such responsibility, but only within a specific context. You might have in one territory a Women's Social Services leader who might be a colonel. You might also have, say, a dozen very capable hospital superintendents or administrators in that same territory. Of these it would be only one or two, if any, who would want to be the Women's Social Secretary because, while having nursing and administrative skills in the context of hospital service, they would not want the headache and the heartache that come with the management of personnel, and complicated administrative responsibility.

Many women in the Army find vocational fulfilment in specialised service. The Army leader often has to be something of a 'jack of all trades', with a fairly diverse range of developed abilities. But many of our women prefer to school themselves in one discipline. Some are averse to dealing with budgets, having to finance expensive operations, managing properties, dealing with 'the awkward squad'. There is also a physiological problem with some women. Women of twenty-five or thirty years of age cannot step into positions of top authority, for this requires experience and wisdom gained over the years. If you can find the person who has such experience and ability before she has lost her dynamic force, then you have the perfect leader. There have been, and are, women who match this pattern and I have no doubt there will be others. But some fall short. They don't know why they are saying 'no', but nature knows why.

Again, it is a mistake to assume that the cause of woman in the Army is deteriorating simply because you do not see fifteen or twenty women wearing Commissioner's trimmings. Look at the large number of women in the Army. See the jobs they are doing. The great majority of them are finding fulfilment; they are working out their vocation of female ministry – this is what Catherine Booth saw them doing. Hers was not a call to authority but a call to service.

What of married women, then? As with married women outside the Army, some women in the Army feel that there should be a change of status for married women. Marriage adds to a woman's capacity, they say, especially in areas such as the Training Colleges and the social services. But many of our most articulate and gifted women officers feel that marriage leads them to the kitchen, the women's meeting, the sort of cul-de-sac said to await the curate's wife. Could the Army appoint a married woman in her own right to the Training College, to teaching, to social service? In the professions and in other fields married women work with great success. They have married, loved and reared children, and now have time, and want to give it. A woman is all the more qualified in some important ways because she is married. One such married woman, an officer, in Britain, studied social service and became a qualified counsellor and social worker at a Salvationist social service centre for men in London. But it was a lonely struggle for her. She felt it was against the tide of Army thought. Should not the Army encourage it?

The Army would encourage it. But the case mentioned is unique. The number of married women who would subject themselves to the disciplines that this officer did in order to get her sociological qualification might be small.

Many of the best women in the Army get married. But, again, we are on the horns of an administrative dilemma. Grant that we have a woman who is capable. Let's say she is fifty to fifty-five. Her children have gone. Her husband does not reach retirement age for another ten or fifteen years. If she has gifts in a special direction, well and good. If she can write, there's ample opportunity for her to use her talent. A woman teacher may have less opportunity, but teaching would not be ruled out. But there is an administrative and psychological problem. If you put a married woman in a position of authority, then you could cause the single woman to be very concerned. She could feel that you have taken away her future. The wife has had husband and home, all the things the single woman does not have. Should she have both marriage and authority? And remember, some women deliberately forgo marriage for the sake of vocation. They could well resent a system which gave a married woman career prospects better than their own.

We can, of course, claim that many married women officers *do* have responsibility and combine specific Army tasks with their marital status in praiseworthy fashion. The wives of Divisional Commanders, Chief Secretaries and Territorial Commanders have many challenging responsibilities. For that matter the wife of the corps officer, social service officer, any officer at all, can find numerous worthwhile tasks if the will to serve is there—as I know it is in most cases. To be an officer-wife is certainly no cul-de-sac!

Can I ask you about the Army's alleged despotism, its censorship, its denial of free expression in its own press and the books written by officers? You will guess I have in mind a recent case which aroused considerable publicity and controversy.

We admit that this is a difficult problem, and since that case, when we lost a very good officer, we have made some changes in our written conditions of service which we think provide a positive approach. The language is clearer, and more time is given for consideration of it. But we cannot have a doctrinal free-for-all in the Army. Even the General is bound to adhere to our eleven articles of faith—our doctrines. They are plain and well tried. They are part of our Deed Poll as enacted by Parliament. No Salvationist is allowed to repudiate them and remain a Salvationist. We do not burn or cause to be shot the dissenter from these articles of faith—but we can insist that the officer or soldier who does not accept them leaves our ranks. They are a voluntary undertaking when one comes into The Salvation Army and they are a voluntary undertaking while one serves, either as officer or soldier. We do not have conscription; one can always leave the Army if one's inclination or one's conscience makes it necessary.

Having said this, it is correct to add that books published by us and about us by commercial publishing houses do show the trend of the times in allowing much more freedom of expression than used to be the case years ago. We now allow exchange of views and differing opinions in our periodicals—a decided advance towards modern tolerance. But we cannot hinder the Army's effectiveness by allowing controversies on the fundamental aspects of our faith which ought to be, and are in most cases, above argument by Salvationists. What may be an intellectual exercise in London could be a gravely damaging experience to the morale of Salvationists in a less sophisticated or even primitive area—and we are a worldwide international Army.

This is not at all to suggest that we are unduly repressive. We have moved into the twentieth century with all that that implies to any religious movement. Our rules and regulations are scrutinised and revised regularly—often in a liberal direction. We have no doctrine of infallibility in the Army. We get hundreds of suggestions for change, and Salvationists are always trying out new tactics and giving utterance to new ideas. We have thousands of articulate and adventurous young people in our ranks—many of them Salvationist radicals. While they are true Salvationists, their radicalism does not worry us unduly. Some of it we can beneficially feed into the Army. It is significant that our young people are normally quite conservative doctrinally.

The present General is Swedish. One does not expect despotic autocrats to emerge from that background. Even if General Wickberg were of autocratic disposition—a ludicrous idea to anyone who knows him—he is subject to a consultative process in the Advisory Council and in other checks and balances.

Can you cite instances of the more liberal approaches to an officer's Conditions of Service?
The Conditions of Service now become Undertakings entered into by an officer of The Salvation Army. We allow ample time for consideration and reconsideration. There is the training period of two years, or more, for further consideration before the would-be officer has to make a final decision. He can be in no doubt. If he signs, it is a reaffirmation. It is voluntary. It is binding. It is clear. No one from the General down to the most recent recruit can be exempt from it.

But why must the Army be so serious, so strict, about this? After all William Booth was a broad-minded and benign autocrat, if he was an autocrat at all.
I agree. But he expected discipline, steadfastness, and the honouring of covenants freely entered into. His own faith was plain, largely Methodist. Essentially it is set out in our eleven articles:

1 We believe that the Scriptures of the Old and New Testaments were given by inspiration of God; and that they only constitute the divine rule of Christian faith and practice.
2 We believe there is only one God, who is infinitely perfect—the Creator, Preserver and Governor of all things—and who is the only proper object of religious worship.
3 We believe that there are three persons in the Godhead—the Father, the Son and the Holy Ghost—undivided in essence and co-equal in power and glory.
4 We believe that in the person of Jesus Christ the divine and human natures are united; so that He is truly and properly God, and truly and properly man.
5 We believe that our first parents were created in a state of innocency but, by their disobedience, they lost their purity and happiness; and that in consequence of their fall all men have become sinners, totally depraved, and as such are justly exposed to the wrath of God.
6 We believe that the Lord Jesus Christ has, by His suffering and death, made an atonement for the whole world, so that whosoever will may be saved.

7 We believe that repentance towards God, faith in our Lord Jesus Christ, and regeneration by the Holy Spirit are necessary to salvation.
8 We believe that we are justified by grace, through faith in our Lord Jesus Christ; and that he that believeth hath the witness in himself.
9 We believe that continuance in a state of salvation depends upon continued obedient faith in Christ.
10 We believe that it is the privilege of all believers to be 'wholly sanctified', and that their 'whole spirit and soul and body' may 'be preserved blameless unto the coming of our Lord Jesus Christ' (1 Thess. 5:23).
11 We believe in the immortality of the soul; in the resurrection of the body; in the general judgment at the end of the world; in the eternal happiness of the righteous; and in the endless punishment of the wicked.

Now these articles are in the hands of Salvationists in India; they are part of the life and faith of converts in Africa; we are propagating them in our newly-opened work in Spain. We may be somewhat extravagant in our behaviour, noisy and even vulgar in the opinion of some, as we bang our drums and march with our banners. But The Salvation Army is doctrinally based on a quite lucid and sober interpretation of the Christian faith. It is not 'way out'. We have our eccentrics, but our faith is 'middle of the road', neither 'new Christianity'—whatever that means—nor sombre ultra-fundamentalism. We know that faith undergoes changes and tests as history and time bear upon it and as new light shines. We are aware of the need to be comprehensible in our 'Articles of War' in certain important respects. This is the basic document of Salvationism. What is there is the residue after revealed truth, tradition and sound criticism have been brought to bear upon it. With this, we can expect the Salvationist who is educated or otherwise, the man who drives the truck and the academic at the university, to adhere to Salvationist doctrine. If he cannot, he knows what to do. It is not a question of despotism, but of simple loyalty. There can be no exceptions to this, although in other matters the Army's rules are much more tolerant than they were. If I could not accept Salvation Army faith and doctrine no one would have to dismiss me. I would accept the inevitable – I would go.

Seeing we are an Army, can we expect an increase in personal initiative and consultation? The British military have had this. This has happened with the military in the United States and certainly in Canada.

We owe much to personal initiative and I spend much of my time in consultation. So do the General and most other Army leaders. But we must also have a chain of command. It is not oppressive or tyrannical. With us there is also a democratic principle at work. A solicitor once said to me, 'The General under law is omnipotent – except for one thing. He's given all his powers away!' There are a few things that the General reserves for himself. He appoints top leaders. He keeps an eye on periodicals – they are the voice of the Army. He watches carefully the training of officers, the personnel of the Army. A great deal of the business of the Army does not go to him unless I take it across to him. He has delegated to the Chief of the Staff and the Commissioners round the world the authority they need. The Territorial Commander in turn gives it to his Divisional Commander. They give it to their corps officers – the Lieutenants, Captains and Majors – all these men are out on their own! The corps bandmasters have tremendous freedom, as do other local Salvationists.

Furthermore, we have corps councils at which the corps officer can be counselled and advised, though I hope with respect and by someone who knows what he is talking about. Now this is the democratic spirit in an Army, and one wonders if there are many precedents in history, even in a quasi-military force which works to such good effect. Our sometimes criticised Orders and Regulations were not invented by disciplinarians; they came out of human experience. The man who first drafted them, George Scott Railton, certainly had great difficulty in complying with them all. He often transgressed, but was as often forgiven by William Booth. Much can be forgiven in one as loyal to the Army as Railton was.

Do you think that the Army's new-found zeal for social service by our 'amateurs' at corps level will succeed? After all, you have done much to bring it about. Are we going to duplicate the State's social apparatus?

As to the last comment, a British prime minister once said to me, 'Democracy never discovers human need. People of compassion discover human need and bring it to the attention of the system.' He added, 'No government has in its budget any money for experimentation in social services. That must be left to people with a social conscience who find the resources and who experiment in new forms of social service. When these services have proved their worth they become part of the Welfare State. There will always be people who slip through the welfare net. The State has no provision for those. The State lives by the book. The State always administers social service by its head. People receiving social service are human; they need the heart.'

CHAPTER THIRTEEN

The New Model Army

COLONEL LAWRENCE SMITH, Director of Public Relations in the United Kingdom, speaks of his work in Britain and makes some comparison with the United States:

It is not difficult to work with British local authorities. You write a brief on the purpose and scope of the project, send it to the town clerk or the chief administrative officer, and ask for a meeting. When the meeting has been arranged, you bring your people and sit down and talk about it. If the project is good and if the local authority has the money they show an interest. Even if they don't have the money, they show an interest. These discussions take place because an established procedure has been developed and there is a place for the voluntary agency in the constellation of community services.

In Britain at one time it was thought that the State would be 'the Father Christmas' and voluntary agencies would be crowded out.
The Minister of State, Department of Health and Social Security, Sir Keith Joseph, Bt., M.P., has shown a keen interest in the Army's work. He participated in the dedication of the new social service complex in Nottingham and he would have participated in the Coventry dedication earlier this year had he been available. He also invited senior officers of the Army to meet him at a conference arranged last year. The Chief of the Staff was present as well as the British Commissioner; Sir Keith inquired about our long-range

plans and a ten-year programme was submitted to him. Part of this plan is being carried out and the ministry has made certain money available to implement certain aspects of the plans. The minister has displayed a keen interest in the voluntary agencies and has met with other groups as well.

We do run into difficulty with some local authorities. Some feel that they can provide essential services themselves; they don't need the voluntary agencies. But these are minority expressions. When a Director of Social Service is appointed, he usually sees the place of the voluntary agency more closely than others do. Some local authorities, again a minority, feel they should build larger facilities, with bigger budgets, and themselves take care of the needs of the people.

Which do you see as likely to succeed in these two schools: the do-it-yourself local authorities, or those who welcome help from others?
Where the local authority attempts to do all the work itself, the rates will so increase that in time that philosophy will inevitably collapse. It will be too expensive. In most instances The Salvation Army can provide a needed service at less expense than a local authority.

The Army utilises its officer staff, and salaries are lower than for other professional workers. Also, we operate with fewer staff. I am not sure that this is good. There have been occasions when a smaller staff creates undue strain on our people. But there are other economies that are a part of our programmes. We are not big spenders and are used to adopting economical measures.

Then there is the matter of dedication, the 'servant-of-all' concept, which motivates Salvationists. This might not obtain in a secular work.

Of course, we must be careful to note that there are many dedicated people working for local authorities. We have no monopoly of virtue! But good salary and working conditions have attracted them, even though they have a true interest in the people they serve. The Salvationist worker is often willing to do more than his job requires. He will spend hours in attempting to work out the personal problems of an individual. Mind you, I see this displayed in non-Salvationists as well. It is what we call the 'plus' quality, something that the dedicated Salvationist can give. It is a spiritual quality; it is giving more time to the person, going 'the extra mile', to work out some problem, whether it be material or spiritual. This is the spirit that William Booth and his successors have desired for Salvationists.

You know of the British 'war' between science and religion: Bishop Wilberforce against Huxley; Charles Booth against William Booth. Do you think there is anything left of this 'war', of this apparent contradiction?

Today there is a difference in approach. In the minds of some, particularly the non-religious, there may be a feeling that a religious social worker is not as competent as the one they consider to be 'scientific'. But we have found that a marriage of the two is possible. It is often accomplished. In New York city, Dr. Norman Vincent Peale has a psychiatric clinic as part of his Marble Collegiate Church. There is a union there of psychiatry and religion. Dr. Smiley Blanton works with other psychiatrists and provides a more complete service than would be possible under wholly Christian or secular supervision.

In America, professional training is normal among your social service officers. Do you have a statutory limitation? Must they all be qualified, professionally?

No, though it may be desirable.

Many of our officers who are not professionally qualified give good administrative supervision to professionally qualified workers, letting them do their work, and yet having sense enough to know when they are on the right track and when they're not. There are some people who are 'naturals' in social work. Others must be trained. I think the 'natural', if trained, and if training doesn't take all the naturalness out of him, is a much better worker than the person who starts with little ability or aptitude. To a large degree it is a matter of will, desire, aptitude; then add training and you get better results. In the American system, if you want to be a trained social worker you must first have a college or university diploma and be accepted by a graduate school of social work. Generally there is a two-year programme, or possibly a three-year programme, for a master's degree. There are specialised areas of social work such as social case work, social group work, medical social work, and psychiatric social work and other categories as well. But the interesting thing is that many religious people, Salvationists and non-Salvationists, are going into social work, taking this training, and are finding it possible to combine seemingly opposing viewpoints. Obviously, if there is a strong Freudian background in the training, this may create problems. Usually the converted person takes what he wants from Freud and leaves the rest.

So you do not think the Freudian concept is totally opposed to the Christian?
Not necessarily. It is the interpretation placed upon Freud which is largely the problem. Unfortunately, many of the modern teachers have insisted that his philosophy is entirely sex-dominated. They neglect to stress other aspects that can be helpful.

We accept such Freudian concepts as better environment and the genetics of heredity. But we would greatly modify the sexual modes in this. We cannot divorce morality from behaviour. We emphasise moral behaviour where possible. Social workers are products of their training. You can foresee how they will think by the school where they study. On the other hand, there are those who go to a Freudian school only because they have opportunity to go there. Yet they come out of it with their Christian principles intact.

As the British pattern seems to be following that of the United States—is there no interference by the authorities who provide what seems to an Englishman to be immense sums of money? It is axiomatic in some fields that he who pays calls the tune. Do the people who find the money for your Christian programme ask you to modify your Christian programme, or wipe it out, or make it Freudian? Do they leave you free to do your Army thing?
There have been instances where they have suggested that we should not proselytise. But in the main they give us a free hand. Our people show good sense in this also. They realise that they are catering to a person's need, including a spiritual need. They tell him about the claims of the gospel. But this is not necessarily sectarian. It should not be our object to make Salvationists out of Roman Catholics or Jews. In this setting our people can preach and practise a gospel which can be non-denominational or interdenominational, and not

anti-Catholic or anti-Jewish. We simply try to explain the claims of Christ, applying them in everyday life.

During the 'War on Poverty' programme under the Economic Opportunity Act, 1964, there was a 'religious disclaimer' clause in which the participant was asked to promise that, in accepting government money, there were certain things that would not be done in terms of propagating religion. In most instances we held discussions with the supervising authority and were given freedom to do our usual socio-religious task. But in certain instances we refused to sign the religious disclaimer and did not participate in the programme. We felt that, as The Salvation Army, we must operate in a certain way, and if the religion is taken from the programme there is not much left to offer. The gospel is part of our programme and philosophy, and enables us to deal with the 'whole man'.

We must be careful that the government does not tie us up by saying, 'We want no Christianity in this. We'll take your social service but not your religion.' Should they do that, we should say, 'Well, we can't do a good job for you under these circumstances.' We cannot tell where spiritual or social services begin or end, as the two are inextricably mixed.

With special problems, such as that of the mentally handicapped, with which the Army is becoming increasingly involved in this country, and clinical conditions such as alcoholism and drug-addiction, can our Salvationist motivation be relevant?

Just as relevant as in any other aspect of treatment. We can often reach a person through the spiritual element of our ministry more quickly than through the therapeutic aspects of it.

Of course, I am speaking of the present day. It is hard to predict what will happen in the future. But the Salvationist lives and works by his Christian dedication and faith. We add to the therapy. It comes about so naturally that, even though we have people who are skilled in aspects of psychotherapy, who know something of psychiatric principles, the Christian aspect comes through most strongly. After all, we perform our work in Christ's name. Anyone who knows The Salvation Army will understand that, when he requests our assistance, the religious aspect will be there.

You know that The Salvation Army in Britain differs in tactics from the Army in the United States. There you have a mixture of evangelism and social service very closely integrated. In Britain they have been run as separate arms of our service; the one had not much to do with the other. So corps work did not 'mix' with social work, as it does in America. Coming from the integrated system to our separated ones must have presented difficulties.

It did not come as a surprise to me. When I attended the International College for Officers I got around a good deal and learned something of the system pertaining here. There have been changes in the British system. More and more we are hearing the term 'community centre' in connection with corps operations. At places like Hemel Hempstead and Clapton Congress Hall, for instance, they are involved in community work. It has its beginnings in an outreach programme concerned with activities outside the corps building itself.

It breaks out, for example, with an over-sixty club which comes partly from within the corps and partly from the community outside. It breaks out in young people's programmes, where we encourage young people, including those of other faiths, to take part in our activities. I'm thinking of the guides and other groups. It can originate when we invite unchurched groups, bringing them into the Army citadel—the physically handicapped, the mentally handicapped, the old and the lonely. We have a building; we have the people who can help with the needs of these people; and we are constantly moving towards providing essential services for these people. Our corps life will inevitably be enriched by these 'outside' forces, by involving ourselves in activities within the community generally.

Would you say that the Army in the United Kingdom after Darkest England *made a tactical error in going separate ways—social service and corps work?*

As far as The Salvation Army is concerned it is inevitable that it should try to cater for those who have been born into it. Our young people and their elders feel that they must belong to something tangible. When they are asked, 'To what church do you belong?' they say, 'I belong to The Salvation Army,' or they say, 'The

Salvation Army is my church.' We have done a service to our people in making them feel that they belong to a vital part of the Christian Church. Their roots are deep in it, and this is helpful. But at the same time, if we had stressed more the existence and need of the outer community, and our involvement with it, the two could have run side by side. These would not be two programmes but one, with the dedicated Salvationist concerning himself with his own spiritual needs and with those of his neighbour. We must not pass by on the other side.

It is possible that we became somewhat ingrown over the years. Now, as our young people, educated differently from preceding generations, are taught to question matters and tend to doubt until things can be proven, it is inevitable that they should look outward and ask if something cannot be done to help the people 'out there'.

One pointer to this change is that many of our new corps buildings, for which this department is asked to raise money, are community-service buildings. They are not walls to shut us in but are havens, centres, call them what you will, to which all sorts and conditions of men, women and children may come.

Some Salvationists cherish the thought of the Army as a church. They are suspicious of any modification of the gospel which seems to be entailed in a coffee-lounge or club for the aged. They insist instead on a 'meeting-centred' kind of programme. As you know, George Scott Railton fought for this. We were a mission to the unconverted. He wanted single-minded, whole-hearted devotion to that one task. But again, do not the two tasks go hand in hand?

Can you see any solution to the lack of officers and other workers which is acute in Britain? One corps near London operates a clinic for the physically disabled, a get-together for young housewives, a similar service for old people and for others who are socially deprived or mentally inadequate. The great need is for workers. Should we recruit trained professional workers, other than officers? Could we afford it?
On a local level a particular officer may be able to work all this out to his or her satisfaction and to the satisfaction of the local authority. But when that officer is transferred, what happens? Such work must have continuity, or the results would be calamitous. Such work must have skilled staff independent of the corps officer, but with the

officer as the administrative supervisor. To provide skilled workers, some of them professionally qualified, we shall need additional money. This is where our proposed annual appeal will help to raise larger sums of money for social service and other necessary programmes in the years ahead. Much depends on the staff, who will be paid more money than the officer in charge. This is inevitable and even right and proper in the Christian context. For even though these people may be people dedicated to a particular task in a particular field, they may not be dedicated in our terms of 'laying up treasure in heaven'. Above all, we must have qualified people to serve those who will increasingly require our services.

Can we manage professional people? In the medical field, for example, we have a poor record.

We have not always been skilled in using professional staff. This is true in many countries. Even though we may have personnel policies, we do not always use them properly. I think one reason is that some of our people try to give professional direction, whereas administrative direction is what they are expected to give. Then, possibly, we have not done enough screening in selecting new personnel. Obviously, if a staff member is not in tune with our principles, and with what we are trying to accomplish, he may impede progress in a significant measure. This is not to say that the Salvationist is always right. There is often another way of looking at it. Yet when a person comes to work for the Army he should conform to what is known as agency policy. Otherwise he may not be happy within our framework.

Could we ever do what you have done in the States—employ a Jewish doctor in a Salvationist social service unit? He worked among alcoholics, but he was not uninterested in the Penitent-form. He did not seem to be the odd man out. Do you agree that a professional man can make this kind of adjustment?

Certainly he can. But it takes a lot of internal and highly-skilled communication to put it over. We have to make sure that our own people understand what the person is doing. I am thinking of officer and soldier personnel as well. If they will accept the worker, and if the worker can feel that he is genuinely part of the team, the 'alliance' will work. His professional ethics will say to him that unless he can conform to agency policy he doesn't belong. It is a two-way street—partly up to the professional, whether he be Jewish or Roman Catholic or whatever, and also up to the Army. But it is not for the Army to have to conform *in toto* to the individual. We are partners, and must not feel inferior. The true professional will not feel that we are inferior. But on the general principle—there is no obstacle. As long as there is good international communication, and as long as the person himself has been carefully screened, as long as he accepts our agency policy, then there is no reason why he cannot fit into the programme.

As an American you must feel diffident about talking about 'Darkest England', but please let me ask: we are not as affluent as the United States, yet even in Britain the standard of living has been raised a great deal. There is not the dire poverty and ignorance of days gone by. Do you think the 'Darkest England' concept has any relevance to our work and to our planning in Britain?
William Booth had tremendous insight. He was ahead of his time in the imaginative programme he proposed. Even though some of his proposals were discarded after a time, each of them, I feel, served a purpose and proved a point. There is the example of the match factory, how it was closed after it had proved its point—that it was possible to produce matches not injurious to health and still provide a living wage. Certainly that is not a story of failure. The Assurance Society similarly proved a point. In the economic social climate of the time it was a valuable contribution and served a great purpose, not merely financial, until recent times.

CHAPTER FOURTEEN

Salvation Army Leadership as Seen by the Young

As a young Captain in The Salvation Army do you find Salvation Army authority irksome?
Not particularly. In a movement such as ours there is need for discipline.

You approve then, of our authoritarian system—the General, the Chief of the Staff, the Commissioners, Colonels, Majors, Captains, down to the newest recruits.
It is a good idea, provided one has good leaders. If you have men at the top unable to lead in a dynamic way, then the whole system would fail. The 'big man' leader of past times is rare today, many feel. This is the age of the ordinary man, yet we seem to do well with the people we get. The ordinary man is having a bigger share in material success, in politics, in making himself heard. The great man has been scaled down and the common man has been lifted up. Four young men, working-class products, the Beatles, took the world by storm. We are now living in the age of the common man.

Are young people in The Salvation Army smothered by 'traditions', by rules and regulations, and agreed procedures?
No. There's an area of youthful drive and individuality in the Army, but too many wait for commands from older people. We become conditioned to this and tend to lose initiative and drive. The Army was made by many young, adventurous 'daredevils'. But now, perhaps, too many of us wait for the words of command. We feel the

need to be shepherded, guided and directed. But we must think for ourselves.

If we 'democratised' the Army would we not be just another sect or church, and have a sort of 'congregationalism'? Surely William Booth saved us from that?
There's very little in the church method that appeals to me. I believe in the Army's demands and discipline. I like the way it gets on with things. I don't want the Army to be 'churchy'.

But you think Army meetings have become somewhat formal, in fact?
Yes, but more traditional than formal. We do things for the sake of doing them. If we did not have singing in the holiness meeting on Sunday mornings, for instance, people would be amazed, shocked. Of course, singing is a good thing. But the reason for it is not always worked out.

But are you actually prevented from holding meetings like this or any different kinds of meetings?
I do often make changes and try experiments. But whereas we began by breaking away from all the norms, we now have stormy traditions or customs. The band and songsters take part in the Sunday evening meeting in such and such a way.

But you are saying that there is pressure from the band and songsters; there is no rule?
No. It is the climate that has developed: the people themselves rather than the Army rules. It is the way we are interpreting the rules ourselves. We make this interpretation in a formal way, though William Booth had no love for formality—he smashed through it.

Do you think the Army is militant enough? Does it pull its punches to preserve public opinion, the City and the big firms, and the well-to-do?
Well, it is a fact that if we offended them gravely it would cause us to be much poorer and it might limit the Army's ability to do its work, but I would deplore any covering up for the sake of finance, for the

sake of shaking the world by the hand. Yet I do not believe it is the Army's mission, nor was it the mission of Jesus, to condemn and go about disapproving of everything and everybody. Our mission is to bring life, and hope, and love. This is what Jesus said.

Do you agree with the Army taking part in the Festival of Light, joining with those who condemned the B.B.C. and the I.B.A., and the pornographers and so on?
I don't think we need other people's band-wagons. We have our beliefs and we are militant and we have a century of our history to prove that we can fight against evil.

You are married. What do you think of the Army's female ministry?
An achievement from which other churches could learn much. The wife is an officer in her own right. It is a joint command. If a woman is shut out of an officer's full service, it will be by the husband's wish or by her own. Children can be very demanding and some women have no vocation.

Some women see themselves as the 'church minister's wife', responsible only for the women's meeting, with the husband as 'the minister'. The Army does not favour this concept of officership.

Some officer-wives, not my own, feel that they are martyrs. Their husbands are out on Army work while they are left at home. But this is not the Army's wish.

What of women officers who do not marry?
Many of them are marvels. It is hard for some of them, and our history is full of the record of wonderful service they have done. Some are alone in commands which are small. But there is deep concern about this. The Army is trying group-ministry to avoid having too many young officers working alone.

What new areas of work should the Army explore?
Salvationists should get involved in community life, providing purposeful activity for young and old. Our involvement in civic affairs is held in suspicion by some older people. They think it can be a substitute for the true mission of the Army, which is to the unconverted.

Do you think the Penitent-form will remain the heart, the 'high altar', of The Salvation Army?
Yes, I think the Penitent-form is a good place at which to make public decision, and to share one's desires and prayer with other people. People still kneel there. But these life-changing decisions can take place in personal conversation, perhaps over coffee, or kneeling in a sitting-room, rather than following an address at the citadel. We should not be so rigid about this, or legislate as to where conversion has to take place. It can be in a home. But, of course, this decision can be confirmed in front of all the congregation at the hall.

When you speak, are you speaking to guilty sinners? Do you tell them they are in danger of hell fire?
Christianity should not create guilt complexes. That is what the law did. Christianity takes away guilt. Therefore I do not seek to make people feel guilty. To frighten people into the love of God is most deplorable, and cannot work. People have been frightened into accepting salvation, but that is not what God wants. There are moments when people know they are not what they should be.

How are young people in the Army affected, do you think, by the present climate of permissiveness?
The family spirit in a Salvation Army corps makes this kind of permissiveness almost non-existent. I would find it hard to think of three or four who were offenders in what the Army would call sexual permissiveness.

How would you deal with a man, perhaps in the band, who for 'social or business reasons' took alcohol?
If it were for social and business reasons and no other, I would kindly and firmly talk to him. If he did not then change his ways and be willing to fulfil that covenant to which he had signed his name, I would ask him to go; otherwise you would have a creeping paralysis of our principles.

What about the man who smokes a cigarette occasionally?
He must be dealt with. If he is a bandsman or other sort of local

officer he must either stop or resign his commission. It is reasonable that the Army should hold men to their signatures. They signed freely in a covenant with God and with the Army.

Technically, you are a voluntary worker. You are not entitled to a salary. You have an allowance. The Army does not use the word salary for various legal reasons. I believe it means we cannot sue the Army if it dismisses us. How do you feel about that?
It is a Christian hazard! It is the Franciscan idea, the Pauline idea, and the puritan idea, of risking all for God. I would like to see more of it. I think we can be too fussy, hold up too many carrots to too many people who want the vocation of officership to be a sort of primrose path. We should give young people a straight challenge to sacrifice.

What would be your attitude, as a Commanding Officer, when two young people anticipated their marriage, with a result that a child is born six months after marriage?
I would be very disappointed, but I couldn't ignore it. I would hope that the young people themselves would be embarrassed by the situation. They would need to be surrounded by love and understanding and made to feel that they still belonged to the loving fellowship of Salvationism. We all sin and come short of the glory of God.

But suppose they were not embarrassed but blasé about the thing?
Then they would be dealt with more firmly. But they would not be automatically removed from the roll. The rules do not insist that we do this. There has been a modification of the old-time puritanism.

But do you find that marriage, morality and family life of Salvationists are of high standards?
Yes. Salvationism can give a sense of purpose which is helpful in binding married people together. There have been difficulties when the partner spends too much time away on Army duties, leaving the wife a 'grass widow'. Family relationships can suffer because of it. There are marriages which are 'Army marriages' rather than marriages. But that was more in the past. In these days there is

recognition of the needs of all the members of the family – children are not so often neglected.

How do you resolve the tension between family life and Army duty? You've just been away to Northern Ireland? Did you take the wife and children?
No. I left them, but I went with my wife's blessing. I asked her, before I agreed to go. If she had not wanted me to go I would have remained behind. We work well together in most respects.

CHAPTER FIFTEEN

Women in Bonnets

As if to contradict Virginia Woolf's assertion that women are a magic mirror which reflect the figure of men at twice their natural size, Catherine Booth, wife of the Founder of The Salvation Army, loomed large in the life of her husband. With better education than he possessed, she wrote love-letters to him which were often reproving lectures. She chided him for lacking the will to succeed; admonished him for taking ale or brandy, so that he became a teetotaller; and resisted his typically Victorian objections to a woman preaching from a pulpit.

Indeed, at Gateshead in 1860, she interrupted her husband's Methodist chapel service with a request that she be allowed to speak. She knew that he would not be pleased, but she had strong views on the subject. 'In Christ there is neither male nor female', she wrote. 'The promise of the outpouring of the Spirit is no less to the handmaidens than to the servants of the Lord.'

The man who became the benignly autocratic General of The Salvation Army gave way. His wife made a triumphant début in the pulpit and afterwards she became well known as a preacher to rich and poor. Known to Salvationists as 'the Army Mother', Catherine Booth is the prototype of thousands of Salvation Army bonneted lassies who pray, preach and sing, and serve the needy the world over. William Booth's natural caution often needed a jolt such as his wife gave him. Many of the innovations which he adopted as Salvationist tactics, with striking success, had to be forced upon him in the manner of his young wife's *fait accompli* at morning service.

Yet Catherine Booth would probably not approve of the 'Women's Lib' campaign of our times. The Army conceded the principle of equal pay for equal work in the 1870s, even when, as is the case with governments of our time, there were financial and other technical difficulties about implementing the principle. It is Female Ministry that interests the Salvation Army lassie. She asserts her equality with men as a child of God, as a minister of the gospel. This means that, within The Salvation Army framework, a woman can be the person who sells the *War Cry* in the public houses; she can sing with the songsters on the street corner, or on the T.V. programme; she can seek to rescue girls in moral danger; she can command corps where she may be in immediate authority over many men. She can be the Captain, Major, Colonel, Commissioner and even the General. The fourth General of the Army was a woman and the office is open to women today.

But any idea that this means diminution of the femininity of Salvation Army lassies would be unfounded. It is part of female Salvationist inconsistency that, when fashion dictates a shorter skirt, Salvation Army hemlines go up and vice versa. The observant can see that the bonnet has become less like a coal scuttle; it is now rather dainty. Hair styles are more sophisticated. Some old soldiers in the Army complain about this accord with trends, but feminine responses to cultural changes are not easily halted.

This does not mean that Salvationist women have abandoned Salvation Army faith and practice. The young Salvationist housewife does not smoke, drink, play the pools, or frequent bingo halls. She pays her debts and she keeps her marriage vows. She sets a Christian example to her children. The divorce rate and delinquency among Salvationist children is extremely low. Together with research into cancer of the lung (Salvationists are non-smokers), cirrhosis of the liver (Salvationists must be teetotallers), and the degree of parental and marital failure among Salvationists, this would make a promising field for medical and sociological research.

Catherine Booth's insistence on the equal merit of women, as ministers of God, enshrined in her 11,000-word pamphlet of 1859 entitled *Female Ministry*, has had its prophetic insight confirmed by the thousands of Army lassies throughout the world who preach, pray and serve God and the people as Salvation Army officers in their own right. Women can be officers with equal status with men when unmarried, and officers in their own right when they are married. It was as a woman with a mind and a mission of her own that Catherine Booth invaded her husband's pulpit in 1860, in England, in a man's world. It was 'Women's Lib' indeed.

By 1878, when Booth's mission became an Army, he could write:

> It has sometimes been said that female preachers would be the ruin of the Mission. On the contrary it turns out that the prosperity of the work appears most precisely where female preachers are being allowed the fullest opportunity. During the past month sisters have taken a leading position in no fewer than nine of our thirty-six stations. We have at present twenty married evangelists and no fewer than twenty wives take a great part in the services.

It was about this time that George Scott Railton, Booth's first and most influential lieutenant, wrote, 'I do not see why women should not have equal pay if they do equal work.'

On June 21st, 1888, Catherine Booth preached for the last time, from the pulpit of Dr. Parker, in the famed City Temple, in London. While for the next hundred years and up to the present, hierarchies of differing churches were to debate, ponder, and disagree as to whether they should allow a female ministry, many thousands of women officers in The Salvation Army made major contribution to the battle.

The 'war of both sexes', joined in love, marriage and Salvationism, has been expressed in poetic terms by a young Salvation Army officer:*

> . . . The bus can wait.
> I'll preach you a sermon if I may.
> See how the twilit river soothes our souls,
> Gliding in silence by the spellbound willows,
> And in the fields the small and weary foals
> Find in their mothers' bodies softest pillows;
> As children wander supperwards from play,

* From *A Girl to Her Love*, by John Coutts, in *The Book of Salvationist Verse*, S. P. & S. Ltd., Judd St., London.

We to the gaudy, loud, exhausted town.
See how the busy woods grow grave and grey,
The gentle covenant of grace comes down
To manifest to our uncertain sense
  The first grand promise ever spoken;
  How the High Father of omnipotence
Looked at the world and saw that it was good.
  We see this sure and certain token:
The Holy Ghost asleep in Wythan wood.
And so the girl who longs to be your wife,
  Yet is not hers to give,
Awaits the word from Him in whom we live,
Yearning, yet full of humble confidence,
Knowing that all our life
Is hid, not darkly, but in providence.
So let us go the way our Master trod,
  And bravely trust
  Our true love must
Find its fulfilment in the love of God.

Every courtship between young Salvationists should be, and usually is, something of a sacrament as well as a romance. The couple concerned in the dialogue from which the above lines are taken were married when the rules and the regulation period of waiting had been satisfied. The bride and groom stood under the Salvation Army flag when the ceremony was performed, and the words they spoke were largely those framed by William Booth about a hundred years before. The promises they made, not only concerning each other, but in covenant with The Salvation Army and with God, were profound. As stated before, Salvation Army marriages are normally stable; home-life is good, children develop in a healthy and happy environment, and divorce among officers is almost non-existent.

What sort of woman Salvationist may be found throughout Britain today, a hundred years and more after the recruitment of The Salvation Army, and in spite of great social changes? Certainly, she is likely to be influenced by Mary Quant's *diktat* on skirt-length and other feminine indulgences, which could include discreet use of cosmetics and spring fashions. She may not be 'of the world' but she is in it, and aware of its cultural and social vagaries, sometimes reacting to it, but never, if she is a good Salvationist, surrendering to it.

One of thousands of such women won a scholarship to the local grammar school and reached her teens in an environment that can be death to the ardent Salvationist spirit, for she was surrounded by quiet, complacent peace, without contact with the ferment of acute human need. She was 'saved' as a child, and influenced by family customs which included regular reading of the Bible, grace before meals and bedtime prayers.

At the age of fourteen Margaret heard the first stirrings of a 'call' to be a Salvation Army officer, all part of adolescent dreams of emulating Mary Slessor, Florence Nightingale, Catherine Booth, and other Christian heroines in those good books published by the Army, which she was encouraged to read and did read.

The Dell family was not well off, for a foreman in a rural factory did not, in those pre-militant A.U.E.F.W. days of the 1940s command a large pay-packet. But as Salvationists neither smoke nor drink, and are not allowed to be avidly worldly, materialistic or acquisitive, the Dells had enough. They were content. They could even find something for those less favoured than themselves. Margaret was reared to remember those 'other sheep' of Jesus, and she prayed that she might one day help Him to bring them back to the fold.

Happy, even on Sundays as she attended Army meetings morning, noon and night, she none the less responded to the built-in biological time-process which was part of her make up. She worked in the rating office of the town hall, a quite respectable background, but every teenage girl who knows the facts of life (and Margaret learned them the right way, at home and at school), is well aware of the perils in a man's world. Salvationists claim no monopoly of chastity, but they are chaste. Margaret's dates with boys were social occasions —and no nonsense.

She joined the local Red Cross Society, the Church of England youth club, and a local music society. Most adult influence upon her was helpful. But, apart from her parents, the people who most influenced the growing girl were The Salvation Army corps officers who commanded the local corps. They were good, and they did good in the town. They worked all day, and sometimes far into the night, visiting the lonely and the aged, ministering to the sick, alert to human need without regard to class, creed or colour.

Margaret was a corps cadet – The Salvation Army officer-cadet-corps. This required her to do Bible study, and entailed practical work, such as house visitation, selling Army papers in the public-houses, and reading through a list of recommended books. She attended Salvationist youth conferences held regularly on a regional basis and there, when she was sixteen, she saw a Salvation Army bandsman in the uniform of the R.A.F. She took a long, long look at him and did not forget him; but she wasted no time in futile romantic dreams when he vanished. She did not speak to him. He did not know her. She did not think she would see him again. When she was eighteen she was accepted for training as an officer and entered the Army's Training College at Denmark Hill, in London.

There, during the first week after her arrival she saw that lad again, not in R.A.F. blue but in the navy uniform of The Salvation Army. But The Salvation Army Training College is no forcing house for romance. One may not begin a courtship during training days and, besides, the programme of study and practical work leaves no time for such a pursuit.

Even by the standards of Mary Quant's world, Cadet Margaret Dell was good to look upon. Not that this was enough for Cadet John Browning. He wanted a wife who could help him in his work as an officer and, by Salvation Army rule, seeing that he was to be an officer, he must marry an officer; no one, not even were she like Joan of Arc or the Queen of Sheba, would do. He had a full year to think it over and so had Margaret, whose eyes, perhaps, betrayed her, for she was admonished by one of the college staff for showing undue 'interest' in the young man over on 'the men's side'. Margaret was hurt by the suggestion.

She had signed agreement with the rule that she would not be party to any commencement of courtship while she was a cadet. But who is to control the impulses of the heart? She gave assurance that she was observing this condition. There was no courtship until after the couple were commissioned as officers at the Royal Albert Hall. Then the rule did not apply.

The day after, the new Lieutenant John Browning and Lieutenant

Margaret Dell permitted themselves the luxury and the ecstasy of a short walk in Ruskin Park. It was May; the shrubs were blossoming, the ducks were engaged in domestic duties about the pond, and the late daffodils were abloom. Though it was not her home or the idyllic country round about, it was spring, and they were in love. So, even in Ruskin Park, Denmark Hill, by Camberwell, it was possible for them not to care that London Transport buses were roaring down the hill, or that the King's College Hospital complex nearby was architecturally so monstrous as to be likely to give John Ruskin apoplexy.

They even dared to kiss each other. Then Margaret took a train to her first appointment in the north and he hied himself to the eastern counties. Margaret's 'parish' was a coal-mining area. The Bandmaster often came to his long Sunday of Salvationist duty straight from bath and breakfast after a whole night underground. The girl preached her first sermons, spoke often in the open-air meetings, visited many homes and public-houses where she sold the *War Cry*.

During this time the two young people, with official permission for courting, were 'corresponding'. In Army jargon this is the stage prior to 'engagement'. Neither of these pre-marriage formalities may be taken lightly by any Salvation Army officer. The couple became engaged in March. After a ten-months' letter-writing stint and rare sight of each other, the marvel is that they could recognise one another in the street, leave alone become engaged.

Yet they did know each other and they were sure when they were married. At her home, the whole town seemed to be interested. She was twenty, he twenty-three and, standing under the Salvation Army flag, they were a joy to look at, especially for their parents who felt the union to be an answer to their prayers. People from the rating office at the town hall, who had come to see Margaret married, marvelled at the way Salvationists would have Bible and hymns, uniform and prayers, yet all so pleasant and happy and good to look at—and Margaret so lovely!

But how did the girl who was called of God to be one of General Booth's salvation Amazons—how did she adjust to being wife and helpmate to her Captain, very much 'a second fiddle' in the band? One thing he did was to ask her to take turn and turn about with the addresses (or sermons, as churchfolk would say) on Sundays and occasional weekdays. Another thing was for John to ask her advice on many matters, and leave many more to her. The people in Salvation Army corps like to hear the woman's voice; they take kindly to women's counsel, and prefer that many matters of pastoral ministry—domestic problems, problem areas concerning women and children—should be dealt with by the woman officer. They did not need to be reminded that young Mrs. Captain Browning was an officer in her own right, just like her husband.

Every mealtime can be a period of consultation. Sometimes the wife's word prevails, sometimes the husband's. There are three children now so that as officer-wife-mother Margaret is a busy salvation warrior. She confesses, with the nearest approach to emotion she allows, that the only time she feels the rub of officership, the hardness of the cross that is, after all, an inevitable part of ministry, whether it be male or female, is when she has to pack her bags and go to another part of the battlefield, another city or town, leave the familiar faces and places, and start again in another house that is not her own. Not a home, in fact, but a quarters. There will be a welcome, and friendly faces. The house will be reasonably furnished and well maintained, but it is Salvation Army property, not modern, not 'with-it'. Some of the people Margaret knows have two cars in the garage, even a second home—a bungalow by the sea—and such signs of affluence as a deep-freeze well-nigh the size of an Eskimo's igloo. But such tokens of the acquisitive society, the treasure laid up on earth, are not for Salvation Army officers. They sing:

> A tent or a cottage
> Why should I care
> They're building a palace for me over there . . .

In fact, the God whom Salvationists serve does not impose such Franciscan poverty upon them. Margaret would be the last to suggest that He does. However, she is engaged in a Christian war. With her vocation, her husband, and her children, Margaret accepts that this is so and she is content. If for a moment she wavers, no disapproving angel is going to make too much of it.

Perhaps, even in the Heavenly Record Office they know of Albert Orsborn, Salvationist poet, worthy of a far wider public than he has so far received. Margaret knows these lines by him:

Saviour, if my feet have faltered
  On the pathway of the cross,
If my purposes have altered
  Or my gold be mixed with dross,
O forbid me not Thy service,
  Keep me yet in Thy employ,
Pass me through a sterner cleansing
  If I may but give Thee joy!

All my work is for the Master,
  He is all my heart's desire;
O that He may count me faithful
  In the day that tries by fire!

CHAPTER SIXTEEN

The Wife Finds New Employment

You are Swiss. How did you meet your English husband?
I came for a holiday at The Salvation Army Training College in London. I met him on the quad.

But the Army college is not a place for holidays.
No, but I had a cousin who worked for the Principal and it was agreed that I could spend a week with my cousin there.

You had been brought up on a farm just outside Geneva?
Yes. My parents were Salvationists.

What was your work in Switzerland as an officer?
I had never been an officer in Switzerland. I came to England to finish learning the language. I asked to stay in England in order to perfect my English and during that one year I met my English husband. So I have never served in Switzerland.

Where did you go?
To the north-west of England.

How did Rhodesia come into the picture?
We both felt, even before we met, that if ever the need arose we would be willing to go. After we were married, we discussed this together and both felt that, although it wasn't a spectacular call or anything like that, we should make this feeling known. So after some

time we were asked to go. We took charge of the Salisbury Corps, Rhodesia.

Salisbury is a 'white corps'?
Yes.

Any tensions about what side to take? Did you take any side at all?
In those days there was not any feeling of tension between black and white. By the time we left Rhodesia after eleven years, there were Africans attending the meeting, usually educated people who felt that they could improve their English, and benefit from our form of worship. We next went to the Howard Institute where my husband became Assistant to the Principal. There was a spell at headquarters, where my husband became cashier. Then the need arose for us to go to Zambia, which was at that time Northern Rhodesia. We ran a social institution at Ndola. Then we came back to Britain for a time. We had problems to do with the education of our three children, and other family ties—my husband's aged mother. One son is now studying for a French degree; the second is at Geneva, working with The Salvation Army for a year. He wants to learn French. Our daughter is still at school and living at home.

You returned to Britain in 1964 and your husband has been at headquarters ever since? You became the 'vicar's wife' sort of officer?
At first the transition of the family was important. I gave my whole attention to the children for the first six months. Once their schooling was settled I began to feel lost. I did my best in the corps, but I did not find it very satisfactory. I felt there should be something more I could offer. I had always felt very committed as an officer and the casual approach to my vocation did not suit me. This created a lot of tension for me. The children would leave for school in the morning and come back at night and the whole of my day was spent alone. I used the libraries to pursue my reading but it lacked purpose. I felt I needed a push. I felt unhappy and frustrated and my husband was aware of this. We talked about it together.

One day, in the library, my husband saw a course advertised for mature students, particularly married women, whose families were at the stage ours was. It was a preparatory course for qualifications for either teacher-training or social-work. This was a dream of mine. I had always wanted to teach, but life didn't take that shape for me. Well, my husband came home and said, 'I think I have discovered what you want!' He gave me the particulars and the very next day I took myself off to the college which was advertising. They gave me an interview at once and asked, 'When can you start?'

But I had to go home to think about it, for although I wanted to do it, it was a big step, with four weekdays at the college and homework at night.

What about the cost?
This was another problem. But the Principal thought that because I was a Salvation Army officer, usually without much means, the local authorities might make a grant towards the cost of the course. We approached the local authority which stated that, provided I passed the exam and showed a good report, they would help with the tuition fees and my books. I felt quite pleased about that.

But what about the Army?
Earlier I had approached headquarters, applying for a job. My idea was that I could do some translation, for I am bilingual with French and English. There was nothing I could do at headquarters, nothing that satisfied my aspirations. I did spend a year packing books for countries overseas. I enjoyed it, but it was not being an officer!

Well, how did you get on at your college?
In the first year I did five 'O' levels and in the second I did two 'A' levels. After this the Principal discussed my future. I was still preparing to go into teacher-training for which the Principal was keen. There is a chronic shortage of French teachers and for that purpose I obtained a place close to our house.

But on reflection, after talking it over with my husband, I changed my mind. Our hope is that eventually we may go back to Africa.* So we looked for other possibilities. I had the qualifications for the diploma course in social studies and I was accepted by the University of London for that.

* Since this recording was made, the Swiss officer-wife has received orders to return to Africa on Salvation Army service with her husband.

This I did as an external student at a college of technology. It took two years. In some ways they were difficult days. The subjects were sociology, social psychology, social history and social administration. You encounter Charles Booth and Sigmund Freud, and the idea that everything is a matter of science and that religion is at best superfluous and at worst even undesirable. Some of my teachers just did not want to know about the religious side at all. They all plumped for the science. In the last two or three years, however, there has been a change of approach, an understanding of the fact that it isn't all a question of improvement at a physical level; there is also a spiritual problem.

Before I reached the end of the diploma course I was assured that there would be a place in the Army's Men's Social Services.

Did your Salvationist faith, your belief that 'Christ is the answer' hold out among the Freudians?
It became stronger. Once I was involved in practical training I very quickly came to realise that there is only one answer ultimately: Christ. Psychology, psychiatry, sociology are useful tools and need to be employed as such.

Although Bernard Shaw made Major Barbara into a social worker at a Salvation Army men's hostel in point of fact that does not or did not happen until lately. It has always been a man's preserve?
Yes. But it was suggested that I could go to Spa Road hostel as a social worker, on an experimental basis.

How many men are in Spa Road?
Two hundred and fifty. They were not unused to having a woman around. The officer-wives at Spa Road are involved with the work. But the men were not used to having a woman inquiring persistently about their personal lives. I have an office where they come when they want to talk. Sometimes they were sent to me. They would find me behind a desk. They responded to this. One advantage was that very quickly the men saw me as being an 'outsider'. If there was any difficulty within the hostel, they felt they could talk to me because I was there only at certain times; they did not feel that I was involved in the running of the hostel.

Suppose they complained about the hostel, would you report them to the commanding officer?
This would never be my approach. I would challenge the hostel if there was any genuine grievance. This is done regularly with any complaint which I feel is justified. It is discussed with the manager and other officers at the regular group meeting.

If there is a straightforward explanation then I will pass it on to the man and say 'Certain things have to happen this way because . . .' Very often this solves the problem. But even if the complaint doesn't yield to this sort of explanation, I often find in discussing it that perhaps one of the officers is wrong, or that one of us is trying to find an answer to our own problem, while creating a problem in the hostel. This is dealt with between ourselves at the group meeting. In fact, we study very much our reaction to certain situations. We ask, why is it we react like this? Very often the solution is in a change of attitude in ourselves, in the Army, in the officers. There is never at any time a feeling on either side that we are being reported on. It is never done in this way.

What about the men? What sort of problems have they?
A number of men come from broken homes and have never known what it is to have a settled life. Over the years this has affected their work and personality.

Some are ex-Navy or Navy men who have never been able to adjust to civil life. Under the strict discipline of Navy life they often reached positions of responsibility, but are unable to cope outside that structure.

A large proportion of these men suffer some degree of mental illness, often an illness which is not diagnosed early enough. They present patterns of behaviour which the wife and children cannot tolerate and which eventually lead to a complete break-up of the family. This happens before the man seeks medical help.

Some of the more serious problems we meet are with men who have been discharged from hospital (often after receiving treatment for a mental condition) with nowhere to go and no plans for future treatment. In cases like this, time spent on gathering the necessary information needed in order to be able to give the help and support they need often means a further breakdown. There is a serious need for more co-ordination and communication between hospitals and hostels.

Drink and drugs are also problems we encounter at the hostel.

What age would the men be?

We have them from eighteen to eighty-five, but the man with mental illness which hasn't been diagnosed (or if diagnosed has not received proper after-care treatment) fits into the thirty-to-forty category. They come to us because they are completely lost. We try to get them a job to start with. This breaks down and gradually the pattern emerges and we see that at this time they need medical help, rather than help of any other sort.

Does this create a sense of despair, pessimism?

As a rule it is not a condition that can be easily dealt with. But while we can give the man support there is hope – not complete rehabilitation, perhaps, but hope that with constant support and constant caring this man will reach a level at which he functions quite happily and finds himself.

One of the problems with these men is that, because of constant failing in their relationships, the whole of their life is failure and in the end they run away from themselves. A man forgets he is a person with an identity.

You have to give them confidence?

Yes. To this end we have created workshops at Spa Road. There we set a man to do certain tasks under supervision with constant encouragement. When he sees the finished article well done there begins to build in him the confidence which he has lost.

In the workshops we try to help the men to make relationships with other people. When these break down we help them again. Once they have managed it, and are beginning to take responsibility for other people, rehabilitation does take place. Some of the men have been placed in outside jobs and they do very well.

Where does William Booth come into this, with his insistence on the need for salvation?

We keep this in mind. The man is looked at as a whole man. We can do a lot of propping up, we can do a lot of supporting, but we can't 'save' a man. He finds himself only when he has realised his spiritual need.

Do you have a Penitent-form at Spa Road?
Yes, and men kneel at it. But in our group meetings we always discuss individuals and their needs as complete entities. We consider the physical, mental and spiritual needs of the men. We discuss whether a man is ready for more pressure, or ready for new activities, or for new kinds of situations and new relationships. The officers watch very carefully. They are very much the pastors or chaplains to the men. Once we have a man who is ready for that kind of activity he is invited to attend a Salvation Army corps. We provide mini-buses for this. He comes to the meeting with a group of other men, but we specify that we are all individuals; you worship with me and I worship with you. There is no question of the men sitting in a separate group. After the meeting they are taken into the homes of Salvationists. There's coffee and conversation. The whole idea is that they have taken part in an act of worship outside the institution and they have mixed with ordinary people. They are getting to know these people and they enter into their homes. Many of the men have not been in a true home for many years.

Do you find 'institutionalisation'—forgive the word— a problem? It worries the Army in America.
Yes. It is usually better for the man to go after the outside job. But sometimes someone hires a man and he is no problem; he is doing a good job. Within hostels there is a shortage of staff to carry out necessary tasks, so the temptation is not to disturb that situation. Then before you know where you are, the man can't go out. That's being institutionalised. It has a long history. Officers of the Army's Social Services are aware of this massive problem, which needs to be looked at seriously.

Do you think there is a place at Army hostels for unqualified but dedicated and sensible workers from outside, both men and women?
Yes, the Army employs women officers (wives) at Spa Road in the workshops, alongside the men. They teach simple skills to the men.

But it is also very much part of the process of observing what happens in the workshop. They support the men and look at every aspect of their needs, but there is an enormous need for trained personnel.

You talk of mental illness being the main problem, but there is also alcoholism and sexuality. Doesn't this present a special problem with men because you are a woman?
I have not found it so. Again it is a question of approach. If a man feels in any way that I am condemning him, say for his being a homosexual, then he certainly would not want to talk to me about it. He would want to hide it. But if he feels that I have an understanding of the problem, and that to a certain extent I accept this as being his problem, then he will talk to me about the difficulties it creates for him.

Do you find that homosexuality causes men to shelter in Army hostels?
Yes, because they do not find acceptance in so many areas of life. Even in Army hostels, other men who live in the hostel will be very suspicious and hostile if they find that there is a homosexual there. Of course, the officers have to be very careful. One cannot have practices of this kind going on in a public hostel.

Are you able to help homosexuals?
Only the sort of help where the man can say frankly, 'Look, I have this problem. I can't move in various circles because of it and life is becoming intolerable.' The only help I would be able to give is to extend the hand of friendship and to say that now I know he has this problem, I can begin to understand. But in the treatment situation I am not able to do much. I look upon the problem very much as an illness. If I can alleviate some of the suffering which is caused by it, by not being shocked or hostile, then I have done something. I am now dealing with two newcomers to Spa Road who have this problem. The fact that they have been accepted with compassion has relieved their minds tremendously. They are happier, better. We do not have the same glib solution for this problem as in other days, when they might have been recommended to go and get saved and leave it at that. If we cannot cure the patient we help him in any

way we can. Sometimes we can assuage his loneliness and lift the burden of his isolation. Sometimes such men are converted and lead blameless lives – indeed, many of them do much good in the world.

Do you have a sense of fulfilment now, a sense of achieving both your tasks, as a social worker and as a Salvation Army officer? You are not frustrated now?
No! Not at all!

Do you think other women, and other men too, who have looked at the Army's social work from outside, and regard it as a separate branch of Salvationist activity, should follow your example?
It would be marvellous! But for this to happen, particularly in the case of married women, a lot more encouragement and understanding from Army leaders needs to be shown. If it hadn't been for the understanding relationship I had with my husband I could not have done it. The situation is demanding and the work takes its toll. So it is very much a family involvement. Unless you have a home situation where this is accepted it cannot be done.

CHAPTER SEVENTEEN

It's a Great Life

Do you think female ministry can apply only to unmarried officers?
No, I do not. If you fall in love with somebody so much that you couldn't live without him then you marry him, but on the other hand you may not marry. Married or unmarried, you can be God's minister.

But some suggest that to deny the maternal drive is to deny the end for which woman is born. Would you agree?
No. I love children. I like men. I like a meeting best if there are both men and women in it. I have loved young people and still love young people, more than any other part of society, and I always will. Some mothers have had five children but I have had hundreds!

In your case female ministry doesn't have implications of women's lib? It is not a form of opposition to men?
No. I think that women are equal with men, but they are different, and I wouldn't want them to be the same. I have always known that there are some positions that I personally couldn't fill.

If you had been asked to conduct a wedding in the Army hall would you have done it?
Yes.

You think a woman's status in this matter, her divine status, is the same as a man's?
Her divine status is the same as a man's.

In your life as an officer you have both been a head of a department

yourself, and have served under men. Were you able to work with them happily?
Yes, I have been very happy working under men, in Australia, in the United States and in Britain. They have always given me my place and I have never found they kept me back because of my sex. Perhaps a few tried to be bullies, but they did not succeed because I do not respond to threats. I also had excellent co-operation from men working under me.

Do you think that unmarried women officers are accepted by our congregations? In some corps it is said that they are not welcome. They say, 'We want a young man officer, or a man and his wife.'
I think this situation does exist in some corps, but I am happy to say it doesn't exist in my corps. We have two women now. One of them is fifty-seven; the other is younger and we were very happy when they were appointed. Everybody co-operates with them. We believe in them because they are good.

This large proportion of women officers in the Army who are not married and many of whom will not marry—do you believe they are happy and fulfilled?
A great many of them are. Some are not. Perhaps they haven't been as fortunate as I have, going early into creative work. This love of home and love of man and love of children, which is a great thing in the life of many women, is a vital subject. Some girls set it as their objective quite early in their teens. They want to be married, and they are married. But it is not the only way for a woman to find fulfilment and happiness. I am grateful for a mother who never made us feel that marriage was the only goal. She wished us to be trained so that, married or single, we had a vocation. You have to give every bit of yourself to your work. I discovered that very early in my life in regard to caring for people. I hesitate to use the word 'love' these days, because it has been so dragged down, but I mean the kind of love that was in Christ. I discovered when I was very young that I didn't care as much about people as I should. It became my aim to find out how I could care more about them. Now if you care enough about people, that is creative and that is why so many women officers of the Army are happy and fulfilled.

But I have great respect for homemakers and mothers. I hate to hear anyone say of a married woman, 'She's just a wife and mother.' There is nothing greater than being a wife and mother. That's what I don't like about women's lib—its criticism of the role of mother and wife—because there is nothing more wonderful. But I do think it is wrong to start out in life with that for a goal. You enter into that because you love someone so much that you want to live with that person. Then you have children and you make a home, but if for some reason or other this is not the way for you, then that can be wonderful too, and happy and blessed by God.

Many women in the Army, wives of officers who have administrative jobs, do not feel that the Army makes best use of their service. They have a sense of vocation equal to Catherine Booth's or yours, but they have to be isolated at home, until the children are grown up and married. Then the officer-wife is a housewife. Some women prefer this; some don't. Do you think the Army utilises fully these married women who have this vocational drive?

I believe the Army could use some of them a great deal more than we do. I think of one in particular, a qualified teacher; she could well be used at the Training College as a teacher. On the other hand I don't think that a married woman needs to feel frustrated. I can't believe that any Salvation Army officer can be frustrated; as long as there are people in the world there is something for us to do. If we care about people we need never be frustrated.

We claim to have led the way in this field of religious 'women's lib', while the Church of England is still arguing about it. Yet, despite this, do we, in fact, practise it with any great zeal, on a wide scale? Just that one woman General, and few women in leading commands. It is very much a man's world in the Army. This is what the critics say.

I would like to see women treated equally with men, where the ability is equal. Sometimes I think a man is put in because he is a man and not because he is specially qualified for the task.

Would you agree with those who say that the obstacle is a woman's weakness in physique, her liability to breakdowns in health?

Of course, women do feel things very keenly. My observation of women leaders, say, Commissioner Emma Davies, is that she really cared about her officers, she really loved them. She would, therefore, be prone to suffer more in herself, more than a man who would maintain detachment. Yet she never broke down.

Did not Catherine Booth, who believed in female ministry, have qualms about women in administration? Was it not a woman's right to be a preacher, a minister of God, that she maintained? I don't think the women's lib movement would regard her as one of their kind.

No. If I had married I wouldn't have wanted to do my husband's job, but I would have liked to make it easy for him to get on with it. One woman may be domestically inclined, happy to be a wife and mother, though an officer. She is just as worthy and important as the woman who becomes a Territorial Commander. It is altogether wrong to suggest that she is anything less.

CHAPTER EIGHTEEN

The War Chest of The Army

WILLIAM BOOTH ASKED for a large sum of money for his 'Darkest England' scheme in 1890, but he did not get it. There was a generous response at first but it soon fell away and he complained that the public were fickle. The book was a nine-days' wonder. Parts of the scheme fell through because of lack of support. An officer who helps to administer the Army's finances is interviewed:

Does finance matter to the Army now?
We should not get very far without it! We budget according to what we think we are going to get. We could have a much bigger budget if we were sure we could get more money, particularly for the social work in this country. Our work is restricted through lack of funds. We are probably the biggest voluntary social service in the country, yet we could be bigger and better if we had more money. Many of our places need up-dating. We made a good start during the centenary celebrations. H.M. Queen Elizabeth opened Booth House in Whitechapel, London, and there have been other new social-service complexes in various cities, but there is still a lot to be done. The public is by and large very generous to us.

In what fields would there be a likely expansion if more money were available?
Eventide work for one. We want to branch out in a more up-to-date

approach to eventide work, with 'sheltered' housing. This demands absolutely new buildings which involve a tremendous outlay, something like £4,000 per person – about £175,000 to build one modern eventide home. Then we want to do more for the homeless, many of whom are suffering from mental stress and other acute personality problems.

One of our problems is keeping pace with inflation and maintaining existing work. Our budget, including overseas commitments, this year shows an increase of £240,000. At one time £240,000 would have been the whole budget. That must be covered before we can think of expanding.

At corps level in Britain we need money for community service. In many cities and towns we have goodwill centres and are being pressed by the local authorities to take on additional welfare work. In Cheltenham we are asked, 'Can the Army do anything for the temporarily homeless?' Well, we could build an annexe to our goodwill centre which would provide accommodation for three or four families – if we had the money. At Wolverhampton the 'sky is the limit' in social service if we can provide a better building. These are only examples in a general pattern in this country.

When William Booth began his work, he approached the Home Secretary of that time and asked for help. The Cabinet was consulted but the reply was that, though the Government was sympathetic, the answer must be 'no'. Yet in numerous countries abroad there is massive Government help, notably in the United States. Has the picture in Britain changed?

Yes. There has been a great change in Britain, and to our advantage. Both the Government and local authorities now help us. We now receive local authority help, quite sizeable help, for capital schemes. For instance, at Nottingham, William Booth's birthplace, we have had £100,000 for the new social-services complex. The Birmingham city fathers have been very helpful. They financed two-thirds of our new ventures in the city – one for men, one for women and one goodwill scheme; in all, their contribution amounted to over £200,000. Some city councils have promised substantial capital grants of anything from £100,000 to £300,000 payable in annual instalments (with interest added) over periods ranging from fifteen to twenty-five years. Newcastle upon Tyne, Leeds, Bradford and Greenock are making such grants, and negotiations are proceeding with other councils. These civic authorities know that The Salvation Army is helping them to solve the problem of homelessness in their midst.

One local authority, having already made a substantial grant, has said, 'We cannot give you any more, but we will lend you, without interest, £50,000.' This is particularly generous at a time when interest rates are 9 per cent plus. That was for ten years.

Then there are cities where the corporation has erected a building for housing the homeless and has handed it over to The Salvation Army to run on its behalf. This has happened in Reading, Coventry and Warrington, and other cities and towns may soon follow suit.

Is the Army hurt by a fairly widespread idea that we are quite well off? Newspapers, particularly when the High Council meets, have said this. In 1890 William Booth was charged in The Times, *with living in luxury. We know that he lived an austere life and died a poor man.*
The Army is a large organisation and its assets are sizeable, but we are not better off than we have ever been in terms of realisable assets which we can spend. We have millions in properties, that are used for the purposes for which they were put up. We have large investments which are mostly trust funds. These give us income which we spend on our work. But we are not rich—we do not have sufficient money for the work we ought to be doing.

For my part I do not believe the majority of people think that we are well-off—that we do not really need their money. After all, they support our work, so they must have confidence in us. In a public relations research survey recently people were asked, 'What is the charity you first think of? Which is the charity to which you would be most likely to give?' The Army came out very well in that public opinion poll.

Do you think Army overheads are reasonable? Are our Headquarters too expensive and elaborate?
This building, here in the city, was erected ten years ago on the site of our old building which had been destroyed during the war. It is purpose-built, simple in design and is run on highly economical

lines. No one gets high salaries—not even the General. The cost of running the Headquarters is met from The Salvation Army's earnings, thus making it possible to devote the public's contributions entirely to the maintenance and advancement of our worldwide work.

Is the Army suitably fastidious about its investments? A T.V. programme recently aired the view that the Army has shares in armament firms.

We have no shares in arms, or beer, or tobacco, or in anything that would not conform to our standards.

We have been caught before now by a merger—as when a grocery combine was taken over by a tobacco company; but we disposed of the shares as soon as we knew what had happened. We think we can claim to adhere to the spirit of William Booth's alleged remark, 'The only taint about our money is that "'taint enough"!'

We are also very much alive to the voices of criticism in the World Council of Churches about investments in the countries where politics and policies are not in keeping with Christian ideals. We are sometimes embarrassed by legacies and shares left to us. We have lately been mentioned in newspapers as holding shares in Consolidated Gold Mines. It was asserted that this company underpay their black workers, that they treat them as slaves. We had critical letters about this. Now, we did own 808 shares, which came to us as a gift. We did not invest in the company. We have already disposed of them.

We are constantly vigilant on this matter to preserve the Army's principles and its good name. It was recently brought to our notice that a footwear manufacturing company, in which we held shares, had acquired the capital of a well-known betting organisation. The shares had proved very profitable but we immediately took steps to sell them—we must pay for our principles!

The Army used to get much of its support from what was called 'the landed gentry' and from some rather lower down the social scale, the well-to-do middle class. There is now an affluent working class. Does that class help the Army?

Financial support still comes from 'the landed gentry' and from the middle class. But we also get help from men and their families who remember what we did in the two world wars—ask any lassie who sells the Army papers in the pubs. She could tell you of continuing generosity. These people give 5p, 25p and even occasionally more, and it all adds up. With some it may ease their consciences, but there is a lot of genuine affection for, and trust in the Army.

Where we feel disappointed is in the amount of support we receive from large companies. Tremendous consortia, with millions in capital and huge profits, give us, say, £20 as an annual donation. Of course, there are many other claimants and it is notable that 'prestige appeals' sometimes receive large gifts—new colleges, appeals for the costs of civic projects.

The Army does get support from organisations like Oxfam, Help the Aged, War on Want and others.

Yes. Very often these expert fund-raisers come to us because we have the know-how and the personnel on the spot where the need exists, particularly in emergencies and great natural disasters such as earthquakes or floods. They have the money, but they haven't the personnel. They usually cannot rush personnel to Nicaragua or anywhere like that. So we provide the service with our people who are there. They very carefully vet before giving, and they are more interested in digging wells, starting irrigation schemes and providing money for capital projects than in helping with temporary relief, the kind of work they did when they began.

William Booth referred to himself as a 'beggar for God'. Is the Army losing out because it is ashamed of this role? Does the General beg? Would he? Have we become too proud to beg?

No. The General has done his share of begging and I am sure he would do it again if the need arose. In William Booth's day it was not conceivable that appeals would be made by anyone other than the General. There was no one else with the Booth mystique. General Wickberg does not beg so much, because he is busy with other, perhaps more important tasks. But he has Colonel Lawrence Smith, who knows how to talk to people in committees, in board rooms, in the Mayor's parlour and even at H.M. Treasury. One thing we have learned is to ask sometimes and be thankful, and then stop until the next time. Oliver Twist's method, always asking for more, is probably inefficient. The best and kindest people can become weary if they are not given a rest.

CHAPTER NINETEEN

The Making of Officers

WHEN I STARTED going to the Army Sunday-school I was a Catholic and attended a Catholic day-school. But I liked the Army.

Why did you like the Army so much?
I enjoyed fellowship. I enjoyed the way they worshipped God. I enjoyed clapping my hands. I enjoyed everything about it. When I left school I was seventeen and I had a fairly good education. I had been head girl but had to hand in my badge because of my attendance at The Salvation Army.

Did the Army 'capture' you from the Catholics? Did they bring undue pressure on you?
No, but the headmaster questioned me about Army beliefs. The officers told me that I must make my own decision. When I left school I went to college to study child care. The subjects were cooking in bulk for the children in care, child-psychology, child-health, home nursing and first-aid.

What did your parents think of this? Did they agree with your being a Salvationist?
My mum said it was up to me. 'If you are happy at the Army then by all means go ahead.'

Well, what happened after your child-care training?
First I received my Child-care Residential Certificate and went to another town to work. I was the Deputy-Matron there, and later the House-Mother at a school for the mentally-handicapped.

You are an attractive young lady. Did you have a boy friend?
No, because my interest was wholly taken up with The Salvation Army. I helped the officers with their duties. Then my studies were important to me, so I never really had any time for the opposite sex. When you come into The Salvation Army you have to accept that you may be single for some time.

The Salvation Army officers you met up to the age of twenty before you came to this college—what did you think of them?
The first officers I knew helped me an awful lot. They explained The Salvation Army and they taught me everything I know about the Army. But when I explained to them that I wanted to be an officer, like they were, they said you have to be called before you can be a Salvation Army officer.

But before you heard or felt that call there were those other things—the example of those officers and their influence.
Yes, it did prepare the way. They were very, very devoted and hard-working.

What do you hope to do when you are commissioned?
My dream is to open corps in Scotland or in England which have been closed down. I want to re-open difficult corps, re-start the Army's work in my own country.

That is a very hard task. Any aspirations to re-start the work in Russia, or China?
No, not there. Not just yet.

What about the child-care training—won't that be wasted?
There will be so many children in the area where I am going to work—mothers who are out at work, mothers who do not care. I will have ample opportunity to give everything I have learned. I want to give love and attention and understanding, just as the first officers I knew gave them to me. I don't think that my child-care training will be wasted.

You understand that any attempt to re-open corps will cause you sometimes to be alone in very hard places?
Yes. But I believe that through prayer and hard work I can accomplish the task – if the Army will give it to me.

Don't you think a woman would be at a disadvantage in such a task? This is still largely a man's world, isn't it?
That's what they say. But I think it depends on the woman. Because I'm not really interested in the opposite sex, I feel that I can do just as much as any man.

You believe in women's-lib?
Yes!

You know about the Army Mother and her idea of female ministry? Then how long do you think this lonely Joan of Arc crusade may continue?
For as long as the Lord will allow.

But supposing you fall in love? That might change things?
No. I would not allow myself to become attached to anyone, to any man outside The Salvation Army. He must be a Salvation Army officer and have strong beliefs, as I do. He must be as strict and disciplined as I am within myself.

He will need to be a special breed – this hypothetical man?
Yes. I don't think the Lord has made him!

And meanwhile, the prospect does not worry you? You will not get much money.
No, but I will work hard and bring in the money. If I am at a small corps I will be on subsistence allowance anyway. If I am having a hard time the Army will give me a hand.

What about the things young people, especially qualified young people, can have that you won't have? Fashionable clothes, and perhaps a car. Do none of these things interest you?

Before I came to college I did have money enough to get a car. But I realised that I could not have a car *and* come to college, so I put the car out of my mind. As for clothes – I am not a girl who goes out to buy 'way-out' clothes.

What if the Army does not take you up on this idea of re-opening closed corps? Suppose it sends you somewhere else – maybe to a place like Basildon, where they have a play-school and where they need child-care specialists such as you are? The Army does not always take account of what we want. We have to do what the Army wants. Will you do that?
Yes. I know it depends on the Army.

In other words, this wish of yours is conditional on the Army agreeing?
Yes. The Army doesn't know about my 'dream' – it is all in my heart.

Aren't you going to tell them your dream? After all, the world needs the dreams of youth. The Army needs them.
Oh, yes. I will tell what I feel God wants me to do. If they choose me to do it, then I shall be thrilled to go and do it.

Don't you think it might pay you to be firm and say I want to do this or that?
Oh, not at all. I won't do that. I'll go wherever they send me. I feel they have prayed about it. They have prayed about each cadet. They seek God's guidance as to where they want their commissioned officers to go. I will go, by the blessing of God, to do the Lord's work.

You seem to be the sort of cadet William Booth would be pleased with if he were here. I think you are likely to have opportunity to make your dream come true. When you are a little older, you may need to 'insist', but in a proper way. One can be a good Salvationist and yet 'insist', not quite in the sense that you must *have your own way. Army leaders nowadays often give young people their head if they really are concerned. The man who started Army work in some areas of Africa was a boy who just wouldn't take 'no' for an answer. They sent him here and there, but he said, 'I must go to Africa, I must go to Africa.' In the end they became rather tired of this. They let him go, and he did marvellous work. He is still there after more than forty years. Perhaps your dream will come true in that way.*

I have faith that it can be done. Women in the Army have done great things. We must not feel that the great work and sacrifice of women officers is a thing of the past.

. . .

A MARRIED CADET speaks of his experiences. He was born in London, and converted at Highworth, a Salvation Army rehabilitation centre for alcoholics, near Swindon.

Were you there for treatment?

Yes, I went there in 1967, and remained about twelve months.

Where had you been previously?

Mostly in London, catering establishments and behind bars as a barman.

How did you get to Highworth?

From a magistrates' court. I had appeared there for offences connected with drinking, not always drunkenness. Sometimes it was for taking money which was not mine from places where I worked, to get drink of course. I had a long history of alcoholism. I had been drinking since I was sixteen, always pretty heavily.

When did you discover you were an alcoholic?

In the Forces. I served in Cyprus for two years. Brandy was six shillings a bottle and I could get plenty of it. When I came back into civilian life I found I had passed the point of no return. I went to the family doctor, first. He put me on antibuse tablets, a form of aversion treatment. If you drink while on the tablets you become violently ill. But I found antibuse was not the answer. I either stopped taking the tablets or I drank enough to neutralise them.

I tried Alcoholics Anonymous. While I would not knock this organisation, it was not the way for me. It does a fine job, and it does help many to achieve sobriety. Yet I feel that those who are on that programme always have the ghost of alcoholism with them. I wanted to lay the ghost of drink, dead and for ever. I believe a man can reach the stage where he finally conquers alcoholism. I was once an alcoholic. I believe that I no longer am an alcoholic.

Are you suggesting that you are cured?
No. I am converted. I am changed and I have not touched alcohol since 1967 – five years.

American Salvationists who do a lot of work in this field won't use the word 'cure', but you can be converted, they say; you can stop drinking. This is also accepted scientifically. Do you agree?
Yes. I agree with those who have special insight into the problem, the medical profession and social workers. I believe a man can achieve sobriety through various means, but there are drawbacks in the normally accepted methods. Many alcoholics are fighting against this thing for the rest of their lives. The only real answer is a religious experience, God. This is what I experienced at Highworth. I had no church experience at all before going there.

You didn't know The Salvation Army prior to that?
Just in the pubs. I was the big-hearted chap who always gave the Army girl money and didn't want a paper, but I felt they had something which I didn't have – happiness.

Did you try other therapy methods before going to Highworth?
I had been in Brixton prison, on remand, for short periods – medical remand. Then I had been sent to a hospital at Epsom where I was to remain for a period of twelve months, on a court order for the treatment of alcoholism. But the group therapy seemed to be putting the cart before the horse. It told me that once I stopped drinking everything would be all right. I knew this was not true as far as I was concerned. Previously I had managed to stop drinking for various periods. But it never solved the basic problem within me.

You thought you ought to put things right first and then you would stop drinking?

Yes, exactly.

Whereas they said, 'Stop drinking first and then put things right'?
Yes.

Was there any particular thing that happened, or any particular person that influenced you?
The officer there, and his wife, Major and Mrs. Barker, helped me to find a religious experience. The programme was spiritually based. There was normal group therapy but the main programme was centred round the newness of life which is the heart of the Christian gospel. I listened and I was interested; it was different. It seemed a way of life that didn't take the problems away; it gave the power to live victoriously in the face of problems. I sat on the fence for a while; I even fell off on the wrong side, and I had a relapse and went out drinking again. That was the time I realised that I was at the cross-roads. With the help of Major and Mrs. Barker I came to a final decision and found God in the quietness of my own room. I surrendered all to Him. From that moment I have lived a new life.

Did you think this would mean that you would become a Salvationist?
No. It was made quite clear to me that Highworth is not a recruiting centre for The Salvation Army. I was simply converted. I handed my life over to God; I asked Him to take control.

How long had you been there when this happened?
I arrived in December 1967, and I was converted about mid-February 1968.

All alcoholics backslide, or become recidivists, so they say. How many times since then have you fallen back?
From that time, when I accepted God into my life, I have not touched drink. Admittedly, in the beginning, in the first weeks, months even, there was still 'the old man' there, the old attitudes. I wanted to drink, but I knew that God was helping me. With His help I overcame the temptations. When I turned to the Bible—'if any man be in Christ, he is a new creature'—I realised that it wasn't only the work of a moment; it is the work of a lifetime. And so, as I

went along with Christ, those first few weeks and months, the temptations lessened, and eventually there was no desire at all for alcohol.

Five years quite sober, teetotal?
Yes. Since my conversion I have just ceased to want the stuff. I just don't want to drink at all. For me it worked like this. When God comes into a man's life, then he is a new creature. He reaches the stage where his nature is transformed, his attitudes to life, his whole thinking. As Paul says, 'Be ye transformed by the renewing of your minds.'

What happened after 'Highworth'?
I began to go to the Swindon Citadel Corps. I wanted to stand on my own feet and I was enrolled as a soldier. I was commissioned Corps Colour-Sergeant and started attending the torchbearer youth club. I met my wife there, or rather the girl who became my wife. She was a year younger than I. All this, I believe, was God-directed. She had eight sisters, three of them Salvationists.

When you became friendly did she know you were a dried-out alcoholic?
Yes. She also knew that I had been converted at Highworth, although I don't think she realised what that meant. We had a short courtship, because we understood each other. When we were married I was thirty and she was twenty-nine. We each felt called to become Salvation Army officers and we decided we would be married before entering the Army's college.

Were you accepted by the Army without delay or fuss?
Yes.

Did you feel you were giving the Army a large problem? It is unusual for men who have been alcoholics to become officers?
Perhaps. But I knew from the time I was converted that God wanted me to work in the Army. I discussed the matter with Major Barker, at Highworth. He explained what avenues could be opened.

Are you ready to do what they want you to do? Have you any special plans of your own?
When I went for my candidate interview, I said that I would go where God wanted me to go and serve wherever He wanted me to serve. But I did feel that, because of what had gone before, the social work of the Army would be the most useful avenue. Since coming into training I feel I would like to work specifically for alcoholics.

Have you grounds for believing that the Army will give you this opportunity?
Eventually yes. We did seven months of our summer-term training at Middlesex Street hostel, and I have referred men to the assessment unit at Booth House. There is a great need in that field. But wherever the Army puts me I will serve.

How do you and your wife like it here in this college?
We are enjoying it very much indeed. We had, as I have said, seven months at the Middlesex Street hostel. It was rather like going in at the deep end, but we managed it. We learned what we didn't know, more than how much we did know! Perhaps I was something of a rebel in my first year here, but having that experience with the Men's Social Services has humbled me, humbled both of us.

What was the difficulty during the first year?
I am all for discipline – I try to discipline myself as much as I can. I think it was just the brigade structure in the first year – doings things which I couldn't see the reason for. It was, perhaps, a natural reaction that I didn't always feel like jumping when I was told to jump. First, I wanted to know why. But I think this second year is turning out much better.

You have one child you say?
Yes, she is just two years old.

Your wife is happy here?
Yes.

PART THREE

Ministry for Women and Girls

CHAPTER TWENTY

But I Always Fail

SALVATION ARMY SERVICE for girls and women began in 1881, though there had been a number of stop-and-try-again attempts before that. The permanent work began when a housewife Salvationist, Elizabeth Cottrill, took into her home a delinquent girl who was in danger of being lured into a brothel. This amateur moral rescue work, at 102 Christian Street, Whitechapel, was too limited for such ministry and, besides, the woman's husband objected. The couple's children were also in the house; pressure on the limited space was intolerable. The Army asked Elizabeth Cottrill to find a separate house which she could supervise as a shelter for the growing number of girls from up and down the Mile End Road and the Ratcliff Highway, a veritable jungle of violence and danger to women, which Jack the Ripper would make infamous. She did find such a place: Hanbury Street. In the first year there she received eighty-six women and girls, some of them prostitutes, other more or less innocent, who were likely victims of pimps and brothel keepers. That Hanbury Street shelter, makeshift and small, welcomed eight hundred women whose past life would raise eyebrows among respectable Victorians. It led the Booth family, particularly Florence Booth, wife of Bramwell, William Booth's oldest son, to a work of moral and social reclamation which is today carried on in a vast network of hospitals, hostels, probation centres and schools all over the world. The cost is enormous, but Elizabeth Cottrill's little rescue home at Hanbury Street operated on a budget of £8 per week.

No knowledgeable Salvationist would claim great success by the

Army in winning the long-term prostitute back to virtue, let alone to that conversion to Christianity which is the great objective of Salvationist workers. The Army has known the saved prostitute—over the years more of them than is realised, for she is one type of convert who cannot shout her past from the housetops, though she wishes to give glory to God. But much greater success has been gained in helping the girl in danger of entering that oldest profession. The Army serves the foolish girl; the girl in need of 'care and protection'; the unmarried girl who is pregnant, often below the age of consent; the runaway girl; the gullible; the mentally-retarded girl. The Army shelters, loves and aids thousands of them. An experienced officer of the Women's Social Services of the Army in Britain speaks of modern-day work and the challenge it presents.

The use of your mother and baby homes is diminishing? That is a fact?
Yes, diminishing over the past six or seven years. Following a change in public attitude and increased provision by the State, the unmarried mother is not so dependent economically. There is also the fact of legal abortion and increased contraceptive devices such as the pill. Also, of course, many girls can now get advice on how to avoid conception. The stigma of having an illegitimate baby no longer exists for many girls. But we are finding that more and more girls want to keep their babies with them. These need support and help over the first year or two. Some of these stay with us. We don't turn a girl away if she wants to stay until she can find somewhere to live with her child.

Of course, there are many helped up to now in our approved schools and probation homes, and there are the young people in our girls' hostels and in children's homes. Many of these have been helped towards better lives; some of them have been converted.

One important change in our work for girls is brought about by the 1969 Children's and Young Persons' Act. Instead of having approved schools and probation, the Act calls for community homes. The Probation Service is no longer responsible for people under seventeen years of age unless a probation officer is already working with other members of the family. All young people of seventeen years and below are the responsibility of the Children's Department of the local authority.

This means that approved homes, probation homes, and our children's homes will now become community homes. There are three types. There can be controlled community homes, which means that the local authority have complete control of the running of the home and its finances, and all that is to do with it. In the assisted community homes we have two-thirds membership on the board of management, and the local authority has one third. The day-to-day running of the home is left to us, subject to arrangements with the authority which are sanctioned by the Secretary of State.

Are you still allowed to run the home in accordance with the first principles of William Booth, to love souls?

The aim of The Salvation Army Women's Social Services is, as it always was, the salvation of the individual by faith in Jesus Christ. That is laid down in our regulations. We have no reason whatever to change it.

You don't find this aim causes derision? Do people in these modern times understand what you are talking about?

It is coming to be realised more and more, by all kinds of professional people, that no boy or girl or older person is simply a body and a mind. There are many sides to their personality. So when we speak of a person's need to be helped, we mean not only bodily and mentally but also morally and spiritually.

Of course, some social workers do not feel able to cater for the spiritual needs as well as the social needs of the young people in their care. But in an approved school not run by The Salvation Army or any religious body, there is a chaplain affiliated to the school to help in that way. There is official recognition of the need of this spiritual care. In *Rules of the Home Office for the Conduct of Children's Homes* it is stated that a child who is away from its parents needs, more than any other, the comfort of a religious faith, and the inspiration to right thinking and training which it gives.

A report issued some time ago suggested that for children there is no substitute for a home, and that institutional life is a very poor second-best. It is said that where you cannot supply a parental home, you should seek a foster-home.

It is quite true that for any child a good home is best and a good foster-home is a good substitute. But, on the other hand, there are many children who are emotionally disturbed. Others have come from difficult backgrounds and they cannot fit into a foster-home. Through the years we have had children brought to us who have failed in not one, but sometimes two or three different foster-homes.

Few foster-parents are willing to take mixed family groups, and if you have, say, two boys and two girls, or a boy and two or three girls, and the authorities want to keep the family together, then they bring them to homes such as ours. There the children can be included in family groups. That is often better than splitting them up into several foster-homes. In one of our children's homes in the north of England we had a thirteen-year-old girl, and two siblings. The mother had been in hospital and when she was due for convalescence the authorities decided to move the children nearer to the mother. They were going to place them in a local authority children's home. But the boys and girls were aghast at such an intention. They asked us, 'Is it true that they are going to put us into a home?' They just had not realised that for the last twelve months they had been living in a 'home' – a Salvation Army home.

How far do Salvation Army Women's Social Service officers in Britain have to be professionals in these days?

Over the years we have tried whenever possible to allow our officers and employees to take professional training. With three colleagues some twenty years ago I took a course at London University for the Diploma of Social Studies. Before that, some officers in the United Kingdom had taken social science studies at Bristol University. Through the years numbers of our officers have taken the Home Office child-care course. At present we have others taking the residential course in child-care. This leads to professional qualifying courses.

As an executive officer in the Women's Social Services, how do you assess the attitude of professional administrators of social security in

Britain? Are they friendly, and understanding of our religious approach?
By and large they do understand and appreciate our religious motivation. Of course, much of the work we do is a statutory obligation on local authorities. They are glad for us to co-operate with them where they need our facilities. They have no quarrel with the way we conduct our homes, although we ourselves would often wish we could do things much better.

Do you foresee that rising standards of living, increased enlightenment (if you agree that that is coming), with improvement in health standards, with other modern scientific marvels, will make your 'rescue' work superfluous in Britain? (For example, it was thought that the discovery of penicillin would cause a great fall in the incidence of venereal disease).
There is no evidence for this whatsoever. At the moment there is great disquiet in the country because of the increasing incidence of venereal disease in children under the age of sixteen. This is quite appalling and is on a par with the fall in moral standards which has been evident. In some schools there are increasing pressures on young people towards promiscuous behaviour. They are given to understand that this is the 'normal way of growing up' and that as long as contraceptives are used there is no reason why they should not do as they want. We feel that young people ought to be warned, not only of the moral danger of promiscuity, but also of the fact that venereal disease is a very real and terrible possibility and that contraceptives are by no means unfailing protection against infection.

The ratio of illegitimate births in this country is still high despite the 'new morality', contraception and increased abortion. Yet these mothers and babies do not so often come to the Army and to other such voluntary agencies.
That is so. Many more girls are now cared for at home by their own parents. They go to a local hospital and have their baby and then they can arrange through their social-service department for foster-parents, or for the children to be taken into care by the authorities, or for adoption.

In spite of the idea among many sociologists that adoption is the best solution to the problem of the illegitimate child, you are one amongst many others who believes that the mother is the best person to have the care of the child?

Yes, where it is possible for her to do so.

Do the Women's Social Services encourage the mother to keep the child?

The Women's Social Services do not put any pressure on the mother one way or other. But they do believe that she should approach the whole position with an open mind, and not be pressurised into giving up her child before she has had an opportunity, after the birth, to consider the situation and decide. We have known young girls who in later life have bitterly regretted that in an emotional state at the time of the birth, when they were not mentally able to cope with decisions of that kind, they were persuaded into giving up their babies. Of course, there are many obstacles in the way of girls keeping their babies: housing, finding a day nursery, the need to earn sufficient to care for the child. The Family Income Supplement now brings help to many girls faced with this crisis.

Young mothers should always be given the opportunity to bring up their children if they want them. We have known young people in their teens who have become emotionally disturbed, and whose lives have been very adversely affected, because of the discovery that they were adopted. Sometimes the adoptive family has not been able to cope with this crisis. If young people find they have been adopted, and they do not know who their parents are, it can be a highly traumatic experience.

On the other hand, children brought up by their own mother usually honour their mother and love her for the fact that she kept them with her. I have heard a teenage girl say, 'My mother did not love me or else she would never have let me go.' The fact that a child is abandoned by one parent, the father, is no reason why the other parent should also abandon the child. I think it should be noted that no one ever says to a young widow, 'Because you no longer have a husband, your child should be adopted.'

We are not an adoption society, as such. But when a girl comes to us, unless, of course, she is brought by her parents, she is quite often in the care of the local authority anyhow. The local authority social worker is therefore responsible for the girl's future and for the future of the child. There are the adoption societies and if a girl or her parents want to be put in touch with them we have a list at Headquarters.

At the moment, most of these societies are unable to take more people on to their lists. There are more applicants for adopted babies than there are available babies.

The Women's Social Services deal with teenage girls in sexual trouble, who are promiscuous. In this area, the Army had its historical role, helping to get the age of consent raised to sixteen.

Do you find that the age of consent matters so very much? Is there not ignorance of the law or defiance of the law—that law?
Yes, flouting the law certainly, and probably ignorance of the law when the participants are both very young. We have had to deal with school-children at the age of thirteen, fourteen and fifteen. Yet we think it is important that the present law should be retained and enforced. Otherwise girls under sixteen are going to be at great pressure from some dubious night clubs, houses wanting call-girls, and other 'businesses' and people. These people are made to pause if they know a girl is under the age of consent.

You know that young people now mature early, both physically and in intelligence. Do you think this modifies or explains the present promiscuity among many young people?
Thirty years ago, when I started in the social services, girls of twelve and thirteen were having babies. This alleged moral revolt is very much over-stressed in the papers. Crowds of young people are not sexually permissive. There is a percentage and this has been high-lighted in the press and by the other media. Some financial interests have a great deal to answer for. The pressures put upon young people in some kinds of advertising films and in books and magazines which emphasise the sex interest put young people at risk. Sex and nudity are used gratuitously in advertisements for drink, for tobacco, and for cars, with harmful effect on many young people. Sex is part of growing up, part of maturity. But the present exploitation of sex suggests that if you don't take part you are not 'with it'. But crowds of young people do not go along with this

pressure. I am sure some sections of the press and other media and advertisers suggest what they do for their own purposes.

What are the factors in English life, or the break-down of life, which have caused your delinquents and 'drop outs' and other sorts of needy women and girls?

In the majority of cases it is the family background: either marital disharmony, or lack of example and discipline within the home. You have parents each going their own way and having no concern for the children. Sometimes the children have been given too much of everything except training and teaching. They come to us emotionally disturbed. They need love, they need control, they need discipline, they need an ordered way of life. They have a basic need for security and they do not get it. Most who come to us, therefore, have that type of disturbed background, family disharmony or broken homes.

CHAPTER TWENTY-ONE

Just for the Kicks

A SALVATION ARMY officer interviews a fifteen-year-old girl at 'Avalon', a community home at Chislehurst, Kent.

Where were you born, Sarah?
In a big house at Hampton on the Hill. In the bathroom! My dad was living away from home. My mum had left him. He used to beat her up. If his food wasn't as he wanted it, he'd throw it at her. He used to go out at night and get drunk, and go out with other women. She went back to him but she left him again. Then she went back and left him again. In the end they decided to call it a day.

Do you see anything of your father?
Up to about two years ago, I used to go to him for week-ends and holidays. He's all right. I miss him a lot actually.

Has he tried to get in touch with you while you have been here?
No, he doesn't know where I am.

What was it like in your early days, at home? Can you remember?
Seven of us children were at home to begin with. But my two brothers and me, and my sister and my big brother left home. They had run away and some of us were in care. But I decided – I was only a kid, about seven – that I wanted to live with my mum. When we were all together we were very happy, except when Dad rowed with Mum.

But apart from that we were happy. My mum couldn't cope with Dad.

We moved to a coastal town when I was about ten to get away from London, really, because I used to keep getting ill. I used to have terrible nosebleeds and be off school for weeks. They said that the country air would do me good. So we moved, just me and Mum; three others followed afterwards, and two of the boys were in boarding-school, which the council paid for. Once they ran away with me, and my mum said she couldn't look after all of us; that's why they went there.

Why did you keep moving house?

I suppose it is in the blood. We just like moving around. No particular trouble. Only bits and pieces. Everyone has troubles, don't they?

What were you like at school?

When I was there I was good; I learnt a lot. But when I wasn't there . . .

Illness? Or playing hookey?

Until about two years ago I used to be away with illnesses. But then I started being naughty and in the end I just never used to go to school at all. I just used to walk about and go to coffee-bars, and stay in. Sometimes I was on my own; sometimes I had friends with me.

Your mother, did she mind?

She minded, but she could not make me. She couldn't get hold of me. I wouldn't let her. Many times we had rows over it, but when she realised that I just wasn't going to school she accepted it. I used to help her do the housework, and get the boys' tea.

Did the school authorities come round?

Yes. When they did, I was in bed. They didn't come back for a couple of months. Then about a year ago they said I had to go to court. I went to court and they put me in a remand home for a month.

You were put in a remand home because you were missing school?

Yes. When I came out I started going to school again. Then I missed a couple of afternoons. I went in the mornings. So they put me in a children's home where I had to be in at 10 o'clock. That didn't suit me, so I used to go to my uncle, who has a bedroom. That was instead of the children's home.

Did you go about with a gang?
I have always gone round with a lot of people, but that's not getting into trouble, is it? For the past two years I have been with one friend. She has stuck by me all the time. I used to be in 'the crew'. My brother used to be the leader of the skinheads, and we used to go around Paki-bashing.

Why did you do this?
Just to get kicks out of it, a laugh, you know. We got fun out of it.

Were any seriously hurt?
One went under a car. It wasn't our fault. But mainly it was black eyes and bruises. I had a fight with a girl. She had a razor blade, and cut my face. Five other girls held me down while she was doing it.

In this Paki-bashing, how many of you were there?
Sometimes only about five or six, sometimes there would be up to twenty-five.

Do you dislike people from Pakistan, Asians and so on?
No. They are a different colour but that makes no difference.

But they are worth beating up?
I would not go out and do it now. Then it was what everyone was doing; you know what I mean.

What else did you do?
We went down to the club and had a fight; chairs and china got broken. We sometimes smashed bus shelters. If clubs said 'No white people allowed' we used to go down. Sometimes they would start and sometimes we would. Then there was trouble.

What did your mum think of this?
She never used to know about it. I just used to say that I'd been in a bit of a fight. She didn't say much about it. I think she knew, sometimes.

Why are you here at this Salvation Army centre?
Maybe because I won't go to school and because I wouldn't do as I was told. I used to stay out at night.

But there must have been a reason stated to the effect that your mother was not able to control you?
Yes. My mum said that she couldn't make me go to school. She had to make a statement. But it got so twisted that it looked like she was saying that she couldn't control me. All she could not do was make me go to school!

But you would not stay in the place to which they sent you?
No. I just used to go round with three or four girls. I never had much to do with boys. I used to go drinking with my friend and a few other girls. Because I wouldn't stay in that home they sent me to Middlesex where I was assessed and then they sent me here. It's all right here.

But you are looking forward to getting out?
Yes. I will go home to my mother.

Do you think it was a bit foolish to do as you did? Would you do it all again?
Some of it, but not all. I would not go round beating people up, but I still would not go to school.

Do you enjoy being aggressive?
Yes, but not all the time. If people are going to be aggressive with me, I am going to be aggressive with them. I like a good fight.

Would you like to be married?
Yes, everyone does.

Have you lacked security?
Yes, in some ways, I have.

I know of your plans to be a shorthand typist. What of other plans? Are you interested in religion?
No.

But this is a religious place?
Yes.

Are they kind to you?
Yes.

Do you like them?
Yes, as people. I don't look on them as religious people. I look on them as themselves, in spite of the fact that they are Salvation Army. Just because they have got 'S' on their collar it don't mean nothing. At times I wish they would stop talking about being saved and all that lot. At meetings, you know, and whenever someone brings it up. They talk about it. Sometimes other girls want to become Christians, you know, and they have a discussion on it. But I can't be bothered. You get a bit cheesed off, you know.

You don't want to be a Christian?
No. I'm too bad. I don't believe in it.

Don't you want to have a home of your own?
Sometimes I think I'd live with a boy friend but it is so insecure. They could just turn round and walk out. My friend is having a baby. The boy she was going to marry arranged for them to get married in three weeks. But two days before he phoned up and said it was finished. She can have an abortion because she is five months. But she doesn't want to give it up. But I have known people that have lived with blokes. My sister did. It turned out all right. They got married in the end.

You don't see anything wrong in unmarried people sleeping together?
No. As long as they are not sleeping around with every Tom, Dick

and Harry. If I fell pregnant and the boy had no intention of marrying me I would have an abortion. I am against abortion but I would never bring up a kid without a father.

Did you never go to church?
Sometimes I had to go every Sunday. But I am really an atheist. Going to church was one of the rules.

Your mother never went to church?
No.

Your dad?
No, he's an atheist, too.

What worries me now is how I can get out of here when I have been here a year. There is a possibility that I might have to stay until next Easter, because the school-leaving age has gone up. Though I like the people at this place, I also hate it—I don't know whether I will be able to stick it for another eight months. The time is really going slow. I want to be happy. I want everybody to be happy. I want my mum to be happy and my brother's life to be sorted out. Is he going to be married or not? My sister to have her baby; my other sister to find the money for her house. It is just one big wish . . .

You come from a broken home and all your dreams are centred in a home?
I have a mum and dad, a step-dad. Of course, Mum's not married, she's living with him. They are getting married soon.

How old is your mum?
Forty.

Your step-father?
Thirty-two.

How did your mum meet him?
In a pub.

But how can he marry your mother if your mum and dad are not divorced?
No divorce. My dad won't.

But divorce proceedings are going on now? The marriage will be presumed to have broken down?
I don't know. Mum was telling me about it on visiting day. I don't understand it all.

So, when you leave here you are going home for a while. Then you are going to get a flat and do shorthand typing?
Yes. I did want to be a journalist, but it is a bit too hard for me. They want me to do O-levels. But I don't think I would pass. But I always fail! Yet I think I'll have a go!

CHAPTER TWENTY-TWO

Jessica's Problems

MY MUM AND DAD left me when I was six months old. My sister is not like a sister to me. If I met my mum or dad I don't think I would want to speak to them. I've never cried about it. I think I must be hard.

My name is Jessica and I am fifteen. In the last year I have been in various remand homes and now here at 'Avalon', the Salvation Army place.

Do you know where you were born?
In London. After hospital I was with my mother and father for six months. But then my mother and father both left me, so my granny had me.

Do you mean that your mum and dad ran away together?
I don't know. But they both went. I had a sister. She was left as well to walk the streets with me and my sister; then she went to the social security. They put us in a nursery. My sister was supposed to go to foster-parents but she didn't want to go. I went instead and Gran brought my sister up. Then my foster-parents didn't want me any more. I was nine. I had been with them since I was two years old. They put me into a reception centre.

Had they any children of their own?
Yes. One of them did not like me at all. She used to beat me up at

night. There were also three brothers. The oldest brother used to like me. The others did not. From the reception centre I went to school outside, with other children.

Then I went to another children's home, a nuns' place until I was thirteen. But I never liked it, so I was moved to London.

The place that you didn't like, why?
I don't know. I suppose it was because it was so religious.

You don't like religious people?
Perhaps now. But at that age I used to resent it. I ran away about four times.

Where did you go?
I just used to walk the streets. But the police picked me up and took me back. The nuns would say, 'Right, you need a bath!'

So they were kind to you except that they were religious!
Yes.

You came to London at the age of thirteen.
The nuns wanted me to leave because they felt that I had been there too long and I wasn't settling in. So I was put in a home in London. I was all right there. At the earlier place the nuns would not allow me out at night. Now I was allowed out until about eleven o'clock. I took advantage of this and stayed out all night.

Literally all night?
Yes.

Where did you go?
To a friend's house or just mucking about. Making nuisances of ourselves roaming the streets. Sometimes got in about twelve o'clock.

I would make some excuse, missed a bus: had to walk home. If I stayed out all night I could use my friend's bedroom. She had an older sister who slept with her boy friend so there was a spare place for me.

What did the people do at the home when you did not get back?
Phone the police who would look out for me. As I was indoors they did not find me.

They tried to punish me by keeping me in the home but I always longed to get out. I liked being in the home of my friend.

Did you ever worry about your mum and dad, your sister or your gran?
They were just people that I used to know. I never look on my sister as my sister.

Does she come to see you here?
She has been once. She is nineteen. She is not married.

Have you ever heard of your mother or father since they left you?
No. When I was about twelve I used to worry about it; now it doesn't bother me.

Have you ever cried about it?
No. But I feel bad about them. I always say that I wouldn't speak to them if I met them.

When did you start going into remand homes?
At fourteen. The people became tired of my running away and the police became tired of searching for me. I was bad in the remand home; in the 'cell' more than out of it. I used to be cheeky to the staff, swear at them.

How long in the cell?
The shortest a day; the longest a week.

What was the cell like?
The first I was in was brick all round, a window at the top. Not much room. There was a wooden bench which served as a bed. There were two doors; if you could get out through the first you could not get through the second. There was a small window high up. You couldn't reach it. The food was rationed. No pudding. I had time to think. Made me think of 'Why I am so bad?' 'Why can't

I be good?' There were no books and radio. The silence nearly drove me mad. I tried to kick the door down. But I never escaped from that place. I was in the cell most of the time.

Why were you sent to another remand home?
Because they could not do an assessment of me! So they put me in a lodge, but I ran away. I didn't like it there. The cell was better. Much bigger with a window you could see out of. The caretaker's complaints helped to put me in the cell so I stuck my tongue out at him every time he passed by the window! That meant more trouble for me. There were a lot of tough, rough girls at that place—I wasn't the only bad one.

What happened to bring you here to 'Avalon'?
I ran away from the remand home. Assessment at these places should take six weeks. I was there for eight weeks. We had a riot. I chucked a table at the window but it bounced back, because the windows are unbreakable. So I stamped on the table and it broke. We got the legs off it and started banging the window. Eventually we broke the glass. After we had smashed the window we climbed on to a balcony, then on to the roof which was quite high. We got down somehow and ran through a farm and on to the main road.

Where were you planning to go?
We weren't planning to go nowhere. We were just running away.

Tell me about the court, will you?
We used to go to the shopping centre to nick things. Half the things I stole I did not want. It was just to see who could get the most. We took cardigans, coats and stuff like that. It was the birthday of one of the girls so I got her a pair of tights under my blazer. As I was about to walk out the Superintendent came up and said, 'Excuse me, Miss, but we have a suspicion . . .'; something like that.

The coppers come round and we couldn't get away with it. We used to put the stuff in a black box and now they found it. I had taken over £70 worth of goods. We had to take it all back. There were eight of us. The manager of the store asked how much pocket-money we had. He charged us the same amount. We got off lightly because we were in a home.

Part of the reason for my coming here was that I took a bracelet from a pub. It was just lying on a table. I pawned it, got £30 for it. One pawn-shop man asked for the consent of my mother and father, I told him I had a crippled auntie, who was housebound. So he said. 'I will come round to her house.' So I gave a false address and went somewhere else. The police found where I did pawn it. I didn't get charged but I was sent here.

What do you think of this place?
I like it.

How long have you been here?
Nine months.

Have you run away?
No, I have never wanted to. It is the only place that made me feel that anyone cared.

Do you still nick things?
Only out of the larder now and then.

Are you allowed out?
Only with the staff.

How long must you stay here?
A year. I went to a hostel for a week; I didn't like it. I knew I was going to get into trouble. So I told Major I didn't want to go there again. Now I don't know where I will go.

Are you learning some trade or skill of any kind?
I do quite a bit of typing but I don't like it.

What would you like to be?
I don't know.

What are you most afraid of?

That my children are going to end up like me! That is what I am afraid of most.

So you look forward to being married?
I don't know if I will get married. But I suppose I am really. My friend is having a baby, and one of my other friends has had one. They are not happier.

Do you think that is foolish?
I don't know. I suppose, with them not being married, they will end up like I have ended up.

Where will you meet the kind of person you will marry?
I don't know. I know where there's one person I would like to marry. He's a Salvationist.

What about your future?
Well, I want to be happy. I don't want to get in any more trouble. If I do, the next place I will land in is Borstal.

Would you like to be a 'goodie' as you call them?
I don't want to be one of these high-class people. I just want to be myself. But when I am myself, look what happens.

But you could be yourself and good?
Yes.

CHAPTER TWENTY-THREE

The Trials of an Adopted Daughter

MY NAME IS JESSIMOND. I am nearly eighteen. I was adopted when I was a year old.

Do you know your real parents?
No. I was told that they were divorced.

Where were you from the time you were born until the time of your adoption?
With my mum who adopted me. My real mum was living with the mum I have now. My father walked out on my real mum and then my real mum walked out on me.

Did mum who adopted you have children of her own?
Yes, two boys, twins, and a girl.

Was it a happy family?
By the time I was able to understand what it was like we were staying in a council house, quarrelling and arguing all the time. Mostly money. My adoptive mother spent her cash on bingo; my father tried to make ends meet but there was always a shortage of cash.

Your adoptive mother, did she go out to work?
She took in foster-children to get money, but she did not look after them properly.

When she was having arguments with my dad she used to bring my name up and say that I wasn't her child.

Because your dad adopted you rather than she?
Yes. He used to say, 'You wanted her as much as I did.' I would be upset, and go to sit in my bedroom. Sometimes I would run away until it had all quietened down. I was very unhappy. Sometimes I would creep out and go to a friend's house and then come back during the night when they were all asleep.

Are your foster-parents still together?
No, they have separated. She often said she was going but we didn't believe her. But she did. He still thinks a lot of her but he said he would never have her back because she left him all the bills to pay. She went off with another man. My dad saw her get in a man's car. Now he sometimes sees her but they just ignore each other. When I first came here she came to see me. But she didn't like some of my friends and she wrote me a nasty letter. She hasn't been to see me any more.

Do any of the family live with your adoptive father?
No. He has a new lady friend. He is going to be married to her. She has seven boys. So he is not going to be lonely.

Was your childhood very unhappy?
The unhappiest part was if I was late coming home at night. Just five minutes and my mum beat me. I was happy when my mum left home. I could have friends in and go out. I never used to have any new clothes so my friend and I started shop-lifting. I was fifteen. My mum didn't bother. If my dad asked questions I would tell him that my friends had given the clothes to me. But one day I was caught and the court put me on probation.

Was the probation officer helpful to you?
Yes. I felt ashamed at first and I still feel ashamed now.

How old were you when this happened?
About fifteen, I think. My father was upset and he told the court he

wanted me home. I knew he meant it, but my mum did not. I had two years' probation. But after a year and seven months I was caught again. The court gave me yet further probation and a fine, £20. My mum said that my real parents were shop-lifters and that I followed after them.

Do you think your real parents were like that?
I would like to meet them to find out. My mum and dad wouldn't tell me who they were in case I went back to them. They are not marvellous; they left me. But I would like to see them.

Why are you here, Jessimond?
Because I ran away from home, from my dad. I got fed up. I went to live with my friend Janet. I wanted my freedom. I used to have to stay in at night and look after the children, and that sort of thing.

What happened when you ran away?
I was caught nicking at a large store and I went to court again. I was to go to a hostel but I didn't like the look of it so the magistrate sent me here.

This is a Salvation Army place, a religious place; does that worry you?
No. I used to go to Sunday-school when I was little.

Do they ram religion down your throat here?
Yes. But they try to help you and try to talk sense to you.

You ran away from home because you wanted your freedom. Did you consider running away from here?
I did when I first came, but now I've nearly finished my time. Only got three weeks left, so there's no point now.

Are you interested in religion now?
Yes, I believe in God, and things like that. They try to get people saved here. I got saved in one of the meetings. When I leave here in three weeks' time the Major is trying to get me a residential place. I would like to work with children as I have done it before, and live

in near my sister, in north London. When I have time off I could go and see my sister, instead of walking about the streets; then I need not get into trouble again. I don't think I will. I have learnt my lesson. I have learned the hard way.

I am going to try to be more sensible. I think I will go to The Salvation Army because the Major at Bromley, which is near here, has written to my sister about me.

Have you a special boy friend?

Not now, but I hope to. I must pick a good one this time. The last one was from Jamaica. But most coloured boys beat up their girl friends. But never again.

Sometimes I lie in bed thinking of the sort of life I'd like. I want my children to be brought up like others, properly. I would try and keep them out of trouble. I will tell them of my mistakes for my friends might go round blabbering.

CHAPTER TWENTY-FOUR

A Case of Depression

YOU CAN CALL ME Clara. I am twenty-one, and I am a Londoner.

What kind of home?
Oh, a council house. My parents are Irish. They were brought up strict and they brought us up the same way. We were all Catholics. Church every Sunday until we were about seven or eight. If we didn't go we would get a belting from our mum. Both Mum and Dad came from Dublin.

I used to think I was hard done by until I was about sixteen. Then I began to realise that my parents had done well for me. It was a happy home, really. There wasn't plenty but we weren't poor. My elder sister and I used to row a lot. Then she left home when she was fifteen. That was an improvement! I left school at fifteen and went to work at a teachers' training college, in the laboratory, washing the dishes! I also helped the man who used to polish the desks. When I took the job they said they would send me to college, but I didn't stay long enough. Then I left home. I was nearly sixteen. I went to the north, to my sister. But I was only there for three weeks. I couldn't get a job because I didn't have cards. At home my parents had the police out looking for me. My sister was on probation because she got into a fight with a policeman. She bit his hand, or something. Then I got into trouble and was put into a hostel for a year. I used to stay out at nights. I had some wild friends and we would go to week-end parties and things like that. My mother wanted me to be in early. One night I stayed out till twelve. I was a coward so I stayed away from home.

I did find work in an animal laboratory. I told them I was at a hostel. They let me go to evening classes. I kept the job for about two and a half years.

Were you at the hostel all that time?
No, they let me go home after eight months because I was good. Then I had to leave my job because the firm went bankrupt.

What kind of friends did you have in these teenage years?
Mainly girl friends at the youth club. I knew the boys there, but I didn't have many boy friends at the time, only one or two. The boys were skinny and I was fat! I danced and listened to records. But many things went wrong. I entered hospital to lose weight. When I came out I fell off a bus! So I was out of work for six weeks. I had depression problems because of my over-weight. I think that is why I used to stop out at week-ends and do daring things. I used to get very touchy with my parents and have bad moods. I had to see a psychiatrist and saw a number of doctors and they gave me a lot of advice and some medicine. Of course, I had to diet.

Was your depression because you thought you weren't attractive to boys?
Yes. I never had a real boy friend, you see. All my friends had special boy friends, and were getting engaged and getting married. I am still here, alone. I did have one boy friend, but I didn't like him much – my mother did because she knew his mum! I went with him for about two and a half years.

He was not the father of your baby?
No. I still see the father of my baby, but he has never talked about marriage and I'm not going to propose to him. He is coloured, you see, and there are a lot of problems. He is at a college.

Was marriage in your mind when you started having the relationship with your baby's father?
Yes, I think so, but I am not sure. I sometimes thought it would be nice to be married to him. But I never mentioned it.

Did you think it was wrong to have such a relationship with men without marriage?
I wouldn't advise it for anyone. I was a big-head really. But I thought everyone did it.

Were you shocked when you learned that you were going to have a baby?
Yes. I didn't know what to do. I didn't tell my mum. I didn't know for about three months. Then I thought I had better go to the doctor's. When they told me I didn't know what to do. It is not so bad now. In a hospital like this we are all in the same boat.

When is the baby due?
The end of this month.

How did your mother react to all this?
Well, I left home. I didn't tell her, directly. I just packed my things and left a note. But she has been really understanding. She's given me everything I need. She said that if I put the baby to adoption I could go home. But my dad would not have me in the house.

What advice would you give to your younger sisters?
If you want to do that kind of thing, be very careful, use a contraceptive and not to end up like me! That's what I'd say!

What about the future?
I've set Sunday aside so that I can talk to my boyfriend. Mum tells me to ask him what he is going to do for me. 'Try and get a flat or a room nearby.' She says she's willing to look after the baby while I go to work.

That would be a bit of a struggle wouldn't it? You are not thinking of adoption?
No. I did think about it but others have managed on their own so why not me?

What do you think of this place? It is very religious isn't it?
I like it. I'm not just saying this. We have prayers in the morning, but it's not a bore. We just pick our songs out and sing them.

CHAPTER TWENTY-FIVE

Life and Sex – But no Love

I LIVED IN THE East End. Mum was born on the Continent but came here as a child. She met my father here; it was her second marriage. She had eight children. Her first marriage ended in divorce. My mother had seven children by the first marriage. I was her only child by the second. Both my mother's marriages were to Asians. All of her children went into a home. She only had one room. My mum and dad lived in one room with my sister.

Did your parents agree?
Well, there were arguments. Sometimes about money. If they had too much to drink they started quarrelling, but it didn't bother me. I have been in a local authority home from when I was about five till I was twelve. It was the same one all the time and it was good. Of course, I went to school.

But at the age of twelve you left; what happened then?
I went to my dad for six months. He had married again. His wife was horrible to me. So I tried it with my mum and then I came here to this Salvation Army place, 'Crossways'.

My father's second wife had seven children by him; they were not married; there was no room for me.

What went wrong when you lived with your mother?
Nothing. I came to hospital to have my baby.

How old are you?
Fourteen. But I know I look older.

Before you went to hospital to have your baby and before you came here, you lived with your mother and your stepfather?
My stepfather is at sea. Mum is going to get another divorce from him. He is horrible. He won't talk to anyone. If he gets extra money aboard ship he keeps it.

Your baby was born when you were exactly fourteen?
Yes. The day after my birthday.

Do you love her?
Yes. She's asleep now, I have just put her to bed.
I always used to look after kids. I used to look after those of the next-door neighbours.

Did you intend to have a baby?
I don't know.

Are you going to marry him?
I don't want to get married so young.

But you are very young to have a baby. Did that seem unusual to you?
No.

What did your mother say?
She did not know until I was eight months. I went to school nearly all the time. The same school down Mile End. Mum went up the wall at first. But soon she was all right. She visited me but not until my baby was three months old. At first she didn't want to know me. Now I go there every week-end. If mum can get more money I can go home. But as it is she cannot afford to keep the baby. They are expensive, you know.

Do you find it difficult with a baby at the age of fourteen?
All my school mates know, and give me things for it. The teachers

know, and give me things for it. At first they used to say, 'That's the girl with the baby,' but now, when I meet them on the stairs, I know everybody and it is all right. Sometimes they say 'How's your daughter?' and I tell them that she is well. I feel proud about it.

Did anyone tell you that it is against the law for a man to have sexual relationships with a girl under the age of sixteen?
Yes. But they did not do anything because I was in care.

Do you sometimes see this man?
Yes.

Would you like to marry him?
No. I don't want to get married at all, not till I'm older. I don't want to get married young. Once you get married, and you want to go out, you can't. My mum and dad were divorced.

But with your baby you would be more or less tied to the house?
Yes, but I'd rather have that than have a bloke nagging me all the time. Better to be happy alone than married and keep having bust-ups. It's all right to live with someone, but not to be married. I am not going to be like my mum, who was married three times.

If you had a younger sister what would you say to her—about your life—your hard times?
Well, when I was a kid I wasn't allowed to go out. I didn't go to school for six months. I wouldn't go in a girls' school, so I did not go to school. That was how I met him. He worked in a shop.

Why did you refuse to go to a girls' school?
There are lots of snobs in girls' schools. I'm a cockney; they are all lah-de-dah's! I didn't want to become all snotty-nosed.

Where was your mother in all this? You were a thirteen-year-old girl?
She was at work. But I never went out in the evenings.

Is your baby being adopted?
No. From the first if I could have her, I wanted her, but they did not tell me whether I could have her because I was so young. They said I could keep her. I wouldn't let her go now.

What are your plans for the future?
I will leave school, get a job, and get a flat.

Who will look after the baby?
She will go to a nursery school. She will be two or three.

What kind of work will you do?
Typing or looking after kids. I did typing at school but I like looking after kids.

Do you think there is anything wrong in a single girl having a child?
No. Many single people are happier than lots of people who are married.

Are you the youngest unmarried mother here?
Yes. There was another girl. She was a year older than me when she left. But nobody knew I was as young as I was.

You do look a great deal older than your years. Is that what other folk have said?
Yes. I could go to the pictures for adults only.

Did the baby's father think you were older than you were?
Yes.

Do you like Crossways? It's a very religious place, isn't it?
Not half. You have a little meeting every day and a meeting on Sunday. But I ain't never here at the week-end. When I was young I went to my Catholic church. A woman took me. But she was bored to tears because they spoke in Latin. From then on I would go to the 'prodigal' church, the Protestants. I didn't go every week because you can pray on your own doorstep if you want to pray. I pray in bed.

CHAPTER TWENTY-SIX

Nothing on Her Conscience

AT THE SAME home for girls, Rhona answers questions:

Where were you brought up, Rhona?
I was born in Wales but I am not Welsh. My mother and father were born in the Ukraine, in Russia.

Your parents met during the war in a refugee camp?
My mother says she wasn't a refugee.

It is not dishonourable to be a refugee. Many good and famous people have been refugees. Where did they settle?
In Wales. They had six children besides me.

Was yours a happy home?
Well, normal. Unhappiness and bits of happiness, all mixed up.

Were there arguments?
Between my mother and father? With seven kids! Every day! Not big arguments but they were enough.

Were they a loving couple?
No. Sometimes my dad might kick the girls, instead of kicking my mum.

Did you have a happy life at home?
To the age of about fourteen. My sister left home when she was fifteen, my brother soon after her. She was sent to an approved school. Later my brother ended up in one. My sister's trouble began with petty theft, my brother's with shop-lifting. I had to do most of the writing to him at the approved school. My father wrote to him but he never wanted anything to do with him. This letter-writing was hard. I was only fourteen. The things my mother made me write upset me.

When I was fifteen I went to work in a factory. I hated every minute of it. But one day I just couldn't stand it no more and did something that got me the sack. Within a half-hour I had another job in a supermarket. It was better than the factory.

What age were you when you left home?
Fifteen. I had a row with my dad and went to stay with my uncle. Then my brother showed up with a girl who decided that I should go to London with her. I stayed at the home of this girl's mother.

Your father did not object to you coming away?
He did not care. I lived at the home of this girl for two months, and then I pinched her boy friend. So I moved in with my sister, the same one who had been in the approved school. I worked in a supermarket. I had a friend in the supermarket and we used to go out together. We used to drink a little. Then I met some drug addicts and I started, but nothing that would make me go mad, just cannabis and a few pep pills. Something I took once made me sick. It was acid and I never took anything after that. I was so ill after it. Then I met a boy friend, my baby's father. I went with him for two years.

Do you love him? Are you going to marry him?
He did not want to marry me though I was pregnant. He asked me after I had my baby because he thinks the world of her. But I could not marry the man who did not want to marry me when I really needed him.

Was he your first boy friend?
No. When I was fourteen I used to go out with a sailor. I told him I

was older than I was, and one night at his house when his mother was out, you know . . . But I didn't know what I was doing.

You were only fourteen?
Yes. He must have been about twenty. I left the house with a clear conscience as though nothing had happened. Then he went away. He got married. I was broken-hearted. I still think it was true love.

But since then you have been with other men?
It's something you seem to drift into. But there was only three of them. When I was back home I was going out with a boy. He was decent and kind. But my mother found out. There was an inquest report in the papers—a girl had committed suicide over the same boy I was friendly with. Anyway, my mother started moaning about this. One night I was late, but only in the next door but one. When I got in my mother pulled the hair out of my head. She said I would commit suicide next.

Did anyone explain to you what all this was about?
My mother said, 'Don't let any men touch you, or kiss you.' That was stupid. I thought that if I kissed a boy I would be pregnant. At school, everybody was debating on whether to show a sex film. I never learnt a thing about sex that would help me, only about tadpoles! I did not know how a baby came. When I became pregnant my first thought was, 'Get rid of it.' The hospital said they wouldn't do it for me. My sister said, 'Go out and get a job.' My sister is a prostitute. She said that if I got a job she would get me money and I could have an abortion.

Then there was this girl Teresa. She was a lesbian. The trouble I had with her. She thought she could take me to bed with her. She could never understand why I wouldn't. But we was good friends. I used to smoke with them, grass.

You said something about having no conscience?
No, I have nothing on my conscience, no. I cannot think of anything. Nothing that I would lose a night's sleep over. I am not bothered a bit about having a baby. Have you seen her? She's lovely!

What about marriage?

Oh, I'm all for it. But it's no good jumping into a thing.

Is he a Welsh boy?

No, he is West Indian. I think marriage ruins a lot of people.

This is a religious place, isn't it?

Yes. I am quite happy to go on Sunday to the service. I quite enjoy The Salvation Army. I had my baby dedicated in The Salvation Army, but when I went home I had to take her to the Catholic priest. Not because I wanted to; my mother wanted to. I sometimes regret having my baby so young. If I was about twenty-seven or twenty-eight it would be better.

CHAPTER TWENTY-SEVEN

A Live Rat for Company

THE SALVATION ARMY'S Cellar, Gutter and Garret Brigades began early in 1884. The training of officers had begun a few years before, and Emma Booth, the General's daughter, had asked, 'Why not take a room, and girl cadets, to live in the slums? Let them dress as the people do, only be clean; let them visit, sympathise, and put before them the example of a good life.' The first slum post was opened in Drury Lane (Seven Dials). The work spread rapidly in Britain and overseas. The 'slum sisters' of The Salvation Army gave a new word to language in Scandinavia, where slums on the London and New York pattern had never existed. To this day in Norway, Denmark and Sweden, in new apartments and among flat-dwellers with reasonable standards of living, 'slum sisters' occupy 'slum posts' where the lack is moral, emotional and spiritual malnutrition, rather than the old-style cold and hunger of London.

In recent times the British public was made aware of the Salvationist slum and goodwill work, by the writings of Hugh Redwood, a Fleet Street journalist who, in 1928 during a Thames-side flood disaster, encountered women slum work officers of the Army. He became involved in the work for flood victims, and for the needy and unfortunate in many other parts of Britain. He also wrote a book, *God in the Slums*, which became a best-seller and which helped to enlist workers and funds for the Army's effort with its new title, 'The Goodwill League'. Often the slum work is now described as goodwill work as a concession to local authorities or citizens who dislike the implied social stigma behind the word 'slum'. Yet, in essence, the Scandinavians have found that the human heart and the human dwelling-place can be as cold and miserable when new and opulent as when old and derelict.

Captain M. has been a slum and goodwill officer for the past ten years. Before becoming an officer she worked for a county executive committee of the National Health Service.

She became a Salvationist when her eighteen-year-old sister heard singing as she passed a Salvation Army hall. Because she liked music she began to attend the meetings and was later converted. She now tells her own story:

As a result of the change in my sister's life I was sufficiently intrigued to want to see for myself what The Salvation Army was all about. I fell in love with it because of its joyfulness, its abandon in worship, the freedom and practical expression of its faith. I was sixteen and still at grammar school. My parents did not object to us joining the Army; indeed, some time later they became soldiers themselves. Initially it was largely because of the love of music we all shared. But there was an element of social life involved. I felt a great change. I had been a regular attender at church but I had never experienced any personal real faith. I soon began to visit the public-houses in Chatham, selling the *War Cry* and singing to the patrons, who usually welcomed the Army.

I was sworn-in as a Salvationist when I was eighteen, and I entered the Training College when I was twenty-one. The conviction that I should be an officer grew steadily and surely; I felt I could go no other way.

Example played a part. As a teenager I thought the corps officers were remarkable people. They were wonderful in their sincerity, in the expressions of their faith, in their caring for the people. They were my ideal disciples of Christ.

My family were sorry I had to leave home. They accepted that I was sure about my decision, but I don't think they appreciated that officership was the natural thing. There was this overriding sadness about breaking the family circle. I was the home-lover; I was the one they thought would never leave home.

Training I found difficult at first. I was not used to public work, mixing with so many people. There was no home life. As to the outcome, I asked for slum and goodwill work; it had long been at the back of my mind. This went back to the time at home when as a

Salvationist I visited the house of a woman who appeared to be very old. But she was, in fact, only in her forties. As her mind was disturbed, her husband had left her and she lived in a hovel, a caricature of what a home should be in modern England. She was so lonely that she fed a rat. This rat came every day out of its hole in the corner and she talked to it. It was company for her, something that was her own. Afterwards I tried, and other Salvationists tried, to be her friend. We took her food and clothing and tried to make her feel that she was not abandoned, that someone cared. I asked God to help me to take to this woman love and understanding. I had never been in a home like that. I did not dream that such awful places existed. The impression was so profound that I felt that this life of service was worthy of the best in me. Part of the shock I felt then, because I had always shared the love of parents and brother and sister in a good home, was that this poor creature had a husband and a daughter, neither of whom had anything to do with her.

The staff in training accepted my wish to be a goodwill officer. They warned me about the practical aspects—it sometimes involves squalor and nauseating conditions, verminous bedding, terrible neglect. They told me I might have to scrub and clean, which had not been my style as a shorthand typist. I had not done manual work.

I was commissioned to Hoxton, one of the Centres that is a memorial to Hugh Redwood, as the fifth officer. We were a team doing social welfare and Christian evangelistic work among the poorest people there. It was not always poverty in terms of money, though some people had very little. But much of the poverty was in poor conditions—old people who were lonely, young families who found it hard to agree on how to run a home. Many people had sufficient income but not the ability to manage it.

The officer in charge had served forty years as a goodwill officer and I had to submit to discipline, especially seeing I was the junior member of the team. One needs discipline if it is fair and I found it fair. She was strict but she was very experienced. While we were expected to work to a standard, she lived by it herself. We had a good home life. We were not just a team; we were a family.

Officially we were allowed Saturday afternoon and evening free, but our first priority was the work. Whether we were free or on duty, if we were needed then we had to go. The first priority was the people. As to money, I never suffered from lack of it. My allowance was adequate. It did not compare with that of secretaries of a county executive committee of the National Health Service, but then neither did my expenses. We had no time for expensive social junketing and no opportunity to wear fashionable clothes, which was just as well for I could have afforded neither.

Part of my duty was the operation of 'meals on wheels', thirty to forty meals a day. The old people often needed more than dinner, and with God's help we tried to provide. Often we were the only visitors they had.

A foot clinic was run by the local authority, but at the Centre, with an officer on duty.

When we met people at the Centre, at the old age pensioners' meetings, women's meetings, or at the pubs, or in their homes when we took meals, we found that they came to depend on us. We sometimes helped to reconcile families. We filled in forms and helped with official business. We learned to become our own citizens' advice bureau. Sometimes people's loneliness is self-imposed; they are often independent people. Sometimes they are lonely and they tolerate their loneliness as a shield – nobody comes and they are proud, and try to convince themselves that they don't care that nobody comes.

Of course, the experience that changed my life is conversion; one does not forget that when one becomes a goodwill officer. I have often had to do tasks that I could not have done before, dirty and embarrassing – duties one can do only because one belongs to God. These needy people are my people because they are Christ's people. One could not find enough compassion and love without His example and His sacrifice, which seem to flow from Him and enable one to surpass oneself.

Sometimes this gospel of Christ, which was rarely preached in words, was accepted by these elderly people. When you were there when they needed you; when they had problems in their home; when they were bereaved; because you helped and because you shared their grief, they thought about it afterwards. We cleaned their homes or helped them in their sickness and they thought about the motive behind what we did. Then some of them accepted the faith of Christ, in whose name we served. We did not go to preach; we went to care. Sometimes young people came to the meetings and became converted because they had looked and listened and eventually been convinced.

PART FOUR

In Darkest England Now

CHAPTER TWENTY-EIGHT

A Changing World

WILLIAM BOOTH WAS many years ahead of his time; his book, *In Darkest England and the Way Out* proves that. He could see into our times, rather than his own. Poverty today has a different significance. It does not come from the same causes as it did in William Booth's day. Residual poverty, after the welfare state has met its obligations, comes from evils such as alcoholism, gambling and sexual maladjustments. There is neurosis, psychosis and psychopathic behaviour.

But though William Booth spoke of the 'submerged tenth' as an economically submerged part of the population, he was well aware of the psychologically and physiologically deprived people who lived in his day. Headings in his book speak of the criminal, and how to help him; the moral lunatic; the drunkard; the children who needed help. Under all of these headings he laid down very well-delineated schemes for meeting the needs of the people. A line stretches from William Booth to us today, and we can still look at similar problems which remain unsolved.

The word 'homelessness' might give us a clue both to the continuity and to the change. When we say 'homelessness' we look at the Men's Social Services of The Salvation Army, and see some 9,000 men who live with us every night. The enlightened social worker asks 'What are the problems of these men?' They are homeless, single men. The reason for the homelessness may be that they are not married; never have married; are divorced or separated.

Then they ask what are the reasons for this. Figures presented by a psychiatrist, who did a survey of two large Salvationist hostels in London, show that some 15 per cent of the men are schizophrenics;

some 45 per cent are men with behaviour disorders. This would include those whom William Booth labelled 'moral lunatics'; it would include about 30 per cent who suffer from alcoholism in a chronic form. 45 per cent are chronic gamblers. Here are reasons for the homelessness, for 'the new poverty', which is discovered when the basic economic needs of those men are met. It is a twentieth-century poverty arising from inadequacy.

Booth House, opened by H.M. Queen Elizabeth in March 1968, illustrates in itself our new way to meet old needs. For though we have new words and trends and much else that is new and different, the basic strategy of the Army is that of William Booth, who phrased it in his well-known words, 'Go for souls and go for the worst.'

Though the work done by the social services of The Salvation Army over the years has been of a high calibre, much of it had to be done in inadequate buildings with limited staff and limited skills. One change has been to set up at Booth House, a referral assessment unit. The unit gathers information from those who would refer men to us. We soon discovered that men were being sent to us by the prison authorities and the probation service, from mental hospitals and from general hospitals. Other social workers, Salvation Army officers, ministers of the gospel, the police and others added their quota. Indeed, our hostels were often being used as dumping grounds. For example, a man was referred to us by a prison social worker. He had been in prison for some time. His offence had been murder. Pressed for further information, the social worker said that the man was very withdrawn and that he was coloured. To have taken this man straight from prison and put him into one of our large institutions, would have been asking for trouble.

So we began to sort out the men who were referred to us. People at mental hospitals sat at the end of a telephone saying, 'We have a man. Will you take him?' That was all the information given.

We discovered that many of the men referred to us had alcoholism problems. In our assessment unit, men with this difficulty come for a period of up to three weeks. We try to find out what the reason is for their alcoholism. What is their physical condition? We now work in co-operation with the London Hospital. One of the professors from the teaching faculty comes in each week, with his team, to examine newly-admitted men.

Following assessment we send them down to our centre at Highworth, in Wiltshire, or to some other facility appropriate to their need.

Besides alcoholics, we assess men suffering from mental illness. An interesting example of this is an Irishman, 'Danny'. He was walking up and down in front of our Victoria Homes when someone said 'good morning' to him. Later we discovered that he had a schizophrenic illness, and tuberculosis. He had merely booked himself into the hostel as an ordinary lodger. But he needed a different kind of care.

There are many like him and with this in mind we have established a therapeutic community at Spa Road. There we have four officer couples living and working. The men are given occupational therapy. Salvationists from round about come in to share activities. The idea of such therapeutic communities is to widen the concept of treatment. It gives a man a share in the process of rehabilitation as well as being the recipient of a serving and caring and healing ministry. Many men have thus been brought to a point where they have been able to leave our hostel and go out to life outside.

One man we received was deaf and dumb. He was an enuretic and also labelled as homosexual. He could have had no place within the ordinary hostel. But the team at Spa Road considered him and decided that they would try to do something for him. In the first place he was referred to a doctor who discovered that his enuresis had a surgical component. After a comparatively minor operation he recovered from his enuresis and was no longer a bed-wetter. But before the operation was performed and before the man's control was re-established, the community had accepted him as a bed-wetter and were willing to cope with his problem.

The next problem arose as to what this man could do. His normal occupation was menial and it was thought that he should go back to that kind of work. Then it was discovered that he had a knowledge of both English and French and also creative ability on an artistic level. He is still at the centre, not only restored physically but also with some measure of religious experience.

One great change since the first *Darkest England* is that there has been a revolution in thinking about social work. We are now dealing with a highly self-conscious profession, and the professionals have sometimes pushed their abilities and their image at the expense of the voluntary agencies. Probation officers, five years ago, might speak of The Salvation Army as the people who, when a man did not have the tuppence necessary for his bed-money, would not accept him into the hostel. People said that our hostels were too large, and dirty, and not well kept. That was the image, and it remains the image with some people.

We could simply inform the probation service and health services that the men are with us because they have been dumped upon us! As an example, the Mental Health Act of 1959 decreed that mental illness should be treated in the community, and not in asylums. This meant that the energetic psychiatrist who simply wanted to rid himself of a great burden of chronically sick people discharged them into the community. The community was not ready to receive them. Many of them ended up in our hostels. They present us with one of our greatest problems. The families of these men have not known them for up to twenty years, and so the men come to us with nowhere else to go. This has been the outcome of the new, so-called 'forward-looking approach' to mental illness. The community has not accepted its share of responsibility for these men. So we take them and are often blamed for the conditions some of them create.

There are also the people who, like the Cyrenians in the Bible, find men living in broken-down houses and say no one will take care of them. But the men live there because they want to live there. Put them in a house, with good surroundings, and they would soon be drop-outs from society.

Television has been a great aid in showing what we are doing. *The Philpot File* has brought us praise and help. In a mid-week series, shots from our Spa Road hostel impressed people tremendously. A man had come from a mental hospital in Portsmouth. He had nowhere to go. The sympathetic hearing he had, and his acceptance by the officer on duty that evening impressed many people. This is all part of a reversal of preconceived ideas which social workers and others have had of the Army work in this field.

There has been a change in the attitude of Government and local authorities to the Army's work. At one time they refused to help in any way. At other times they tried to soft-pedal or back-pedal the soul-saving aspect of our endeavours. Now they do help us with grant aid and they do not as a rule interfere with the spiritual side of our work.

In all our approaches they need to know that we are doing work which is their statutory responsibility. We usually find that we are doing it more cheaply than they would be able to do it. Money comes to us in various ways: from central government funds, from the Department of Health and Social Security. Some men are sent from hospitals and so the financial burden is met by the N.H.S.

Sometimes we do a specific task, such as the care of old people in eventide homes. Here the local authority meets much of the expense. Work we do for delinquent youth in Scotland is a charge on the tax-payer. It is on a scale that enables us to have highly-skilled workers in Scotland; none of them is an officer but all are Salvationists. The salary is paid according to the appropriate scale. Increasingly we are asked to do work for the Government. We have recently received grants for our Spa Road Centre's work for alcoholics. Most government officials believe in what we are doing *because* it has religious motivation.

We are, of course, entering into this world of professional social service with increased emphasis on training. We now look to the treatment concept of social work, rather than to just the housing and feeding of men. In Greenock, Scotland, we are now taking men into a reception area where there is a condition that a man is willing to be expertly taken care of. This, of course, requires a staff of qualified social workers. The Director of this work in Scotland has a Residential Care Certificate and also a diploma in social work administration from the University of Glasgow. He is highly competent in this field and regarded as something of an authority in Scotland.

In our Scottish units for young men and school-boys we have a training programme, and we are now beginning to staff our centres in Scotland from the trainees who have gone through this system.

We believe that if God means us to do a work, He will provide us with the money and with the staff. So there has been very little advertising. We have with us officers who are professionally qualified and of experience. One, with a degree, is notable in that he walked into our hostel straight off the street and began work by scrubbing floors. Gradually he came to the place where he was ready for officership. When listening in officers' councils to the Governor of the Social Services speaking of the need for trained social workers, he felt he should equip himself in this way. He set about his 'O' levels and his 'A' levels, and recently he finished his external degree from the University of London. He is now a B.Sc. I believe that it will be within our social services that we shall discover our social workers.

The programme of training in the Army's International Training College is geared to new demands in social service. Intensive training for social-work officers takes place in their second year. They visit prisons; spend time in residential homes; are exposed to mental illness in the sense that they meet people who are mentally sick, not as mentally sick people, but just as people.

It seems that in the future there will be a dual approach to the work. There will be those who will be trained for managerial posts, and others who will be trained for social work posts. Besides this, we are now able to employ social workers and nurses and, because of government grants, we are able to pay professional salaries. Recently, following the presentation of urgent needs, we received a grant for salaries of £12,000 per year from the Department of Health and Social Security. Another grant of £10,000 per year comes from the Home Office for work we are doing among offenders and ex-offenders.

There is no limit to the possible expansion of our work except our lack of faith. Perhaps we take heart from William Booth, who did not look at obstacles but went right through them. He was also willing to make tactical retreats when he was so obliged, but he was sure of ultimate victory.

CHAPTER TWENTY-NINE

Going for the Worst

Is the 'Darkest England' scheme still in being legally and actually?
Yes. William Booth ensured that the financial and legal aspects of the scheme were protected. We operate today with a social fund that grew from the 'Darkest England' appeal of 1890.

We are only now beginning to realise the Founder's wise conception of social work. His views on the clinical nature of alcoholism make one realise how far he was ahead of medical thinking of his day. In his book he states that alcoholism was probably a disease. That is a statement decades in advance of expert opinion in 1890. His great 'dream' has not gone into history as far as we are concerned. There is much of his great vision that we must yet try to achieve for this and later generations.

Yet there were men in his time, cleverer men I suppose, like F. D. Maurice and Charles Kingsley, who talked much about social science. The Founder's idea of salvation went deeper than this!
There is a question of genetics here. You have the sociologists and the medical profession and perhaps the humanists and plain 'do-gooders' like the Webbs, like Charles Booth, the Fabians, and socially-conscious politicians. The Founder spoke the language we understand. He used the message of the gospel. In the early days of the Army very much was done by direct intervention of God. Booth believed he could do 'at a stroke' what we sometimes do in other ways. Because he believed he could do it, he did it. We can advise, give psychiatric treatment, medical treatment, and so on. We do speak about conversion, but it has become more complex for some

people. In the early days Salvationists dealt with the alcoholic, the drunkard as they called him. There was no psychiatric service or medical service to precede salvation or to follow it through. Many of these people got through to a better life without our modern aids.

In these days I think God expects us to do as much as we possibly can, with all our available skills, to help the man. So we speak to him about deliverance and see that he gets the necessary treatment – salvation is the over-all priority – psychiatry if it will help to that end. It is all part of a whole treatment.

In the United States there was a proposal at one time that government aid would be given only if the Army would undertake not to do any kind of proselytising. If such a proposal was made here, what would your feelings be about that?
We certainly would not undertake any work that limited our freedom to work in Christ's name and to offer His salvation to all who needed it. But, thankfully, we can say there is no interference with our preaching the gospel. None of us would participate in merely humanist endeavour.

Yet there are many humanist organisations in the field, more than there used to be: Help the Aged, Save the Children Fund, Shelter, Oxfam. These are not avowedly Christian. Does there still exist a requirement for Christian service?
There is certainly something about the Christian experience that radiates compassion far different from that of the 'do-gooder'. A recent programme on T.V. the other evening brought in many donations for our work because of what viewers saw at our Spa Road centre. This is compassion that goes beyond social service as such. There must be a heart of love as well as a head.

In the nineteenth century we had rough beginnings, with people like Elijah Cadman who had a maxim, 'work or starve'. We had those terrible coffin beds in which the poet Francis Thompson slept at the Blackfriars hostel. There was subsistence supply of food, hunks of bread and margarine and cocoa. Have we moved on from that?
Alas, some of the buildings are still with us. But the facilities are

better and the conditions have improved greatly. We used to call the centres 'elevators'. If a man could not find work he would be employed by us chopping wood and so on, to pay for his shelter and food. Nowadays, a man does not have to beg – Social Security sees to that. We have new facilities that are really superb. But in the older centres we try to lift men to better levels of life. We give them a better environment and we help them in other ways.

We have been blamed for having no 'purpose-built' hostels. On occasions, local authorities have complained, as in Glasgow at one time, about bad conditions in some of our hostels.

Our hostels are open to inspection at any moment. That is the law. Fairly strict conditions are laid down. In these days we do not have serious problems, which is amazing when one considers the type of men in some of our centres. Here at Middlesex Street in back alleys you can see men lying around at any time of the day – groups of them, drinking meths. They are absolutely knocked out. Many of these men come here. To keep that place clean, to keep these men clean is something that only a person with a big heart and great energy could do. Yet if you went into the hostel and looked at the floors, quite clean and tidy, you would never realise that such men slept there. There is a legal standard, quite high, even in an old hostel. Go to others here in the city, like Westminster or Blackfriars, which are quite old. It is amazing that they are as clean and efficient as they are.

You are now dealing with drug addiction, the 'hippie' problem, and mentally sub-normal people. Are these problems worse than they have always been, or are we more aware of the problems?

We are more aware, because of recent legislation which has the effect of turfing out such people from mental hospitals, without any follow-through. One new problem for us is that we have so many mentally-handicapped men to care for. What can we do for this type of individual? Are we just going to give him shelter? Having been given shelter, what is he going to do during the day? Often he goes out on to the streets and gets into trouble. The much-talked-of increase in the prison population has something to do with the fact that mental hospitals have been forced to reject people with these mental conditions. They merely get into trouble and may go to prison.

But William Booth would expect us to do our best—these men are with us in our hostels. What can we do for them?

It is a tremendous problem, but we have now developed complexes of social work—at Booth House in London, for instance, where we have a referral centre and a rehabilitation centre. At Spa Road we have similar work going on. Sir Keith Joseph has shown interest in this work and the Government has said that it will pay the salaries of the professional staff. Government grants have enabled us to use a mini-bus to collect men from various hostels for various sorts of therapy. This work is also developing in Liverpool. There the local authority have asked if they could move into our hostel and help with professional staff. There is tremendous development in this area, which does demand professionals. Numbers of Salvationist professionals are working with us, and, as the complexity of the need increases and as standards rise, this professional element will increase.

This is as it should be. But we are not moving into mere professionalism. We want all engaged in the work to have that basic 'call', to believe in the power of Christ to help in every situation. This is the important plus-factor in Salvationism. This is what appeals to most people when they come to help us: the spiritual drive through the whole of the social services.

Has your experience with this modern 'submerged tenth' called into question your Salvationist belief in redemption as being possible for every human being? Do you still believe that everyone can be redeemed?

If I did not believe it I could not take the platform at any meeting at any hostel. When I look out at the sea of faces, when I see their look of hopelessness, they seem to be looking up to me to say, 'Do you believe what you are saying?' If I didn't believe that any man in that congregation who came forward to the Penitent-form could be saved, then I could not go on. But I do believe! Having seen remarkable transformations in many lives among such people, one cannot doubt God's power to save.

Men seem to lose their will, lose their ability to do anything. Yet there is a glimmer within them of hope and desire for something better. Sometimes it leads them to believe that what we are saying is true. There is deliverance for them! Many of these men become truly converted; some work with us, new men; others go out into the world to a new life. Many of these men have been in deep trouble. Many of them have resolved their problems – by the blessing of God.

You spoke of lay-Salvationists working professionally. Are you willing to take lay-workers who are not Salvationists?
We do not say they must be Salvationists. Whoever comes, we feel that the test is that there should be a religious experience. Our youth work in Scotland is run by lay-Salvationists, at Mount Bruce and Kilbirnie. The Probation Officer in charge is a Salvationist.

Do you suffer from a shortage of officers?
Yes. This is one of our great concerns. Our problem now is to get assistants, to avoid the strain of an officer being kept at his hostel morning, noon and night, seven days a week, with no relaxation. We get quite a large number of lay people as assistants, and we are thankful for them.

Yet when one thinks of the work in the future, if we don't get officers what are we going to do as far as leadership is concerned? Where are we going to get our directors, our sectional officers, our divisional officers, our departmental heads?
I cannot say that the solution to this is the lay-Salvationist. The solution to this is the young Salvationist, with the necessary qualifications for the task and the deep sense of vocation.

Is this a greater need than money? William Booth was rather disappointed in the results of the 'Darkest England' scheme. He hoped it would produce more, financially. Now are we better served with Government help, local authorities and so on?
We still need money, but I agree that we need dedicated workers even more. The Army has continued to benefit financially from the Founder's long-term plans for his 'Darkest England' scheme. Some assets we have, such as properties in the city, and very valuable

indeed. We might create a new social service complex at Spa Road from the sale of a site here at Middlesex Street. This is a project very much on the drawing-boards. When the property was bought in the Founder's day, no one thought that in years ahead there would be such city development that it would become so valuable.

We are thankful, and we are prepared to cash in on it, to develop a far more modern social centre at Spa Road. This goes, of course, for a number of new hostels about to be built at Cardiff, Bristol, Manchester and Newcastle. There are important and expensive additions at Birmingham, at Coventry and at St. Helens.

When one realises that it costs something in the region of £3,000 per man to build a hostel, one has some idea of the amount involved in a centre for 150 men. Something like half-a-million pounds or more is required to build one new hostel. Finance for such schemes involves discussion with local authorities. They do help with grant aid towards the tremendous costs.

We now have quite a number of these purpose-built new properties. Bradford is one, Leeds is another. We are at the moment involved in property extensions valued at something like £8,000,000. Think of that! William Booth asked for £100,000 for his 'dream' and £30,000 per annum for maintenance. He did not get that much.

Can I ask you one last question? William Booth said, 'Go for souls and go for the worst.' Do you feel, in the Men's Social Services, that your officers still have this aim?

Yes, I am sure of that. But I sometimes wonder what William Booth meant by 'worst'. Is the man in our hostel the 'worst'? There are others who have not been brought within the scope of our work in Salvation Army hostels. Our men are not the most wicked; they are perhaps the most unfortunate, the least endowed with education and good social background. I can think of many of 'the worst' who never come within range of the Army—the criminal, the pornographer, the betrayer of the innocent—they are also part of 'Darkest England'. Yes, we believe that salvation is for the 'whosoever', the 'worst' of any kind, whether it is the vicious or the weak.

CHAPTER THIRTY

Keeping Men out of Prison

THE FIELD WING EXPERIMENT at Booth House, the Salvation Army social service centre for men in Whitechapel, East London, is an alternative to Brixton Prison for first offenders; Mrs. Xenia Field's campaign, with co-operation between magistrates, probation officers and The Salvation Army, prompted the Home Office to consider a new chain of remand hostels. The officer in charge speaks in particular of his work in the Field Wing:

As the first officer of Booth House I am responsible under the director for the running of Booth House, a hostel for men. 211 men are accommodated. Within the hostel itself is the smaller unit, the experimental bail hostel which we call the Field Wing, named after Xenia Field, who was the main inspiration for the idea and who provided some of the money for maintenance. Also, the Army social service here is responsible for the feeding and living accommodation of all the men and for Rawson Home Hostel, which is the eventide home here, and the alcoholics' assessment unit which is also housed here.

The Field Wing is an attempt to prevent men being sent to prison or to a remand centre, when possibly they have done nothing which warrants their going to prison or even being convicted. It hinges on the problem of 'no fixed address'. A man wanders about London and, because he is short of money and has nowhere to live, it looks as though he might get into trouble. He is apprehended by the police, who take him before the magistrate as a suspected person. The magistrate may wish to have medical or other reports on him. He therefore places the man on remand to appear before him in two, three, or even four weeks' time. But because he has no fixed address the only place where the magistrate can send the man, to ensure that he appears again before the Court, has been either the remand wing of Brixton prison or, if it is a young man, Ashford Remand Home.

In the case of young first offenders, particularly, this has been done reluctantly by magistrates and probation officers for years past. Yet the Courts have had no alternative. In the end, when they come before the magistrate again, prison forms no part of the actual sentence for some of the men and sometimes they are actually acquitted. Yet they have already been to prison. A man in work, so accused by the police and brought before the Court, may lose his job and even the place where he is living—perhaps a share of a flat with his friends. He is thus classified as having 'no fixed abode'. He comes out of this custodial remand, having lost his job and perhaps his digs, in a worse position than he was before he went before the Court, though he may have been innocent or at least not guilty of any offence that warranted such punishment.

Xenia Field was for some time a magistrate. She felt that something ought to be done about this problem, especially as it affected young people. She asked The Salvation Army for help and Booth House was set aside.

The bail hostel was opened by Mr. Reginald Maudling, then Home Secretary, in November 1971. At that time it was intended to take men from two courts only—Bow Street, where the Chief Metropolitan Magistrate, Sir Frank Milton, is extremely interested in the experiment, and the other was the Inner London Court, at Great Marlborough Street. The Home Office provided a research team. Each man was interviewed as he came in and before he left. The idea was that the project could be reviewed after six months, with an interim report, and then after twelve months a final report would be made on the first hundred men. In the initial stages our daily attendance was something in the region of four or five and after a while it was decided to open the hostel to other Courts in Inner and East London. In September 1972, it was opened to all Metropolitan Magistrates' Courts; the Guildhall and the Mansion House Courts;

and the North-Eastern Courts area. The intake now is almost up to the possible maximum.

The men concerned with this important experiment live in our hostel, very much like any other men. They share the dining-room and two television lounges, the recreation facilities, paying their way over the counter. The only difference between such men and ordinary residents is that the men on remand have to report at 11.30 each evening. If we find that a man has not come into the hostel for – say – two nights running it looks as though he may have absconded. We then have to contact the nearest police station. Magistrates are concerned to ensure that a man is going to turn up at the due time at Court.

Most of the men are young, ranging from seventeen upwards. Many of them are greatly relieved that they have not been sent to Brixton prison, or (the young men) into Ashford. The man over thirty appreciates this even more than the younger man, who may have little idea of what prison means. Booth House is a well-established, modern hostel with good facilities. The older man who has been living rough in a disused house, or sleeping under the arches, may feel strange when he comes here but he does appreciate it. There is always hot water; he has a room to himself. There are bathrooms available.

There have been a few who have absconded and we are hoping that the final report of the Home Office Research Team will reveal why this happened. Some men who came from Scotland felt that they would 'beat the rap' by going back to Scotland. But, of course, this does not happen. On my latest count, twenty-two who were sent by the Courts just did not turn up. The *Guardian* said, when commenting on the opening of the hostel, that the only thing that could ruin the experiment was the discovery that the absconding flesh was weaker than the grateful spirit! This must have something to do with it in the case of some men. They have left the Court; no one escorts them to the bail hostel; they are just told where to come. We want to know why some did not arrive and why some left after they did arrive!

Criteria for admission to the Field Wing were agreed by the magistrates, by the probation service and by The Salvation Army. These are:

The man has to be seventeen and over.

There must be no condition in the bail order to report to the police.

The man must be on remand from a magistrate to return to a Magistrate's Court. This excludes anyone who is remanded to appear before a Crown Court.

He must not be addicted to drugs or alcohol.

He must not be mentally disturbed or mentally ill.

Also, he should not be a sexual offender or charged with offences involving children, or have a history of such offences.

He should not have been sentenced nor known to have had a previous custodial sentence, a sentence of imprisonment, or a period of training in a Borstal or detention centre.

You see, the prime object of the Field Wing is to try to single out the man who has committed only one offence, or who has never been in trouble with the police before, and shield him from the bad influence of those who have been in prison before. The Field Foundation is firm on the custodial clause. We have to turn down any man, even though he may have had only a fortnight's custodial sentence twenty-five years before. For at present this rules him out completely. This does not meet with the full approval of magistrates or the probation service. When the progress of the experiment is reconsidered this is one of the principles we hope to change.

The Home Office judges success here under three headings: minimal benefit; normal benefit; maximum benefit.

The first means that men have derived something by living here, something better than living in prison or having 'no fixed abode'. We say that for a man to live here is obviously better than to live three in a cell at Brixton prison, where they are locked up for twenty-three hours out of twenty-four. Here they live in clean surroundings with their own room, free to come and go as they wish, free to find work or to continue with the work that they have, free to go out and visit their friends.

'Normal benefit' is when the man is out of work when he first came here, and of 'no fixed abode'. But during his time here he finds work and he finds accommodation. When he reappears before the Court he is able to say that since he has been living at the Field Wing he has found himself a job and he has a place to live.

'Maximum benefit' relates to people who came in here with a number of personality and social problems, not merely being out of work and not having anywhere to live. Through interviews with the officers here and with the probation officers, these men are often able to resolve some, if not all, of these problems. When they go to Court again they may have a job and somewhere to live; family differences with wives or parents, or both may be settled.

As far as magistrates are involved, they are concerned with getting people back in Court on the date set. We are much more concerned here with helping a man to resolve his personal and spiritual problems. A probation officer visits the hostel every weekday from 9.30–10.0 a.m., or later if necessary. The men can talk to him as well as to Salvation Army officers. One man, a government official, had had trouble at home, he had been pushed to his limits by his son, a sixteen-year-old. In a flash of temper the man had drawn a knife on the boy and slightly wounded him. The son took the father to Court on a 'grievous bodily harm' charge. The magistrates were concerned that the man should not go home for a while, until the thing had been sorted out by the probation service. The man came here for three weeks. He had never been in trouble at all with the police before. Because he was living in the hostel he was able to carry on with his job; his wife visited him and by the time he reappeared before the Court the whole matter had been resolved to the satisfaction of the Bench. He was allowed to return home.

Another man here had misappropriated some of his firm's money. He had never been in trouble with the police before. There had been a broken engagement, which had preyed on his mind. Imagine the effect of sending a man like that to Brixton! Instead, he was sent to us. We managed to get him a job working at a Salvation Army headquarters. When he went back to the Court, he was also placed on probation, and was able to continue living here, but in another part of the hostel. He continued at work and when he had found his feet once again he found another job for himself. The latest report we have is that he is working and is married and has settled down very happily.

The Government has now decided that it will do something to extend the idea behind the Field Wing. One newspaper stated that Xenia Field was a perfect illustration of the power of the individual to affect the course of legislation, as shown by the success of her experimental wing at Booth House in Whitechapel. The Government seems to think that this kind of social reform can be put into practice elsewhere.

One word concerning the Army, and the Men's Social Service in Britain, came from the *Sunday Times*, which said of the Field Wing experiment at Booth House: 'Mrs. Xenia Field, life-long penal reformer, set up a foundation to finance the scheme and fairly naturally turned to The Salvation Army for help. They can be relied upon to give any experiment a try.'

CHAPTER THIRTY-ONE

Sigmund Freud Helps the Salvationists

COUNSELLING HAS BEEN given by Salvationists for about a century. Christians have felt able to offer counsel, to those in great need, for a thousand years or more. But now the need for a more specialised service has become evident. The ailments of our time, including depression, alcoholism, homosexuality and various manifestations of neurosis, are dealt with in confidence by Salvationists who have training for their task.

An officer is pioneering a counselling service within The Salvation Army. He works through the Army's Men's Social Services, but the development is not simply a Men's Social venture. It is hoped that the counselling service will meet needs not only in social centres but also at Army corps in London and the provinces.

The project aims to provide guidance, and assists with the training of Salvationists as counsellors. Personality and emotional problems, with marriage difficulties, increase. It is hoped that Salvation Army officers can be helped to a better understanding of counselling needs. A course in pastoral counselling is attended by a group of officers of the Army.

The pioneer officer answers some questions.

Would not Salvationists argue that if one goes to the Penitent-form and

gets saved, one does not need to have a lot of talk about it? It's done, isn't it? Or is it?
The idea that religious experience solves all a person's emotional problems is mistaken. Religion can be linked with mental illness. In fact it sometimes causes mental illness. It all depends what kind of a religious experience one has. Christian experience can be an aid to mental and emotional stability. But there are vast areas of need in the lives of many who profess Christianity.

What are the causes of these stresses and inadequacies you are seeking to deal with?
This is a disturbed age. We are living in a pluralistic society. Previous generations did not know the mixture of cultures and religions that is a part of life in Britain today. We are in the wake of two world wars, in a time of chaos and change that creates disturbance in people's minds. Most people love the *status quo*. They don't like change, which makes for uncertainty.

Am I to take it that when people come to The Salvation Army some of them still require counselling, even though they may have knelt at the Penitent-form and claimed this once-and-for-all salvation that William Booth was so insistent upon?
There is no doubt in my mind. There is so much that needs clarifying. So many people have been deeply and emotionally hurt. They need healing that may take time. Counselling offers a relationship. It is therapeutic. It is not judgmental. It is an accepting relationship.

Non-judgmental acceptance! A woman or a man with these problems of more or less severity will come to a counsellor and have the same sort of relationship that one might have with a psychiatrist?
Yes, this is so. One of the facts of today is that people with emotional and personality needs may fight shy of the minister or the Salvation Army officer. They go to a doctor or a psychiatrist, a psychotherapist or a social worker. They do this because they know that they are not going to be judged by the doctor, the psychiatrist, or the social worker. They are shy of the Christian because they expect moral judgments or even censure from Christians.

But can a Christian deal impartially with sexual delinquency, or dishonesty, and other moral offences, which the Bible and evangelical Christianity condemn? How can you suspend your Christian judgment?
One does not suspend one's Christian judgment. What one offers is acceptance. This does not involve approval, but the professional approach to the client. One attempts to help a man to see the origins of aspects of his own life which are disturbing factors. The very fact that he comes indicates that he is aware of a need. He doesn't need to be told that there is something wrong with him. He is probably condemning himself and does not need the counsellor to add to his self-condemnation. He already feels isolated. Condemnation simply increases his sense of isolation. The important thing is that there should be a bridge built between counsellor and client. The attitude of acceptance need not include approval. What the counsellor sees in the quest of the client is that this quest, even though he may not always recognise it, is in fact a religious undertaking. He is seeking for a philosophy of life. He is looking for truth.

How would you differentiate between a 'philosophy of life', as you put it, and what the early-day Salvationists called a satisfying religious experience? Are they not one and the same thing clothed in different phrases, a matter of semantics?
We all have higher and lower phases of experience. What is important is that we should understand and rightly evaluate the higher and lower planes of our experience. This can go on in a counselling relationship.

How long does this counselling process take?
Some folk are helped in a single interview, or a weekly interview over a few weeks. For many it may be a very long-term process.

Are there technical rules for the relationship? A framework of procedure? You are getting near to the relationship between a patient and a pyscho-therapist?
At the beginning of a counselling relationship you need to know about the person's home background, the place in the family, the kind of social setting, the kind of home life. It helps to know what happens at crucial times of adjustment, at school-leaving age, sexual

adjustment, marital status. There is a general building up of, to use the awful words, the case history of the person. This, in a long counselling relationship, is of the utmost importance. That is all the preliminary. What the counsellor is seeking to do is to enable the client to understand his own experience and to decide the ways and means whereby he can make necessary adjustments to bring to himself a more rewarding experience of life.

How do you deal with the more difficult problems?
The course we are running is comprehensive. One series of lectures is being given by the Army's Colonel William McAllister, L.R.C.S., L.R.C.P. (Edin.). He deals with medical aspects, homosexuality, alcoholism, anxiety and depression. There are studies on all aspects of counselling: the structuring of the relationship; the safeguards that are needed; the use of the interview hour. We have to deal with the suicidal and despairing; with preparation for marriage; and with marriage counselling. We have speakers from Alcoholics Anonymous, from the Samaritans, from other counselling services, and from St. Christopher's Hospice for terminal patients.

Isn't it true that some of the officers attending this course have been attempting counselling on their own?
Oh yes, this is so.

Can we assume that a Salvationist marriage is almost wholly stable – that divorce is non-existent in The Salvation Army?
The incidence of divorce in The Salvation Army is very small.

Is this Hobson's choice? We don't accept divorce easily?
In some instances, yes. But there are Salvationist marriages where there are acute stresses. But I think the fact that many of the parties concerned have made a Christian announcement, by the wearing of their uniform, by their Salvation Army witness, does tend to keep them together. Without this kind of sanction, as you might call it, they might have drifted apart.

A counselling service might help a couple whose marriage might otherwise break on the rocks. It might bring them to a point of self-understanding and mutual understanding. There are numerous

Christian couples – I would not want to isolate Salvation Army couples – who need counselling at some stage in their married life. Though we can still maintain that the Christian concept of marriage is the way to fulfilment of the human personality.

You are for marriage, and not for divorce?
Yes. Although, under certain circumstances, I see there is no alternative to divorce.

What about The Salvation Army officially? Does it allow officers to be divorced?
No. The Salvation Army cannot happily accept the idea of divorce for its officers. There have been a few cases where a married couple have separated and then the 'innocent party' must sacrifice rank during the process of divorce, though it may be restored after the proceedings are concluded. We have a greater measure of understanding towards people with these tragic problems than we once had.

Remember that marriage is facing stresses and strains that it did not face in the Victorian era. Yet one can still believe in the future of marriage. Three-quarters of the people who seek divorce seek it in order to re-marry. They recognise the failure of one marriage but not the failure of marriage as such. Then, in recent years new divorce legislation and easier divorce mean that many couples who were kept together artificially – who were not really living together though still married – now avail themselves of the relaxed legal attitude.

Does The Salvation Army do more to help people with sexual problems, not only those of divorce but in the age of the pill, with free contraception on the National Health Service, does it help young people in pointing out the dangers of promiscuity and the perils of abortion?
Every Christian denomination should do much more than it is doing to prepare its own young people for marriage, and to understand their own sexuality. We are seeing a great degree of pre-marital sex in the world today. But it is wrong to identify pre-marital intercourse with promiscuity. Many young people are concerned with the quality of their relationship with their sex-partner. They have sex with the person they eventually marry. So while there is increase in pre-marital sex it is still only a minority who indulge in promiscuity.

Do you not, as a Salvation Army officer, have to be severe and censorious about pre-marital sex?
Not severe or censorious. We need to educate Christian young people to see that the sexual relationship should come as the climax of a growing dignified relationship. Young people should learn to wait for sexual experience so that it takes place within the marriage relationship. This is because sex is good and not, as previously suggested by many, that it is bad.

Does The Salvation Army allow you to counsel the use of contraception?
The Army does not prescribe anything at all within the counselling relationship. It is our Christian understanding that we take into the counselling relationship. We do not need to uphold any rigid set of morals.

With tremendous population pressures, many people feel their responsibility for the future and the need for family limitation for social reasons, for health and family reasons. Surely The Salvation Army has something to say to people who seek counsel on this urgent intimate matter?
The Army has never been opposed to contraception as such. It has left it to the private conscience of the individual. So we need not argue any particular 'party line' with regard to this matter.

You deal with each problem on the merit of each particular case?
This is true in any area of morals. One has to start with the 'client', just where he is. You hope that, because of his increasing understanding of the issues involved, he will make the right decision. But it is not for the counsellor to make the decision for the client. It is not for the counsellor to become the conscience of the client. The counsellor must help the client towards a greater degree of personal 'autonomy', towards a better understanding of what his life is all about.

Many people have money problems—mortgages, jobs, cost of education and so on. In The Salvation Army these tend to be taken for granted.

Do you put this area high in your counselling—material things? The acquisitive society; the commodity society?
These are part of the complex situation, but I doubt whether the economic factor is often the basic factor. What worries most people is much more basic, anxiety about life itself. For many, life has lost significance, meaning and purpose.

Does your counselling service assume a widespread sense of guilt, a guilt neurosis?
We cannot help being what we are. We are frail and faulty human beings and guilt is part of human experience. What the counsellor must not do is exploit the client's sense of guilt. The function of the counsellor is to recognise the quest for a meaningful life.

But the old-time Salvationists made more use of the sense of guilt: indeed, his purpose was to help people to repent, to pray, to kneel at the Penitent-form, to seek salvation?
But that salvation meant living life at its fullest; it meant meaningful relationships with other people and with God. Counselling serves the same evangelical purpose. But what the counsellor must not do is manipulate the client with this over-all purpose in mind. This is not the function of the counsellor.

Is alcoholism one of the problems encountered?
We are linked with an assessment unit at Booth House where there are always ten alcoholics in residence for assessment purposes. Counselling is linked with the alcoholics assessment unit.

Is there any evidence of anything permanent being done to rehabilitate these men?
The assessment unit has been functioning for five years, in conjunction with the Harbour Light Home for Alcoholics at Highworth. One can never say that an alcoholic is 'cured'. He is never cured, but he often remains sober. I have heard that a third of those who have been through the unit and through Highworth are well on the way to sobriety.

Are some of the problems you encounter caused by religion?
Some varieties of religious experience can do real harm. There are some people who for psychological reasons feel happy only within an authoritarian structure. Now more and more people want to feel free, autonomous. This is one of the problems confronting us as an authoritarian movement.

You are not counselling the 'down and out' in the William Booth sense? Does that submerged tenth still exist? I suspect that people come to your counselling centres in their motor cars?
Yes, they come in their cars. But we are thinking in terms of percentages. The 'tenth' applies to those with some understanding of the significance of life. The submerged are the 90 per cent.

William Booth was referring to poverty. On his scale, it is a condition which has largely been removed?
Yes, although there are still areas with that kind of poverty. The alcoholics we are seeking to help at Booth House are somewhere up the social scale. We are less welcomed by the vagrant on the bomb site. I understand that there are about 30,000 of these and most of them are mentally affected in some way.

Can you see a future for The Salvation Army in terms of William Booth's original 'Darkest England' dream? He said, 'Go for souls and go for the worst'. Is there any future for that?
The development of counselling is certainly within the framework of going for souls, and of going for the worst. It all depends on what you mean by 'the worst'.

What do you think William Booth would think if he came back and knew what you were doing? What is 'the worst' today?
We have to see 'the worst' in terms of human needs, human suffering, human despair, rather than in terms of moral depravity. All the counselling centres opened in recent years are overwhelmed with needy people turning to them. This is quite in line, it seems to me, with the original purposes of The Salvation Army, to enable people to find themselves, to find God, to find fulfilment in life.

You do counsel homosexuals? What is the Army's view on this problem?
Within the Army there is still a great deal of horror at the thought of homosexuality. We were against the Wolfenden recommendations, which led to the present-day lifting of legal sanctions against consenting adult homosexuals. But I believe we are moving towards a greater understanding of this situation. We can recognise the homosexual so long as he is not a practising homosexual.

Of course, children and young people must be guarded, as they are still by law. But the fact is that the homosexual needs activity that helps to sublimate his sexual urges.

One of the basic problems of the homosexual is that his homosexuality sets him apart. He becomes more and more introverted and more and more alone. Yet four out of five homosexuals are not recognised as such. I am at present counselling three homosexuals. You would not know that one of those three was homosexual from his appearance.

What about practising homosexuals?
I am counselling practising homosexuals.

How are you inhibited—are you inhibited—by what is in the Bible when you speak to practising homosexuals?
I am not inhibited by the teaching of the Bible. The teaching of the Bible in its deepest sense is always ahead of our human 'illumination'. We are in fact only just moving away from a total condemnatory attitude because we are understanding to a greater extent the origins of a good deal of homosexuality. When we see how homosexuality has arisen in specific instances, we learn that this is a part of man's fallenness—man's fallenness that takes this form in certain lives. All men are fallen. We share a common, fallen human nature. The homosexual is unfortunate in having to suffer, it seems to me, often because of unhealthy relationships in the early years for which he is not responsible.

It is not a matter of genetics?
No. The percentage of folk who are homosexuals for genetical reasons, by imbalance in hormones and that kind of thing, is very

small. The attempt to establish that it was genes or hormones never succeeded. Most authorities now think that 99 per cent of homosexuals had faulty relationships in infancy.

You go on to say it is the mother, mainly?
Yes, but not that it is the mother's fault. The switch is not made from the mother to the father in the fourth, or fifth years, for some reason, because the father is absent, or because the father is feeble, or because the mother is dominating.

CHAPTER THIRTY-TWO

Policeman and Ex-con in the Army Together

THE FIRST SALVATION ARMY work for prisoners began in 1883 in Melbourne, seven years before William Booth's social service blueprint, *In Darkest England and the Way Out* was published. This was giving history a push for, as we have noted, William Booth had long insisted that it was not part of The Salvation Army's mission to become immersed in sociological effort. But the Australian experiment was so successful that the following year the Army began operations at Wandsworth gaol in London.

At first the work was carried on solely from outside. The *War Cry* reported that a 'saved thief' had no difficulty in catching 'one and another as they came out'. There was nothing in the way of Prisoners' Aid in those hard times and the Army arranged for released prisoners to have food and shelter: 'We have no idea of providing for any man to live in idleness . . . as we have arranged for temporary work at chopping wood whilst other employment is sought for.' But getting The Salvation Army into British prisons was almost as difficult as for prisoners to break out, and for a time, in 1888, the work in Britain was discontinued. Abroad, the authorities were more ready to allow access to prisons and even to help with grants and premises. In South Africa in 1889 a Salvation Army corps was started inside the gaol. Prison work inside the locked gates began as early as 1885.

Quite naturally, as a man of great compassion, Booth believed that prisons should be reforming institutions, and in his book, *Darkest*

England, he said that in Britain they were often the reverse of that—they made bad worse. He had many proposals for work outside the gaols and indeed, by 1890, much was being done by the Army as prison gate work. But he insisted, 'We shall seek access to prisons . . .' 'The Bridge', a Salvation Army half-way-house for ex-prisoners was operating at Argyle Square, London. In 1894 Herbert Gladstone, the Under Secretary at the Home Office, in a speech at the Mansion House spoke of the Army and began the process of opening the doors of the prisons to Salvationists on the same terms as to Anglicans, Roman Catholics and other churchmen.

When General Booth himself gained access to Portland gaol in 1901, admission for other of his officers could not long be denied. William Booth later visited Dartmoor prison, Inverness, and Aylesbury women's prison. But, more to the point, he gained access to the seat of power itself—the office of young Winston Churchill, then Home Secretary. Not long after, Churchill announced that in furtherance of his policy of more humane treatment for convicted prisoners the Home Secretary had granted permission to The Salvation Army to hold mission services at the various convict prisons, in addition to the quarterly musical services which had already had excellent results. It is said that Churchill had been moved towards liberal reform of the prison service by Galsworthy's play, *Justice*. It is also likely that Booth's prayers and compassion had affected him. 'Am I converted?' he had asked the General as they had parted.

From that time prison work by the Army has continued and expanded. The Army has helped in the rehabilitation of many notorious ex-prisoners, not excluding murderers. Visitation to the 'death cells' in those countries where the death sentence still obtains is still carried out. The Army's work on 'Devil's Island', the penal settlement on French Guiana, was a major factor in the decision of the French authorities, first to ameliorate the conditions there and then to close it down as a prison settlement. Commissioner Charles Péan of The Salvation Army received the Legion of Honour, numerous other awards, and world fame for his heroic and devoted labours in bringing about the end of Devil's Island.

For obvious reasons the identity of ex-prisoners is strictly protected, but sometimes they give permission for details of their lives to be revealed. One such man has been a Salvationist for fourteen years. He works as maintenance engineer in a hotel. He tells his own story:

I was converted in prison. A third of my life was absolutely thrown away. At the time I was converted I was serving a seven-year sentence. An Army officer regularly visited the prison, for two or three chaps were registered as Salvationists. I had been playing the organ for the Church of England services and on one occasion the Army ran out of pianists. The Salvationists asked if I would have any objection to playing for the Salvation Army service. The officer came from a nearby corps. As time went by we talked and he began to influence me. I began to listen to him and believe in him. As a result of his influence I and six other men were 'saved', as Salvationists say.

(He was asked why he had been in and out of prison and in again.)

Basically because I had no roots of any kind. I lost my mother when I was nine. My father and I were not close. As any habitual criminal will tell you, if you start it is easy to go on. Prison has become less and less punitive. It can be a 'home from home' for a person who reads, or for a person who can enjoy some hobby, for that man who can separate himself from the rest and shut himself up in his cell. That kind of chap can easily live out a prison sentence with hardly any worry, provided he has no wife or children or relatives that he loves—'I care for nobody, no not I, and nobody cares for me!'

For me prison was not a deterrent, and it does not work the other way round either; there is no rehabilitation. Very few prison officers seem to care two hoots about the rehabilitation aspect. Perhaps they cannot. They are there to look after the people who have done wrong. Some do try to take interest in some prisoners who are not hardened and who might be helped. But the prison system is not suited to that attitude, really. Many men, once they've been, go again—there is not much interest in 'turning over a new leaf'.

My belief is that there's only one answer to the question, 'What makes a man stay out?' It's got to be a change of heart. Nothing else will do.

No, I was not a violent type. I never planned serious crimes. If there was money about for the taking, I took it. I began as a lad. I ran away from home three times. There was no proper home life.

The last time I ran away was at the age of sixteen. Then I met a chap who told me a tall story. He was a representative of the North West Canadian Mounted Police. He said he was going to Liverpool. We booked into private lodgings, digs, and on the second day I came downstairs expecting to find him at breakfast. But he'd vanished. He had given me a wrist-watch, his own, he said. When the landlady had a quick check she found that a number of her possessions were missing, the watch included. I was wearing it! Looking back that long way I think I was innocent, but the police didn't believe me. Certainly I had been a fool. That time I got probation. If at that time someone had said, 'This lad needs looking after', this might have worked out differently. I went on the road looking for work, but once you get a police record, and when you are without guidance as a youth, it is easy to fall into bad company and bad behaviour.

I first went to prison at the age of eighteen – six months. In those early stages there were about eighteen-month intervals between sentences.

When the war came and I went into the forces I managed to get through as an N.C.O. and warrant officer and with an exemplary character. This is significant, for I had work to do, discipline and oversight. I was in the Middle East most of the time, in the engineers.

But I came back to Britain with a fat gratuity and soon I was like the prodigal son in the far country: I was soon broke and alone, so that the same pre-war folly started all over again.

No, I did not have a steady woman friend. In essence I was a lonely man. Never was a good mixer. A long, sad time went by, and I never learned the art of making friends and being friendly.

Meanwhile I continued with my life of thieving. The amounts were never more than people left lying around, never enough to make it worth while really – it really is stupid. There were a couple of breaking and entering jobs.

The longest sentence was five years. These longer sentences were because I was incorrigible. There were spells of two or three years when I was out and went straight. But sooner or later the old difficulties would crop up. You very often have to lie to get a job, though references are not so important in that kind of more or less casual employment. I was a good signwriter and, in the years of working in the building trade, I picked up other skills. I could get jobs even if I lost them because of my record. Many people are out of work because they want to be.

After I became converted I worked for The Salvation Army and they watched me carefully and prayerfully, and befriended me. I married and my wife became a Salvationist.

For my present job I advertised in a trade magazine and I had fourteen replies. But, of course, I could supply references. My employer likes The Salvation Army. I became a Salvation Army bandsman, having learnt to play while I was in prison. The Army Captain taught me. He persuaded the Governor to requisition the Prison Commissioners to allow a sum of money to buy instruments as a rehabilitation project. They were given enough to buy ten instruments. I bet Winston Churchill would never have anticipated that. I have also been commissioned a songster and I am very happy as I sing. I have been asked to be the Band Sergeant of the young people's section.

I really believe that the old life is over—all things are new! The only solution for a man who has been in and out of prison, to keep him out, is for him to have a change of heart. We hear a lot about the rising prison population—well, for my money, one should get them all saved; they wouldn't need to be three to a cell then.

The Captain led six men to conversion, in addition to myself. Four of them are still Salvationists like myself. One went back to his own church, though he married one of the songsters of the Army and he is now an office manager.

I go to the Salvation Army meetings all day Sunday and I have many friends there. The people at my corps know about me. If I give my testimony it comes out. I never wrap it up. We have had a policeman in the band and we also had a probation officer. The Clerk of Court at my home is the Band Secretary and the Sergeant-Major is a solicitor, and one of the songsters is an instructor at a prison. When I get up to speak in the meeting it is a sort of family joke. Sometimes after I testify the policeman testifies, or one of the other members of the legal system. The policeman, the prison instructor, the solicitor and the others all understand. They don't look down on me. I am a comrade in the Army of God. They know that Jesus saves solicitors and ex-cons.

CHAPTER THIRTY-THREE

The Man at the Door

YOUNG JIMMY, AGED twenty, from up north, gets on well at the Army hostel at Westminster. He throws out the drunks and the fellows with bottles and he says 'No more' when the place is full up. Also he's lately had a bath and been saved and he's doing nicely, thank you.

How old are you, Jimmy? How long have you been here in the hostel?
I'm twenty. I have been here three weeks. I wanted to come down to London to see what life was like. I came down from Newcastle. Life in London has been all right, up till now. The fellow at the Employment Exchange sent me here.

Did you know The Salvation Army up north?
I stayed in the Newcastle Army place for about six months. I got on all right.

You have a home and parents somewhere?
Yes, but I left home when I was sixteen. I had a row. I have been back a few times but I have not really made it up. I don't get on with my mother and father.

You would probably find you could get on better with them now that you are older. But you have left home now; you wouldn't want to go back?
No. I am too independent now.

What work are you doing?
I'm on the gate, just now.

Is it difficult? Do you have to keep people out?
I throw people out regularly. But it is not too bad. I let them in until the hostel is full and then I have to turn them away.

That's not a very easy job.
No. And I have been in that position myself.

Do you have to turn many away?
We try to keep out those we think will cause trouble. People who are drunk, those with bottles—we chase them away. Bottles are not allowed in. They are dangerous.

Supposing a man is difficult, violent? Would someone help you?
We don't have many like that. I try to manage myself, but I can get help.

They know it is not your fault. What is it like being so young and at one of these places?
It doesn't bother me. In May I would like to get on with my own life. I don't let anybody bother me; I don't bother anybody else. I have a few friends on the staff here.

Do you sleep in one of the dormitories?
No, I sleep downstairs, where the night men sleep. There are about six beds. The first night I came here I was in a shocking state. I had no decent clothes; I had not had a bath for weeks. I had been refused a voucher for Blackfriars. But when I came here they took me in and gave me work. They have a woman working in the canteen and when I went for meals I was disgusted with myself being so dirty and ragged. I had been sleeping rough. Then I went to the meeting and I was saved. This made a great difference. I feel more respectable. I have something to hold on to. I have a Bible and I can read all night if I want to. I want to become a Salvationist.

Your mum and dad—do you drop them a line?
I have thought about it, but I will try to prove myself first.

Have you any brothers or sisters at home?
Yes, six brothers and four sisters. A brother and sister are married. Another brother is engaged. I wouldn't have thought of going with a girl before, but now I feel different about that.

PART FIVE

The Soldier

Salvation Army soldiers have always been our greatest strength. Our work would be impossible without them. From them our officers are called and trained. They are the bands that play and the brigades that sing. They teach our children, lead our youth, witness on the street corners and engage in a thousand part-time, unpaid, but highly valued tasks. The interviews that follow indicate the faith and opinions of some of them though, as mentioned earlier, not necessarily the official views of The Salvation Army.

CHAPTER THIRTY-FOUR

No Trouble with Teenagers

You have family associations with the early-day Army – could you tell me what these are?
My grandfather was a well-known Salvation Army officer, a revivalist; my father was an officer decorated for his service with H.M. Forces in the Second World War.

Tell us something about your own family beginnings, could you?
I met my wife when her parents were officers stationed at Rochdale. We are both children of the regiment.

And do you want your children to be Army, too?
Not necessarily. I want them to find Christ as I have. Where they go then, is up to them. I know if they know Christ, then whether it be in the Army or wherever, is not the most important thing.

What is your occupation between Sunday and Sunday?
Wholesale greengrocer, in a management capacity. I have thirty wagons altogether. My work is mainly organising the distribution of fruit and vegetables.

Does your religion interfere with your business?
It interferes and it helps! Before some decisions I have to make, I have to stop and think what the right thing is to do as a Christian. When I am dealing with a client, or a problem with one of the staff, I try and think what is right, the best way, the fairest way. I have to be

firm, sometimes, and a Christian commitment works for and against at such times.

What are your duties within the Army?
Torchbearer youth group leader and youth club leader. I am, therefore, involved with young people, not only those with Salvation Army backgrounds but many other types of young people.

The torchbearer movement is making a tremendous impact on non-Salvationist young people.

Any special tactics?
Well, before you can get to know people properly, you have to spend time winning their trust, making them feel you have no ulterior motive, proving that you care for them. Managing our football team during the course of a season you might get into conversation with a young fellow, and that could mean something.

Have any of the young people been brought into the Army, or become Christians, through the work?
Several have become Christians and two are in Salvation Army uniform. One youth plays in the band. Some of our young people are carrying out social service by their own wish on a Sunday afternoon. They are a mixed company in our club. They include immigrant Pakistanis who go with us to old folks' homes on Sunday afternoons. From there some go on to a children's hospital. There they spend time playing with the child patients.

What are your views on social drinking? Is it a problem?
Under no circumstances would I agree with social drinking for Salvationists. It would not interest me at all. Any Salvationist who is not going to observe the Army's teetotal principles would not be welcome by us.

What are your convictions about personal giving to God's work?
For me 10 per cent is right. This does not mean 10 per cent in the Sunday envelope. There are many ways by which we can help people who are less fortunate than ourselves. Of course, regular personal gifts finance the local corps. This is sound and essential.

Do you think our system of regulations is good? Should there be changes in Salvation Army administration?
Nothing very strong. Perhaps some of the regulations are a bit old-fashioned. I don't particularly feel smoking is wrong, but if you are going to be a leader you must set an example.

At your youth club, you have snooker balls in use since the club was opened. Many other clubs in the area have periodically to replace much of their equipment and restore their property. Can you give any reason for your freedom from this sort of trouble?
Yes, the leaders in general have the respect of the young people who come in. We care for them. We pray for them, and are prepared to do anything to help them. We get them to work with us. We re-decorate the club, and they do it themselves and it becomes their club. All these things help them to feel it is their club; it is something going on for them. If a new member comes in for the second week, get him over the first week, and then he begins to work with us. You have to keep an eye on them until they realise the set-up. After that there is no problem at all.

CHAPTER THIRTY-FIVE

Man and Wife at the Penitent-form

I COME FROM the Midlands but, as you hear by my tongue, I was born in Scotland. I never met The Salvation Army until I came here. When I left home I must have been about eighteen. I wanted a change, I wanted to break away. I was married, but my wife didn't know where I was going. 'I will write every day', I said. This is where I landed thirty-three years ago. The first morning, a beautiful morning, the sun was shining, and I walked along London Road, just followed the crowd. The people were walking to Whitley aerodrome. I followed and I thought, 'I will try for a job.' I waited till the office opened and I got my job. Motor mechanic. I sent for my wife and set up home. Four children. A boy and a girl, both married. I am a grandfather now.

What made you go to The Salvation Army?
I was always fond of bands. At work I got friendly with this chap who was a trombone player. He said, 'We'll go and listen to the Army band.' So we went. They used to play in the market square, before it was bombed. We went six or seven Sunday nights and eventually we went inside.

I drank whisky and used to smoke maybe forty cigarettes a day. I must have been about twenty-five. We continued to go. Eventually my wife came too. There were many nights when I should have gone to the front, to the Penitent-form, but I didn't. My wife was like me, she felt that her life was incomplete. Then one night the preacher was Colonel George B. Smith. I never forgot his words. He said, 'I tremble when I think of the responsibility that Christ has placed on my shoulders.' Then he spoke the message. My wife rose and I rose and we went together to the Penitent-form. That is how we became Salvationists.

One night the wife of one of the Army people had an accident with a lorry; the driver was drunk. I took the woman to the hospital. That started me visiting the hospitals. I used to go and say, 'How do you do?' I would hear remarks like, 'Don't you worry, dear, the chap from the Army will be in. Somebody will come to see you.' This opened up an avenue of service for me. I have done it ever since. I go every Sunday from 2 o'clock till 5.30 and then if I am required during the week I go. Sometimes I go every night, sometimes twice a week, sometimes once a week. They say, 'You will come and see me when I get out?' That takes up time.

Have you ever been disappointed with the Army?
Sometimes. We have an old Commandant here, a Scot. One of his sayings is, 'They used to have the clocks outside to let the people know when it was time to come in. Now they have the clocks inside to let them know when it is time to get out.' Another time he said, 'Now, laddie, you'll be faced with the devil many a time, and maybe he'll sit beside you. But always remember this: it is Christ you come to worship. Always keep that in mind and never mind the other things.'

Sometimes the people do not get saved. Does this worry you?
Yes, it is a bit dismal. But then I open the *War Cry* and look and see six seekers here, and three seekers there, and two seekers at this place. That puts new life into me. I hold the position now of Welcome Sergeant and do lots of jobs in between hospital work.

As a motor mechanic you are a trade unionist. Any conflict between your Christian faith and trade unionism?
Not the basics of trade unionism, but sometimes the expression of it.

Would you always obey the union?
Not if I felt it was to do something morally wrong. Mark you, I have

never been placed in this position. Where I work, union relations are excellent. In my hospital visitation I have a relationship with the union whereby they notify me if there are any union people or workers in the hospital. The unions are no threat to my Christianity.

This permissive society, does it worry you?
The Army ought to say something about the evil side of it. When we are discussing things at work, things that come on T.V., they ask me what I think. There's that picture that opened in London. But they are grown adults and they say they have a right to see it. It's when you see a young girl of sixteen or seventeen who is going to have a baby it is really sad.

The Army is at the bottom of the pit picking up casualties. Do you think we ought to be at the top of the pit stopping the people from falling down? Shouldn't the Army be more forthright? If the British Commissioner asked Army soldiers to write to the newspaper, theatre, T.V., or film people protesting about degrading shows or features, would you be prepared to write?
I could write in my own words but I am not a very clever man in putting pen to paper. But it would be good to demonstrate against these things. To me the most corrupting thing is that young people pick these things up.

Do you think it is right for folk to have sexual relations outside marriage?
What respect can a bloke have for a girl if he does that? What faith can he have in the girl or in himself?

Contraception for the unmarried?
We have turned it down once in my town. But it is a good thing if it avoids illegitimate children coming into the world.

As a Scotsman you must have views on money. Do you regard it as your own? Do you give to God's work?
I'm in a good job and I am fairly well paid. Of the money I have I like to pay my dues to the Lord. We often say, the wife and I, 'Well, this week we can afford another fifty pence or so . . .'

CHAPTER THIRTY-SIX

Children of the Regiment

You, as the wife, were you a 'born' Salvationist? Here, in Wales?
Yes.

Did you go reluctantly to Sunday-school, and all that?
With two sisters and a brother I enjoyed going. I had a strict upbringing, strict parents, but despite that I was happy. We were not allowed to read comics, or see *Cinderella* or films or anything like that. Yet we were quite happy. It was not harmful in any way. We have more understanding now as parents. We can compare our childhood with how we bring up our own little boy. We are not as strict as our parents but still quite careful. We still do not like films excepting something special like *The Sound of Music*. We would not go once a week or even once a month.

You, sir, as the young husband and also the child of Salvationists—was your upbringing as strict as that of your wife?
Yes, but I had a happy childhood.

What sort of education?
Secondary modern and then down the coal mine as a surface worker until I was turned seventeen.

Was it hard to be a Salvationist in the pit?
No. The first morning I was sent underground I went to a miner who knew me. He said, 'You are a Salvationist.' After that everybody knew about my faith, and I took my stand.

You met your wife at the corps here?
Yes. Our courtship had to fit in with Salvation Army activities. It was a very happy time. We were in love and went off to youth chorus practices, youth band practices, open-air stands and indoor gatherings. We have one little boy, aged eight.

Did you ever quarrel?
Well, I wouldn't say quarrel. Differences of opinion. We argue sometimes, but we do not quarrel.

You have differences of opinion—about the Army?
Sometimes. I feel that my husband is too busy; we may have only one free evening together. You can feel you are not noticed, and feel a little lonely.

What about leisure?
We rarely get any. I play brass band records. When it's fine I like walking in the country.

Wife: I go to a flower-arranging class occasionally, but mostly it is Army activities. Sometimes we have friends to supper or we go out to friends. Mostly they are Army connections.

Husband: I like a rugby match sometimes down at Cardiff. Being a Welshman I like to see Wales beat England.

Smoking or drinking a problem?
No, never. Never started—what you've never had you never miss!

What about the facts of life?
Wife: Yes, I learned some of 'the facts of life' at school in my final year. When I went nursing I learned much more. My mother would not speak of such things. My sister and I would talk about what we had heard in school but we would not dare to mention it to our mother.

Husband: My Salvationist parents did not tell me much, either. I just got to know one way and another, schoolboy talk and so on. It is not the right way, willy-nilly. I think parents should tell the children.

As typical young Salvationists, do you believe that family planning is a good thing?
Wife: Yes, most definitely. If people with this problem went along to their health visitor or doctor, it would avoid many serious problems. We are both in agreement about this.

Do you think Salvation Army marriages are strong? Do you know Salvationists who are divorced?
Wife: Yes; two couples. It is not common among Salvationists. Most seem to be happily married.

Have you any religious objections to divorce?
Wife: It is better to be divorced than to live unhappily together. But sad when this happens and it could have been avoided.

Husband: By and large a real Christian faith is a great bulwark against divorce. If the couple are Christians before they marry they can talk over their problems, pray about them and seek help. That helps a marriage to survive.

Does your boy take to the Army? No compulsion?
Every Sunday morning he's up like a lark—10 o'clock juniors. All day, in fact, even up to the night meeting. He enjoys everything.

What about law and order—mugging, bank robberies, the use of guns by criminals? Would you favour the re-introduction of capital punishment?
Husband: People are getting away with too much far too easily these days. Young people have much more money; they pay a fine, and then go and do the same thing again. I think they should be punished more severely.

Wife: I think they are too lenient, also. Often they come out of prison and do exactly the same thing. Perhaps they need special kind of treatment.

Rehabilitation attempts to create a conscience; the Army has a part to play in this kind of thing. We have been reading about the goodwill work by the Army down at Cardiff. That is for 'down and outs'. If we also had a place for the after-care of prisoners it would meet a need. I believe that we have such places abroad and in other parts of Britain.

Do you think we need changes in the Army to meet modern needs?
Wife: We should be very careful of some of the recent gimmicks. I wouldn't like to see dancing brought into the Army. Have that, and gradually anything might come. Soon we'd find that Salvationists were not different from anyone else. For myself, I say, keep the Army as it is. Salvationists should be separate from the world. People expect something different from you as Salvationists. They think highly of us and we have to live up to it.

CHAPTER THIRTY-SEVEN

Colour Blindness

MY FATHER WAS a Salvationist and so was my grandfather. My wife joined the Army when she was seven years of age. We met each other at the Army, married at the Army. Our whole life has been built up around the Army. The Army has taught us the way to live, has governed our life from early childhood. We have slept, eaten and drunk Army! The only thing one may miss by such early conversion is that one does not feel the drastic change from bad to good – one's whole life is sheltered.

What about your children?
As parents it is our duty to lead them in a religious way of life. For us the best way of worship is the Army. So our boys are encouraged to attend the Army at all times; they are not forced, but encouraged. The older boy now seriously wants to come. He talks to us as Salvationists talk to one another about what he can do for the Army and for God. He is active in the scouts. The younger one, with a handicap of deafness, has a sense of wanting to belong.

Do you think Salvationism helps people to stay married?
It seems to be the trend for marriages to break down and I know that Salvationists are affected by this trend, though religion does give added strength.

Can I ask your wife – this demand for equal rights for women? Do you want equal rights?
I am quite happy as I am. I don't think, frankly, that we should be the same. I do not feel that I am discriminated against.

You, sir, what is your weekday job?
Site manager for a building firm.

Building sites are 'tough' places. Do you make a Christian witness?
I do not find it hard. From the first I let everyone know that I belong to The Salvation Army. Now I cannot be there long before everyone knows. I do not tell them; someone else will. They say, 'Oh, he goes to The Salvation Army.' It is no hindrance to me.

Sometimes swearing is purely working jargon, and it has no effect on me. (A term like 'bastard', which is used as a measure in the printing trade.) Of the more offensive terms, like using the Lord's name as an expletive, I will say, 'When I use that language to you, you use it back. Until then, shut up!' This pulls them up with a jerk.

What is your attitude to drink, social drinking in particular?
Some people will have a pint, or half a pint, purely for social reasons. On the building-sites we find that we have some real drinkers. When these fellows come on the site on a Friday afternoon, after a visit to the pub, they must sit in the mess hut or we tell them to clear off. We won't have them on the site because they are a danger to themselves and other people. Like any other Salvationist, I promised I would abstain from intoxicating liquor and I do abstain.

Would you approve of throwing someone out for this?
They should be warned about it. We should say, 'Look, you have agreed voluntarily to uphold the regulation.' If they persisted after that, then I think the rule should be applied.

Christmas time, everyone in the building-trade goes round handing out bottles of whisky. The sub-contractors come in and get the foreman or site managers in for a drink. I am left out of the party. The other day I went to the firm's dinner with about 250 other men. The head of the firm welcomed us at a hotel in Mayfair.

The bar was open and most went to get drinks. I had to sit on my own – I felt out of it. So the big man sent his son over to ask me to have a drink. I said, 'I am a Salvationist; I don't drink.' He said, 'Well, just have an orange with me and let me introduce you to the other people in the firm.' Now, I am a new boy in the firm, but I was taken to the top people! 'He doesn't drink; he's a Salvationist.' And you found you were a marked man, but acceptable.

Trade unionism. What is your attitude? Are you a member?
No. They have lost their usefulness. They are little dictators. They don't get us better conditions, now. These we get by law, and by the work people have done in the past.

Would that apply to a textile worker, for example, who takes home about £17 a week?
If the textile workers threatened to leave their jobs, then the employers would soon put up their wages.

But suppose the firm then hired immigrant labour on the cheap?
Immigrants soon find out the conditions in England. They can come to this country. They are welcome here as long as they accept our conditions and our standard of living. The numbers of new immigrants should be limited. This is an island and we can only support a certain size of population. But when I talk about immigration I am not talking about one race: I am talking about everybody.

You would not mind living next door to a Pakistani?
No. We have been to their homes; we have some of their children as scouts.

Should Salvationists be involved in politics?
As representing The Salvation Army, no. But privately, what difference does it make, provided they uphold Christian standards? No double-dealing or back-handedness. But not to represent The Salvation Army, which is non-political. But a Salvationist with a sense of civic responsibility is the ideal man for the local council. It does not matter which party he belongs to. His Christian principles will dictate to a certain extent what line he will take.

Could a Christian be a communist?
Christian views are more liberal in my view, more like the radical wing of the Liberal party. One needs tolerance of other people. You must appreciate the other man.

Would you favour a return to capital punishment?
Personally I would not like to be the man to condemn another man. If we have done wrong I think we have to accept punishment. But such severe punishment! I wouldn't like to be on record as advocating hanging. But criminals should not be pampered. I have often thought that these people should be brought back to a sense of living. The punishment I would dream up for them would be a compulsory term serving in a hospital or a mental institution – some form of social usefulness. We could make offenders repay in kind. A drug addict would be sent to serve at a social service centre. It is far better than locking a man away indefinitely.

Do you think law and order has deteriorated?
Young people are not watched or disciplined enough. They are allowed to do what they like. Parents should take more interest in them. There would then be fewer young people getting into trouble with the police. There should be more discipline.

What do you think about morals and our alleged permissiveness?
It has always been the same! We hear about it now because of television or radio and the newspapers. Back in the old days, the 1800s and thereabouts, with no T.V. or radio and very few newspapers – and when most people could not read – all this bad news was unheard and unread. The village people knew what went on in the village and that was as far as it went. Today you hear of it from all over the world, so it seems to be much more. But we don't know. We are simply told it is more; they bring our attention to it.

Do you approve of sex education in schools?
Yes.

At what age?
About eleven or twelve. My own children saw a series on school

T.V., 'The birth of a child'. It was explicit, but I think it was very good. They asked questions. It is not a good idea just to show films and not talk about them.

What is the size of your ideal family?
Two.

What about hire purchase? Do you think that Salvationists should get into debt?
I don't think it is wrong to use hire purchase, providing you take care. There are some people who take on so much that they are crippled by the weight of repayments.

Gambling?
I have been grounded in the Army and have the Army view that gambling is wrong. Our 'win' is someone's loss and anyway we have not earned it.

Premium Bonds?
I won't have any but my wife differs from me on this. She sees no wrong in them but she does not buy any!

How much should you pay to support the corps?
I have never met anyone who gave a tenth, but I believe in stewardship. When I receive my wages I go upstairs where we have a box. Into this I put a tenth of the money. That is the Lord's. I do not give that full amount each week in the personal envelope because the Lord's work goes on in many fields. But the biggest percentage goes to support the local work.

CHAPTER THIRTY-EIGHT

The Progress Chaser

I WAS REARED in a Salvationist's home. My father was the Corps Sergeant-Major. He had a great influence on my life. I met my wife when I was in the Forces. She was in the Pentecostal Church. We have one daughter who does not attend the Army. The biggest disappointment is that she does not go anywhere at all.

What about the Army in general?
It is not progressing as it should here. And other corps are having hard times. The bigger centres seem to be holding their own.

Is the average Salvationist as good and sincere as he was, say, thirty years ago?
Older Salvationists that I remember seem to have something of religious experience that we do not see so much today.

As far as this corps is concerned, any converts we get are new people. The young people's corps which normally feeds new soldiers into the corps is at a low ebb. We are situated in the centre of the town. Areas round about have been redeveloped. The people have moved to outer areas. We are still in the middle of the town – minus the people. Children have to travel quite a distance to Sunday-school. Some go to churches near by in their own district.

Apart from that, why do you think so many young people do not attend places of worship?

They are faced with far greater pressures than we were. They are better off financially and there is much advertising skill at work to separate them from their money. This creates a variety of interests and indulgences, many of them opposed to religion. The mass media put across a concentrated diet of crime, sex and glamour. I do not see how we can do anything about this, short of censorship.

Do you think young people's moral standards are lowered as a consequence? Do you think this damages the Salvationist way of life?
I have never found that this is so.

Do you think the use of contraceptives, family planning, is permissible for God's people?
Yes. It is better for married couples to have the number of children that they can afford to raise properly. Too many children mean that someone suffers, both physically and in other ways.

What do you do for a living?
I am a progress chaser.

Do they know you are a Salvationist?
Yes. After a short time people discover when a man is a Christian. They soon realise that there is something different. People come to ask questions. I try to help to the best of my ability. I have had people say they admire the way a Christian acts, but I have never heard anyone say that it is foolish to have a Christian faith.

As a Christian workman do you think you earn enough money for the work you do?
None of us thinks that we are paid too much! It is probably fair pay for a fair job, £40 a week.

What would the average person bring home each week?
The clerical average is, I suppose, £35–£40 a week. Under present circumstances that would be about right.

What do you think of the strike weapon in industry?
The strike should be used only as a last resort. Some people are too

ready to strike. We don't have excess militancy in our union, and relationships with the firm have been good.

Do you think that the Army rule banning all alcoholic drink should be changed?
I hope it will be left as it is. In days gone by, drink seemed to be a bigger evil, yet even today it causes domestic trouble and worse. We are a temperance organisation; let's keep it that way.

What about smoking?
Our prohibition of smoking has been shown to be wise from a medical point of view. Events in recent years have shown that William Booth, who made this rule in the early days of the Army, has been vindicated by time. If I had my way I would bar smoking completely. Nowadays the smoker can be a soldier. This should not be.

What about Sabbath keeping?
The country seems to be drifting towards the continental style Sunday. I regret this. People have more time than ever; they should give some of their time to the worship of God.

How do you spend your time after working hours?
I either read or watch television.

What do you think of programme standards?
There has been a deterioration in the programmes from our viewpoint. Of course, one can either turn it off or watch. We certainly have to choose our programmes more carefully than in days gone by.

What about the Salvationist and politics?
I have never been much concerned. Christians should take up local work. That gives them the chance to put a Christian's view and a Christian's action into their town.

What local issues do you feel strongly about?
Religious education in schools. This should not be entrusted to people who say, when they start to teach, that they do not believe in

it. Religious knowledge should be taught, but by people who believe what they are teaching. We still say that we are a Christian country. The Royal Family acknowledges itself to be Christian. We should try to hold to these things. Even the Houses of Parliament are opened with prayers. We are still recognised as a Christian country. As a Christian country we should try to teach our children the basics of Christianity, and the teachers should be Christians—there are plenty of them.

How much money would you consider proper to give to the Army each week? As between your wife and yourself, bearing in mind that your gift to the Army would not be the only money you give?
About a pound a week.

Do you think Salvationists give enough?
Speaking generally, probably not.

Are we too Victorian? Too strict?
Well, people have said to me, 'Relax your rule on drinking; relax your rule on smoking; then you will have a better organisation, and bigger.' But I doubt it.

Why are you a Salvationist?
Because I feel that is the way that God wants me to express myself. In the Army I have opportunities to witness for God for right and decency that I would not otherwise have.

In your opinion, do Salvationists pray?
I don't know about a specific time, but from my own experience I always try to pray in the mornings. I reckon to read part of the Scriptures before I go to work. At the end of the day you are tired; you cannot find as much interest as you ought to.

CHAPTER THIRTY-NINE

Politics and Religion

As an engineer, what is your attitude to trade-union methods?
There is nothing wrong with the trade union movement as such. I believe in trade unionism. The fact that certain elements have got into it is something quite different.

Is there a class struggle in our society between those who have, and the lower paid, the 'have nots'?
Not necessarily on the old class basis between those who had and those who had not. It is more than that. In days gone by it related to money and to possessions. Now it is very much deeper than this—to do with changed social habits and the power struggle.

You are often exposed to what is euphemistically termed 'social drinking'. Would you compromise your Army principles on this?
No. My wife would confirm this. Those disappointed most, if we did transgress on this, would not necessarily be myself and my wife, but those people who expect us always to live up to our Christian philosophy as interpreted by The Salvation Army.

Do you think that our teetotalism and non-smoking rule is outmoded and narrow-minded?
I can only say that I see no need to drink. My impression, when talking to many people, is that drinking for enjoyment is a myth. If one is drinking because of fear of embarrassment if one doesn't drink—social pressure—on that basis I think the Army's principles

are right. In my work I deal with drug addiction and alcoholism in a group of hospitals for which I am engineer. It confirms my view that one should really keep away from all appearances of evil. As to smoking, in my workaday life I see the effects in cancer and other results of smoking. I have had many discussions with eminent medical authorities on this and to them, apart from the Christian aspect, it seems to be great folly for people to do these things to their own body. As a Christian I take an even stronger view.

Does being a Salvationist affect your political life, if you have any political life?
As I work in the public sector there is a restriction on activity in party politics. In the twenties I was a member of the Fabian Society. The salary I earn now ought to mean that I am in the Conservative camp. But I don't think I am. My background, in my home town where I saw much social distress, stops me taking any step to the other side. It would be better if Christians took more active part in political life. In some places it is said that you should not discuss your religion and your politics. I completely disagree. One's political life is that area which governs one's physical situation, and the spiritual life flows into this physical side. If one cannot discuss these two forces, which completely govern one's life, that is absurd.

(*to wife*): *Do you share your husband's Labour views?*
Yes. I went through similar hard circumstances years ago.

You have enjoyed a happy married life but generally there is an escalating divorce rate. Why, do you think?
Wife: We have had a very happy married life. One should not consider marrying one who is not of the same belief and the same outlook on life. A lot of marriages come apart because the parties do not believe in the same things.

But this is happening between Salvationists. Do you think that this is a sign that there is something wrong?
Not a sign that there is something wrong with the Army. It is people who are wrong. If they truly believed in God and prayed together it would be different. We as a family prayed together and we still do,

even though the children have left home. We always pray together before we start the day. If everyone did this, if husband and wife did it, then there would not be so many divorces.

Sex before marriage is another problem these days. Do you feel that is permissible under any circumstances?
Husband: No. But if people give the impression that there is never any deep emotional involvement between a couple before they are married I always doubt what they say. There were times when we were courting when we got very 'het-up'. But we always had respect for ourselves and, I suppose, respect for those people who had to do with us in earlier life. We felt that premarital sex is not for the person who wants to base his marriage on a stable Christian foundation.

What about the availability of contraceptives under the National Health Service?
If people are going to live this way, we have no control over their private lives. Perhaps they should use contraceptives to save bringing unwanted babies into the world.

We live in an overcrowded island. Family limitation is much recommended. What do you consider is the ideal size of a family?
Two, unless one has multiple births. Two, to replace yourselves.

What are your feelings about the punishment of criminals? Should there be a death penalty? Are sentences too severe?
Husband: Speaking for myself, I feel that the taking of life is no answer at all. I talk with psychiatrists. I feel they go to the opposite extreme. In certain circumstances the punishment doesn't fit the crime. The death penalty doesn't bring back the person who was murdered, so there's no point in taking another life. But in child cruelty cases the sentences are very low.

There is a great increase in vandalism, and juvenile crime. Is there a lack of discipline in bringing up children?
Husband: Yes. The home background is a major factor in this. We tried to make our home a stable home, a home where the children could always come and where they could feel absolute confidence.

In many homes there is no stability. The children just go out. We have two teachers in the family, our younger girl and her husband. They tell us it is extremely difficult to discipline children. Children need discipline, but it must stem from respect.

Some Salvationists are reluctant to collect money for the movement. Do you have any objections?
Husband: Oh, not at all. Quite the reverse. The Salvation Army contributes much to the community which the community does not appreciate. In talking to people I find that they are only too pleased to give to The Salvation Army. Sometimes, I suspect, they think The Salvation Army is doing what they should be doing.

Do you agree with our method of appointing officers?
Yes. The way an officer is appointed is generally right. The system whereby a church congregation chooses a parson would not do at all. If they do not like him they send him away. This is terrible. If we have a fault to find it is that at some smaller corps a young officer is appointed. It would be a good idea to try experienced proved officers at some of these places.

CHAPTER FORTY

A Keen Salvationist in His Way

Have you been in the Army all your life?
Yes. My parents sent me to the nearest Sunday-school they could find – The Salvation Army.

Your parents were not Salvationists?
No. But as early as I can remember I have been in The Salvation Army.

Were you converted?
Not before I went in, no, but as a result of joining the Army, yes. I went into the junior band and all the way through to adult activity.

Were you converted before you went into the boys' band?
No.

Then that was an irregularity – William Booth would not have approved!
But I would have said I was converted if I had been asked, wouldn't I?

Then when did this conversion take place?
It is very difficult to put a date on it, except to say that in my late teens I came to the time when I said to myself – it has got to be one

thing or the other. I was about nineteen or twenty when I really felt 'converted'. Prior to that I had been playing in the band and singing in the songsters—a keen Salvationist in my way.

Then until that time you had been something of a pretender—you had been in the band, and presumably engaged in other Army duties, yet you were not converted—this is something of a contradiction in terms. One cannot be an unconverted Salvationist.
Quite. But it is perhaps only my greater understanding of things now which brings me to admit this. If you had asked when I was sixteen or seventeen I might have said that I was converted and felt that I was.

This experience, which is now memorable, when it did happen, what was it? Where did it happen? At the Penitent-form?
Oh yes, at the Penitent-form. One Sunday morning I walked forward and the deed was done.

One wouldn't have thought in those conditions, a Salvation Army bandsman, that a sense of guilt, a sense of sin, the need to be converted was strong?
No. But it was at a time in the morning meeting which particularly appealed to me. It seemed to fit into my mood. There was not a great feeling of guilt. But I felt there must be a time when one was able to say, 'From now on there is no doubting.' That was the time.

You never felt then—in your late teens—that you might be a Salvation Army officer?
No. I often considered this but I never felt any 'call'.

Yet a youth of that age must have been subject to pressures?
Yes. I was in the corps cadet brigade for a number of years and that is a recruiting ground for officers. Yet there was never a time when I felt I should be a Salvation Army officer. One of the reasons was that I felt I was inadequate—I had come from a very poor family, and I always felt a sense of inferiority.

You stayed at home and married. Tell me about that.
I worked on the Men's Social Headquarters – I was in their band. I was there for three years, up to the time of the war, then I left to work in local government. Later I went to work with a relative who had a garage. I have been there ever since.

Were you a keen brass band man?
No. I have always been a 'second' man. I have never been a virtuoso soloist.

The garage – has it prospered?
It has, just. It would be a long story, really. I and a member of the family to whom it belongs are now the two directors. We run it and it is, at the moment, really branching out into something. The Army has done everything in my life. The family to whom the garage belongs is a Salvationist family – I married a Salvation Army officer's daughter and doors have opened for me in a remarkable way because of The Salvation Army and the training I had in its ranks.

Four years ago I was appointed to the Bench as a Justice of the Peace. I believe that was because of my association with the Army. I have been president of numerous bodies in my home area – Chamber of Trade, Council of Churches and other groups. All this I believe has been because I am a Salvationist. Army service made me learn public speaking. I have never felt it was my merit which caused all these doors to be opened.

It is possible that I am wrong about this. There may be more of my own merit than I admit. But one should not be asked to judge that – 'judging one's own case' is not allowed, especially in a J.P.!

You married the daughter of a Salvation Army officer. You therefore have a Salvation Army home. No drink?
No, thank heavens.

No smoking?
No, never.

No sexual permissiveness, anything like that?
No, nothing of that kind.

Committed Christians have a low divorce rate, you would think?
Yes. Among the problems brought to the courts these days, because of unhappy marriages, there are rarely cases where the folk have been brought up in a Christian background, but where there has been a lack of it.

Reverting to yourself again—this, what some people would call, narrow-minded outlook of Salvationism—no drinking, no smoking, no gambling, a puritanical zealous Sunday observance. Did you approve of it?
I had no difficulty in living up to these conditions. As a Rotarian, I have been to many cocktail parties and similar functions. There has never been the slightest embarrassment as I observed the conditions expected of me as a Salvationist. When my colleagues and friends have an alcoholic drink I have a soft drink. Everybody knows why—I am a Salvationist.

Have you found certain tension in being a successful business man and a J.P. and also a Salvationist?
Perhaps. But I have known it otherwise. I was brought up in a poor family, and I mean poor. Eight of us in a four-roomed cottage. My father was never out of work; he was always on the bread-line. There were times when we hadn't a meal and when Christmas dinner was a piece of bacon. I find no contradiction. I always feel thankful for what I have and what I have accomplished.

What do you think will be the Army's role as more people are socially up-graded? Shall we lose this image, 'the Army of the helping hand', which has been associated with poverty? If affluence becomes the rule, do you still see a place for The Salvation Army?
Yes. There will always be people who need help. The Army's new bail hostel at Booth House, the only one in the country so far, is a good example. Folk on bail are sent there rather than to Brixton Prison. Good influence can be exerted on them there, helping them with their problems. There are many aspects of social need in the country today which I think involve the Army or should involve it.

But if it becomes the policy of the State increasingly to cushion all deprivation, won't this make the Army superfluous?
No. Many excellent people who are reliant upon social security payments, who live properly and within bounds, still need help. The Army runs a very efficient goodwill league at my home corps – I help with it. We spend a lot of time talking to elderly people, lonely people, and other needy types. Then again you get people who misuse what money they do get, who neglect their children and get into debt and other difficulties. There are thousands of people who are short of money and who suffer because the bread-winner has spent his money in a way he shouldn't. Anyone who has any connection with court work knows there is a tremendous amount of unhappiness caused by poverty. The Salvation Army will always be needed to work in this connection.

Do you think that it is not only poverty, but a kind of emotional and social and spiritual distress?
Oh yes, most certainly. That is why I think the Army's goodwill league is so helpful. We are in constant touch with the local authorities and all aspects of the local set-up, and the Secretary has a note of each member, and what help they can give to people in need, and there is a constant flow from the local authority, through the goodwill league, to the people in need.

As a J.P., do you find that Salvationism affects your work? You have to administer the 'letter of the law', whereas as a Christian you are supposed to forgive 'seventy times seven' as the Bible says. Is there any incompatibility between the office of a J.P. and that of a Salvationist?
There is no incompatibility. One is constantly reminded of the saying, 'There but for the grace of God go I.' It is not a problem. It is more difficult to relate one's Christian faith to one's actions in business. My company has eighty people in its employ. They have been with us a long while, most of them. We have a responsibility to keep business going and keep them in work. There it is very difficult not to compromise. The temptation is to shut one's eyes to certain things – this is a problem a Christian must always face.

Do you think the Army's emphasis on social service at Barking carries the judgment of the majority of the Salvationists there? Sometimes the Army corps can be a self-contained fraternity—brass band, songsters, pious worshippers and all that?
There has been no difficulty at all in getting goodwill service going. There are one or two, of course, who say there is no need for it, but in the main they agree and they help.

Strangers? Are they welcomed?
Oh, yes. Good numbers of them attend our meetings and soon cease to be strangers. One problem is that outside folk are willing to accept all that the Army offers in the way of help but they are not interested in our spiritual motivation. Christianity is all right, within bounds; some think we carry it too far!

But as a public man you would subscribe to the idea that a little religion is better than none at all?
I am Chairman of Rotary Club's Vocation Service. This seeks to relate the standards of Rotary to business. Rotarians are expected to accept the ethical and moral standards of business which one would attach to the Christian or at least to the religious. But I find that people tend to think that religion is all right within bounds. They don't want to throw overboard that which religion stands for, that holds social and material life together. But if it is going to involve them too deeply, and if they are going to lose out in anything because of it, then they don't want to know about it! Yet I think, in Rotary, they know what I stand for. One must not discuss sectarian religion, but over the last three weeks I've organised debates with Brian Cooper, a regular contributor to the *British Weekly*. He came along to give a talk on religion generally, and its place in secular society. We are having debates on how we are affected by religion in society and what it means to us.

Do you share the Army's neutrality about politics, party politics?
I think individual Salvationists should get involved as much as they can locally. If I could get involved as a councillor, without joining a political party, I think I would have done it. But I do not care for the party set-ups.

Do you approve of the Army's authoritarian set-up—the General and the rest of it?
I think I stand for it more than the Army does itself! To break away too much from the original set-up of the Army would be much to its detriment. For instance, corps councils to me are irrelevant. The Commanding Officer is in command. He is the Commanding Officer and he must have full control.

In theory the corps council does not rob him of that control. The corps council is consultative. But in practice it does. It is not necessary and it is non-Army to meet, and have committees, and take minutes. If the Commanding Officer wants a thing done he knows whom to approach. Let him call a soldiers' meeting if there is some matter that affects the whole corps. We are trying to become democratic in an autocratic organisation, which is a contradiction in terms. It is absurd.

Some types of Commanding Officers, perhaps unconsciously, may want someone to take their responsibility away. But the Commanding Officer must be in command.

How do you see the Army's prospects in the salvation war in the years ahead?
We are there to try to fight for God. It is not promised that we shall win on every battlefield. I have known dear souls, ministers and officers, who have committed suicide or fallen into mental illness because of lack of results. This is understandable and sad—but it is wrong. We must stand up to be counted, do our best. Beyond that we shouldn't worry.

OTHER DISTINGUISHED SALVATION ARMY BOOKS

The Armoury Commentary

THE FOUR GOSPELS

Edited by

GENERAL FREDERICK COUTTS

The first volume of a new series of hardback commentaries based upon *The Soldier's Armoury*, The Salvation Army's six monthly daily Bible reading plan. The Editor has drawn from the best work of Lieutenant-Colonel Harry Dean, Fred Brown, Bernard Mobbs and Major William Clark, creating a chapter by chapter devotional guide that has respect for biblical scholarship and is closely related to daily living.

---

320 pages, £2·50 net

HODDER
CHRISTIAN
PAPERBACKS

Catherine Bramwell Booth

CATHERINE BOOTH

This definitive life of the Mother of The Salvation Army, written by her grand-daughter, is based on much hitherto unpublished material including Booth family letters and papers.

'Profoundly moving and intimate biography . . . a worthy tribute.'—*Church Times*

'What shines through this book is Catherine's indomitable faith.'—*Methodist Recorder*

JOY WEBB

This Praying Thing

PRAYERS FOR TODAY'S YOUNG CHRISTIANS

Keenly observing the way teenagers react and think and feel, Joy Webb has written prayers for every mood—excited, elated, amused or hurt, depressed, angry. She believes that prayer can bring spiritual meaning to the most trivial incidents and unlikely situations, and her subjects include the first job, parents, the wrong girl friend, etc.

Flora Larsson

JUST A MOMENT LORD

Honest and to the point prayers
revealing with a poignant frankness
the ups and downs of life.

'With characteristic forthrightness,
linked with a caring compassionate
spirit, Mrs Larsson talks to God about
her own shortcomings and deep
longings that they should be overcome.'
The Deliverer